# Love,
# Travels
# and Other Memoirs
# of a
# Filipino Writer

## *Edmundo Farolan*

PublishAmerica
Baltimore

First printing

PublishAmerica has allowed this work to remain exactly as the author intended, verbatim, without editorial input.

Hardcover 978-1-4512-7867-5
Softcover 978-1-4512-7863-7
PUBLISHED BY PUBLISHAMERICA, LLLP
www.publishamerica.com
Baltimore

Printed in the United States of America

# PREFACE

I don't how to classify this work. Is it a novel? Is it a diary? Are they memoirs? I'd say novel in the sense of newness, something new, different, and in this particular work, I am poetic, because I'm a poet, and I reflect on so many things, at a young age of 23 till 26 (1966-69), when I was a student in Spain and Canada, when I wrote these "reflections", or this so-called "poetic novel", whatever nomenclature can be tagged to it. It expresses the pains of loneliness, nostalgia, homesickness, and internal debates, dialogues on the meaning of love, life and death and so on.

Then there's the second part I call "the flow" written in the summer of 1972 in Bowling Green while I was working on my doctorate. I came across two students from Iceland, and another from Austria, and together, we wrote this absurd madness of the meaningless scholarly works we were preparing—a tongue-in-cheek approach to the madness and futility of writing poetry, dissertations, and even a poke at the superficiality of media, especially TV.

Finally, the last part written in 1993, Palali, my maternal grandfather's country home, and the nostalgia surrounding it.

It's not a conventional novel. There are dialogues, but dialogues of memories, or internal dialogues. Some dialogues are in quotes, others aren't. You could say the demons or angels in me spoke with each other/to themselves, dialogues of the mind, dialogues of the soul, dialogues/monologues with friends/family/lovers in search of so many things about life. EF

# INTRODUCTION

I'm a writer. I'm a teacher. I'm a lover, or used to be in my younger years. I'm 67 now. Romantic, the romantic in me, always looking for perfect love and when I don't find it, I move on. I'm a gypsy, or a wandering Jew. Thus a traveler.

I was born in Manila, Rizal's execution day, and 47 years after that fateful day. I'm told by mom that dad was reading The Count of Monte Cristo, and he named me after the hero, Count Edmond.

I was born when the Japanese occupied the Philippines. I was living in Ermita as a baby, where all the old rich used to live, in the early 1940s. My dad was a military man, a graduate of the Philippine Military Academy. He met my mom when he was a cadet in Baguio. Then he went on to Flying School. Then my dad told me that when he was flying on December 7, 1941 he noticed that the tarmac was full of holes. He tried his best to land, and landed safely, but the plane fell on its side because it hit a big pot hole. Then he found out that the Japanese had bombed the air base. It was too late for him to have dogfights with the Japanese. Basa and other air heroes did that and were killed by the superiority of the Japanese zeroes. Dad ended up fighting with the ground forces that retreated to Bataan and in April, 1942 the Japanese overwhelmed them.

Dad said that he was leading a platoon, and everyone else had retreated except his platoon. The next day, when the firing finally stopped, he joined the rest of the forces, and they were surprised to see him alive: "Farolan, buhay ka pa?" (Farolan, are you still alive?) was a joke from one of his comrades.

7

He ended up in the "Death March" from Bataan to Capas, Tarlac, where he was one of the few survivors. The others died along the way from starvation and disease. He was in the camp until his release a year later. He married mom on March 19th, St. Joseph's Day, in 1943, at the Ermita Church. Tita Luisa was the godmother, and lolo Modesto was the godfather. Before he left for the United States in 1944, to train as a fighter pilot (I guess they took him out by submarine to Australia and flew him the USA from there), he worked for Jai Alai in Taft Ave. Jai Alai is now the Casino Espanol and the Instituto Cervantes.

I was born nine months and a half after my parents married. I don't remember my infancy except what my cousins, Inday Alunan and Angie Mata tell me. Angie told me that she would take care of me because mom was nervous with the bombing when the Americans started bombing Manila in 1945. So Angie would hold me and I'd stop crying.

My dad didn't come back in 1945 with the American fighters and bombers. They were the back up squadrons in case they couldn't wipe out the Japanese with their first attack. But they did. After the first wave of assaults, the Japanese gave up. So dad came back, still a hero of the war, even if he didn't have any flight fights, because he did fight in Bataan with the Americans until they surrendered. My sister Nena was born in November 1945, around 9 months after dad came back from the States.

What I remember is my childhood in Fernando air Base. My brother Ferd was born there, that's why he's called Fernando. I remember my dad was a Major, but that was probably in the late 40s.

And in 1950, he was sent to the Command and General Staff School in Leavenworth, Kansas. My sister and I went with dad and mom, but Fernandito (that was his name as a child) stayed behind and tita Luisa took care of him in Baguio. Ferd was only 2 then.

We came back in 1951 by Philippine Airlines; we went a year earlier by boat, the SS President Wilson, a luxury ship just like the cruise ships of today. It took us around 30 days, passing through Guam, Honolulu, and then San Francisco. From there, dad bought a green top-down car (that's how the convertibles were called) in San Francisco and from there, we drove all the way to Kansas.

I went to school there, Grade 1, and I do have fond memories of the snow and the nice Grade 1 kids in school.

In Manila, the next year, I was enrolled in Grade II at St Joseph's College in Quezon City. My teacher was impressed by my English and reading skills, and I remember one day she took me to a Grade 5 class to read to them. I remember an accident I had in school. I fell off the school swing and my fingernails bled. I think I had a fingernail or two that broke and were bleeding.

I went to the Jesuit school, Ateneo de Manila, after St. Joseph's. It was still in Padre Faura, on conset huts because it was just 5 years after the war and we were there for 2 years before we moved to Loyola Heights. I got accelerated from Grade IV to VI, but then my dad thought I was too young and let me stay on for Grade VII. My other classmates went on to High School.

Grade VII wasn't too bad. I played Prince John in a Robin Hood play, my first experience in drama. After that, I became active in Dramatics and Speech. I participated in Elocution contests and drama when I went on to High School. Mr. Pagsanjan trained me, and then in College the national artist Rolando Tinio made me the First Actor of the Ateneo Experimental Theatre. I also won a lot of speech awards under his tutelage, especially in Elocution and Dramatic Reading. I graduated in 1964.

After college I taught English at Araneta University and Baguio Colleges, and then went to Spain to live there for two years. I took a Teachers' Course in Spanish at the old Instituto de Cultura Hispanica, and after that got a Teaching Assistantship in Edmonton, Alberta, and the year after, in Toronto where I got my MA.

In the next chapters, my life journey continues. The diaries of my travels in Europe from 1965 to 1967 and my diary from 1967 to 1969 in Edmonton and Toronto are in the next few chapters, and then I got a PhD fellowship from 1969 to 1973 in Bowling Green. In the summer of 1972, I wrote "Flow of Experience", a somewhat unconventional diary of that summer.

In the last part of my memoirs, I tie everything up, somewhat. I talk about my grandfather, then my dad, then some other memories I had in Chicago, in San Francisco, and my other travels, my loves, heartaches, and everything that makes life what it really is and was for me. 67 years. The memoirs continue.

# CHAPTER 1

*Berne, 1965*

The rooftops were painted by a thin white film of ice. The sun was out and speedily descending, but the ice that had settles over the grass and rooftops remained the whole day. The sun this noon commingled agreeable with the frosted air. Standing alone outside in the lawn, I felt that cold stillness in the air and the warm touch of the sun shining clearly in the blue sky. A thin white mist still hovered between the sun and the earth; a cold white mist that made the air chilly. Standing still, I could hear the grass, stiff with frosty ice, make melting noises from the sun's crunching rays.

My aunt Estella had given me the bonbons. I didn't know how to thank her for her kindness. I simply smiled and said thank you. I guess no one can truly express what's in one's heart or mind. Amboy, the houseboy, didn't like my aunt. He thought she was crazy. He told me many weird stories about her; that sometimes, she would tinker with the old piano and just stare at nothingness humming meaningless tunes. That started when her son died.

My cousin Marcelo was only 24 when he died. Some say he committed suicide; others, that it was an accident. They say he was drunk one night and he went to his balcony to take in fresh air, and he must have fallen from dizziness. But others say he jumped. I didn't want to ask my aunt about him because I knew she would feel pain and hurt, opening a memory wound that has just been recently closed and healed.

In a way, I was afraid of my aunt especially when I saw her without her false teeth and her thin grey hair all scraggly and crumpled on her head. But I liked her because she cooked very nice Ilocano food, and I like Ilocano food.

The smell of melting snow and the crisp cold breeze that limped through my open window into my room brought back nostalgic memories of those short days of winter in Leavenworth, Kansas when I was seven. The image of freckled Tom came to mind, and his sled. I remember he visited Manila three years later when his dad was temporarily assigned with the US Embassy there. He was a good neighbour, and that was a nice sled he had.

I now go to the open window to smell the hush of snow, remembered snow, and my memories now bring me to that ship the S.S. Wilson we took from Manila to San Francisco, and those American girls, little girls who bullied me in the playroom of that ship. Then, during lunch, I remember asking the waiter in the dining room for *patis*, a Philippine fish sauce, and he didn't know what it was, so he went over to my parents to ask what that was. I remember those movies they showed for children. I was afraid to see them alone, particularly The Wizard of Oz. I was afraid of the witch in that movie, and I asked for my mother. I was with my sister, and I remember her brown, tiny little milk teeth.

In school, Jefferson Public School, in Leavenworth, I don't know whether I was popular in school or whether my classmates were just kind to me; yes, probably just that. But I remember receiving so many cards during Valentine's day and Christmas.

The snow outside has partially melted. The reality of melted snow now manifests itself: black, ugly, crooked branches reaching out for the grey sky; dirty colored roofs of Swiss cottages with yesterday's snow still clinging madly to the edges; greyish black streets with traces of snow side-swept along the walks. Empty sidewalks, very empty and naked, snowless, devoid and silent.

The vague mistiness of the falling snow has now disappeared. I feel that the sky is a little higher; I can see the Alps now, not very far away from here: pieces of white icing against the background of leaf-denuded trees spotlessly sparkling in the slopes, very deep dayish slopes.

Today is Friday, another redundant Friday, half-meaningful, half-senseless. I read now, I eat, I live slightly restless thinking of the very near half-hectic few days I am to spend here.

I rush back to suddenly remember the Cathedral bells of Baguio calling me for Mass as I lay half-asleep in Abanao's big bed; the air is Philippinely cold, humid and bad for my sensitive lungs.

The cars pass by breaking the stillness of the air. Suddenly, quiet; a certain quietude, a quiet stillness that expresses a mountain town far away from the roaring humid heat of a city's life. Now children's voices; now distant dogs barking. Occasionally, floating, roaring steel flying over Muri's naturally soft and quiet atmosphere.

11:50. I feel myself existing vaguely, that certain versatile feeling I always feel when everything is now like the train that took me here. I watched the people, a new and different kind of people with sleds and skis and all. Yes, this is Switzerland. I thought of Juanito at that moment, that sun guardian sent to protect me.

Black birds, probably ravens or crows, with yellow beaks, bathing faces in the cold, melted snow that had now turned to ice-water. A white dog color of snow passed by, white moving fur against the white unfurlike flaky snow.

This is my first Christmas vacation away from home. Far away, far so different, cold dry snow, white Swiss sky against the humid tropical heat of a remembered dark Manila night.

This morning, I went to Mass still feeling that certain vagueness, the newness of the snow, that strange blowing wind in the distance, that melting mistiness of the clouds from the mountains framed on my window. More tree branches starked in the grey naked deadness of winter. The sun has now dimmed its rays. Clouds. It will probably snow some more.

I woke up and realized I slept for two hours. My stomach ached. Funny dreams I had. Sort of nightmarish. I was directing JULIUS CAESAR and it was opening night. The actors weren't prepared. The audience walked out in the middle of the play quietly and disgustedly. I went up the stage and shouted at the actors at the top of my voice: "Close the lights and get out of the stage, all of you! The show's over!" I then yelled some more reprimanding them, shouting my head off, but no one listened. No one minded me. In fact, some actors just walked away as though they didn't hear me at all, as if I weren't there. I was so furious that I challenged each of them to a fist fight. But no one gave a damn. My nightmare ended there.

I went back to sleep after a while and another dream started but it was too vague to remember. I woke up again and noticed the pitch darkness around me, suffocating me. My stomach was grumbling and aching all over and I thought I had appendicitis. It turned out I had eaten too much and had indigestion.

It is night now. The snow magnetizes me, perhaps because it has been so long since I last saw snow. I was seven when I last saw snow in Leavenworth, Kansas. I felt a kind of a dizzy thud in my head. I then fantasized an adventurous escapade to a snowy refuge that turns itself into tropical Philippines. The vague thud of Zen's Satori of feeling joy in the midst of inconsistency, of the "je ne sais pas", of the angst and absurdity of being a Filipino.

Those Spanish songs that once inspired me to think thoughts that smiled by themselves mysteriously, funny, secret thoughts about Filipino values described by authors like Sionil Jose, and the stream of thoughts continue with the Jesuit theme, "What does it profit a man if he gains the whole world but loses his soul?"

Then love's loss, tiny pains as I look back now, those sentiments, those lost meanings, the anxieties of youth, those tropical kisses of summer, the sweetness of her face, her soft *kayumanggi* hands. A love half-realized with hands holding and lips kissing on warm, summer, windy days.

It was five in the afternoon and the unseen sun descended slowly as she looked at me and smiled:

"They call this lovers' lane."
"Why?" I asked.
"Because we walking here", she subtly answered, looking at me.

Very abruptly, my mind travels fast forward, two or three years later, and Darwin from Gerona, my cousin Phil's friend shows up like an angel to help me that hot staggering afternoon when my jeep got stuck there on my way to Baguio from Manila. I felt desperate because I knew no one in Gerona and all of sudden, Darwin shows up, kind, and understanding. It felt like a prearranged play where *deus ex machina* all of sudden appears to save you. Only an angel can say, "Nothing at all, you owe me nothing". You wonder and ask yourself how someone can go out of his way to help others. How strange, how lucky that I made it to Dagupan with an almost dilapidated jeep with wrecked spring joints, an empty gas tank, no lights. And Dagupan was another saving grace because my cousin Boy was there and he owned a car repair shop.

When I look back now, I feel the summers, those Philippine summers that were happy summers. The winters that now I feel are sad hopes of anxiety, that certain feeling of what-will-be, a dim, undiscovered sentiment of the novelty of tomorrow's moments. In a poem I wrote, I said "To be once again redundant and at loss with meaningless words. To say what I have always said. To say what I will always say in so many senseless ways."

# CHAPTER 2

*Madrid, 1966*

Back to Madrid, the Colegio Mayor de Guadalupe, back to my room, an artist's room, a bright day, a day of life. Yes, truly another day, another newness...

The mirror reflects a buri hat shaded by a red bedspread on the table. An empty wine bottle reading CASA VINO BLANCO, and beside it, a wine glass used the night before.

Three bottles of photo chemicals, four cans of screen color paint, papers, photos, folders, coins on the floor and on the table, a Yogurt Olympia from the dining room downstairs, photo negatives, a SAS handbag, a jacket, a white shirt, a green jersey hanging on to a chair; walls with posters of Spain and the Philippines, an empty, thinner bottle, a plastic cask with turpentine, a dirty yellow sponge, chemical powder for paint labelled "Oxido de Bierro Negro Sintetico"; two pipes, two cardboard round cubes; books piled in a corner; Sartre, Historia de España, Relatos (Hemingway), Antología Griega, Crestomatia Árabe.

An old 100 peseta bill no longer accepted by banks; a plastic blue glass with an almost empty tube of toothpaste, a green toothbrush used and overused; an empty matchbox, a glove from Switzerland; papers, more papers on the shelves; zapatillas, shoe brushes, my bed with drawing materials on top, sweaters, socks, a wet towel, a blue pair of pants, laundry soap "ESE Super Limpieza"; an empty green hanger, unused ash tray, candles for blackouts once in a while in the Colegio, a half-empty cask of honey; a semi-sketched self-portrait; canvases with absurd paintings for the Guadalupe painting contest; a letter with flowers from a woman half-loved; a green piece of paper bearing a telephone number; brown shoes, sandals, a map of Spain and France.

More empty hangers, a Swiss calendar, wooden closets, an old umbrella, a comb, a bar of soap, an unpredictable radiator, the bill for the month, the dripping faucet, the buzzer, the toilet paper, a rosary, a play by Jacinto Benavente beside a sewing kit, a crumpled coat, a raincoat, dirty underwear, carbon paper, keys and a chain, a used bed, paint brushes…an empty room, an empty day.

I thought of Lita. She reminded me of Natalie Wood. I remember thinking so much of her when I saw the film West Side Story, Lita as the simple Maria. She's married now.

My life now is travelling and seeing new faces, new places and reminiscing…Fr. J. in Nichols and my early adolescent years…I was his altar boy…a womanizing priest and a drunk…he called me "kid"…then Eiffel tower I thought was black but it's rusty brown… the girl from Ipanema: wasn't she the same one from Cebu?

My thoughts fly and scatter. They jump, discontinue, dream of the "I love you" written on a piece of paper as I looked for her, and she wasn't there. Only a cigarette between my fingers, but once upon a time, lovers hand in hand, close to each other, on that beautiful sunny Sunday afternoon…

Bells, gongs, piano music. A man lives his life and then comes memories. Nothing else. To love life and not to belong. Loving with music, dreams, and happiness ending in the fullness of tragedy.

There is so much to say goodbye to. Remembrance once again of something lasting and then, the fullness of nothingness. Life. Try to be happy. Happiness is within and not without. Love, tension, climax, denouement, conclusion, fulfilment like the notes of a classical piano piece.

In June of 1966, practically all of my friends were leaving Madrid and going away, most of them back to the Philippines, others to Europe, and some to the US. I captured their dialogues, as we sat in Tony's room drinking cognac:

"The songs and the wine and the mystery. There is so much to do. Yes, to capture. "
"I will never be able to understand why discotheques symbolize the destruction of life."
"The destruction of all".
"Iconoclastic."
"Vermouth is preferable to anything else."
"I was overjoyed with that song once: "From Russia with Love".

Then inner dialogues begin to brew inside me:

"It was really funny that they met here."
"So far away."
"And they would make love."
"Sarcasm would sometimes be construed as sincerity."
"Youth was never once again believed to have escaped the oldness of time and of everything that was accentuated and filled with the grandeur of a well-dressed and well-shaped excited man."
"I don't know what you're talking about."
"Me neither. I'm too drunk to think."
"Here's another profound philosophical statement only drunks can think of: 'To be was that most problematic situation where once deciphered reality that excluded the sameness of inconstant life.'
"Too profound for me."

"It's nonsense. Dadaism."

Then dialogues I wasn't sure whether they came from within or without or both:

"Visayan noises and beautiful music."
"Tagalog disillusionment."
"Freedom and goodness, life and establishments, escapes from reality, the obvious confirmation of sight and words."
"Deserts. There are still a lot of people left living there."
"A man of this world, a poetic man, that guise of a practical dreamer…was he from La Mancha?"

My thoughts stray away from the dialogues as someone plays some *kundimans* on his guitar. I continue looking back, homesick, the music brings back the fragile past, everything comes back again, and the whole impractical past that was a projection of a dream. A dream of insolence that cannot any more fit into philosophical realities. And I would keep on repeating to myself that thoughts and depths were nothing else but the separation of body and soul; that platonic grabbing of haunting ideas, that running into poetic confusion, into metaphysical impressions, that wanting to run away and yet run into something, to a non-reality perhaps, a reality painted with dreams that cannot be.

I looked for the dream. I couldn't find it. She was not there. I hit the dirt like hitting all that is. Perhaps that's what it is, all there is to it.

I wake up happy despite the hangover. I find myself loving and joyous once again. The power of a new morning has made me happy. I love the world today. Today I think that I will be the most content man in this world despite all the absurd philosophical thoughts that brew within me.

My studies of philosophy at the university has inspired me to create philosophical experiments and theories. I invent, for example, a treatise, a philosophical treatise called the "Theses and Antitheses of Interior and Exterior Sentiments". My theory begins thus:

"The most profound sentiments are divided in two: the exterior sentiment and the interior sentiment. The exterior sentiment of our most profound sentiments is the sentiment that shows only part of our true sentiments. This type of sentiment can be expressed in any manner so long as it is expressed externally, like body language. For example, crying without knowing why is an external sentiment. Expressing our thoughts in the vaguest and most incomprehensible way or the difficulty itself when expressing our person to others without seeing the why or the reason for its incomprehensibility is an external sentiment.

An antithesis to the external sentiment is the internal sentiment. This sentiment is more profound than the first because with this sentiment, we look for the reason or the why of the first sentiment. Here, the conflict begins. In the first place, the incomprehensible leads the person to a vague and confused light (of understanding). On the other hand, the search for the why or the reason for the incomprehensible puts us in a difficult situation because we do not really find the reason or the why. We only ask why we cry, why we express our thoughts with great difficulty, why we talk with vague and confused words when our ideas are truly very clear. The search for the answers to these questions composes the second most profound sentiment called the interior sentiment.

Conclusion: Both sentiments are profound because they express something human. Anything human is profound. The human being is a profound being. And only the human being can express himself/herself in sentiments that are meaningful.

Rebuttal: No we arrive at this point: What happens is that we cannot really decipher the why and therefore, we return to the first sentiment. Discontented and unhappy, we try again to look for the reasons of the why, and not finding them, we return to the first and so forth and so on. We are caught in a vicious cycle, a vicious circle where there is no escape. The only escape left is resignation, a kind of resignation called the simple, thoughtless life."

I try to understand this experiment and see its fallacy. And the fallacy, which is the universal fallacy of all philosophers, is asking why when the question should be what to do and the answer is simple: live life, listen to music, smoke a good cigar sometimes, make love, drink. The Arabians like Omar Khayyam were better and simpler philosophers.

I won't say, though, that I will never ask why again, nor search for my soul or for God, as Western theologians have done through the centuries. I still hope, but now, it's a different kind of hope. It's a hope that seeks more concrete things in life instead of just thoughts.

My words will still rattle but I know they will be more definite, more precise. Maybe broken dialogues or novels within novels, maybe characters drifting in mid-air. But all these will have essence. I will create essences in them.

# CHAPTER 3

*Madrid, June 1966: A Novel within a Novel*

## *FOREWORD*

Yes, something in me says: Someday, that moment will come. In the midst of confusion, in the midst of abstraction, something concrete will come about, concrete and comprehensible. In the confusion will surge an order undefined where all dissipation will give in to a God-given solidarity. Material things that make this reality complicated will somehow artistically and philosophically merge with a simple unity, infinity of blue skies and the inexistence of undefined limitation. Life then will reach its fullness in time, yet time will no longer exist: a beginning and an end, yet no beginning and no end will exist; rather, an inspired infinity patterned by existential thoughts that make more thought the essence of reality.

These words will come into effect when I will open my eyes to feel the absoluteness of my senses. It will come efficaciously through the analysis of limitation, spreading wide abstract inconsistency, projecting self images threading and burrowing from out to in and from in to out, into the innermost depths of existence; the constant being that motivates all beings for what we are, a cold reality which, in its simplicity, is complex to the human mind.

An unevenness communicating to itself through everything uneven, the inequality of society, uneven; dreams, uneven; inspiration, uneven. Different inspired stimuli brought about by a past that once existed, that once was in a continuum that is no longer a continuum but expressive only in words.

I wonder at this moment what happened to Albert Camus. Can he be redeemed? Was his search a futile one? Was he sincere in his absurdity, in a sincere victim who runs away from himself to look for infinity in his own life, coined by limited expression, exhumed by harsh reality?

Dead, we still linger not forgetting this world because reality must have a meaning, whether it be surreal or super real, as every intensity in life after death has to have magic. Is there freedom after death? An unseen freedom that has no dependence on life, on words, on commitments? Are commitments absolute and therefore, the answer to one's existence?

<h2 style="text-align:center">1</h2>

I don't know who I am but I will write about myself and my reality. My reality is a certain blueness I wear. My reality is the smell of onions on a table with a matchstick and a chain of keys. The windows twitter with the birds and the greyness of the sky predicts a gloomy day.

The day begins early in Spain. At 9 or 10 in the morning. It also ends early. At 12 midnight or one in the morning. Life is like fire. It is full of books and machines that tell of greatness. Fiery visions of the apocrypha appear before me. Vicarious. Days pass into months. I find I become more absurd each day. A metamorphosis of scholarship. All that is from the outside of me gets put inside.

My life now projects itself into the future. The events of my life are the events of every dying second of the day, the week, the month, the year: the street noises that come and go, a gloomy spring day, the coolness of a summer with the scent of onions in the air, the cold and then the heat of the day.

There is an undefiled letter written with misconstrued evil in a forgotten language, a dead language, that foretells of delights in new-born days, new-born hopes. Boredom can no longer exist. The days are no longer boring. There is so much to do in a limited word that makes you hear street noises outside or onion-smelling rooms that inspire you to tell stories of fun-filled days where certain persons click and others don't, and if they don't click or vibe, they end up living in a misconstrued reality.

Conventionally funny, I imagine a series of half-delighted reactions to the world that is nothing else but an industrial machine. But one must be a machine these days in order to feel human, to exist worldly. If a machine existence does not remember the past, then it cannot long for the past, or feel nostalgic about it. The machine will record as machines do and parrot conversations such as:

"And then there is this brother of mine. Son of a gun, I never thought he could do it, guy. He went to machine city and was restored to himself. My brother-in-law was supposed to own all of these lands… whatchamacalit….well, anyhow, this fellow had a lot of foolishness. My gosh, it was really funny."

"Yes, go on." I told the machine although I was bored but tried to listen. I needed to be bored at this junction. I was tired of being bored by myself and I thought that someone boring might change the picture a bit.

"…and this is a lot of foolishness. You look sleepy." He suddenly laughs. "…because whatchamacolit, it doesn't count…" And so forth and so on. I was trying to listen until I decided to leave his room. I thought I felt sleepy. I was just bored, I guess, and I couldn't stand it anymore and so I left. He had an ugly laugh. His room was always full of cigarette smoke. I felt a sudden blackness, a stupid, senseless blackness, like when you say "goodbye" and then life continues, and it's not really goodbye. The endless goodbyes of life. His ugly laugh contaminates me, it makes me sick, it was black and hateful, but somehow, I liked him.

## 2

I want to write now but with short words and phrases, incomplete sentences, poetic and non-poetic, non-existing words, get rid of words like "search" and delve more perhaps into philosophy and my innermost thoughts without knowing why, therefore it is, not the language, but the absurdity of self that cannot communicate with any language…

## 3

What is a Bohemian? Am I a Bohemian? Did a Bohemian say that tragedy is life? The Spanish doctor gave me an injection. The needles here are big, and I hated that. I'm leaving for a walk in the park. \I wear decent clothes despite my scraggly beard. Don't expect too much, they say. So sanctimonious. Bastard!

Exam results out. I passed. Aprobado. Influence protection. Atmosphere of creativity. One can create in his own way but no one can really create. I remember J.D. Salinger's "fat lady". She minds a lot.

## 4

Then tea was served. He could not forget who he was. He met himself in a town where all the quietness had turned to a certain kind of lostness that built itself into hope, a dream:

"I came home that day. It took me only 20 hours by plane. I arrived. It just seemed like the Manila I left years ago. It was quiet. I thought of how my parents would react to my coming so unexpectedly. I just arrived all of a sudden. I wiped the perspiration off my face. I was not used to the heat. I said to myself, 'Maybe they'll be happy, very happy.' I walked fast; I was excited to go home. But it was three a.m. and I would wake them up. The city was warm. Even the morning was warm. Europe was cold. The colors of the neon lights that still flickered were warm — red, blue, green — full of life. I lived here long ago when I felt like resting from it all. It was January. I felt cold.

I walked faster and faster. The streets reminded me of a cigarette I lit with my tears. The cigarette drowned. And I drowned with it.

I knew I was home but home was something strange. Something I loved but could not understand. It was not as easy as all that. Yesterday I was in Spain; now I'm here. What am I doing here? I felt numb all of a sudden. I had lost myself. Everything seemed mysterious but it was all there.

I wanted to run. I ran. But to no place. I got tired of running. I felt a breeze. Suddenly I felt lonely and I wanted to go back to see once again the faces of my childhood.

A few hours later, I found myself with my parents. They were happy to see me. They asked me why I didn't come home directly. I told them I didn't want to bother them because it was very late. They didn't understand, naturally.

Actually, I didn't go home because I was trying to understand why I decided to come home all of a sudden. I was roaming the streets looking for an answer. I realized I couldn't find the answer for some reason or other. Anyway, tea was served.

## 5

Dialogues of the mind…

"That meaningless drift disturbs you, doesn't it?"

"Well, words usually don't sharpen the mind; they sometimes dull the mind, believe me. Take words like hypothesis, idiosyncrasy, similitude, Vero similes, equivocal…do they mean anything? All academic."

"I see what you're getting at."

"Who cares what you think? Results are what you need, and not thoughts and impressions."

"You remember that day you came? You saw yourself wandering up the stairs in a maze. The library, the smell of the park, the law books — all reflecting that small city where you thought you could roam freely. But there was no freedom. Everyone knew you. Small city, small town, everyone knows everyone."

"I felt lost in that city even if it was small. But you were there. You always helped me in strange cities. I wanted to thank you but you disappeared all of a sudden. But then I found you again."

"Strange but miracles do happen. Sometimes in unconscious, subtle ways. Ways we don't understand. Omens, unanswered omens, but they were there."

"There are a lot of things that are unexplainable. True."

Distance. Dialogues. Monologues. All spoken at once…

"Did he remember how to play golf?"

"He was punished for being himself."

"There was no way to meet the deadline."

"There were only repetitious moments."

"I hope you'll understand all these events, all these useless events where everybody would rush in to capture the cold night and the many days that followed those nights; those nights turned to days; suddenly, oblivion."

"Oblivion seemed to be the clue to those obstacles."

"Those misty eyes were always bothering you."

"He never understood me, that was why. He felt he wanted to be free, but freedom for him was acting like an animal. In his freedom, he bored himself. Sometimes when the boredom was too much, he took naps. He rested. Just rested."

"He tried to sleep but he could not. He would just daydream and discover in his dreams the quietness of life."

"There was that car with all those girls bringing us home, remember?"

"I wonder how we met those girls."

"Davao. It was Rudy's car. Then the girls came."

"How about that whorehouse? There was a 16-year old girl."

"I was sick to my stomach. We almost missed the flight the next day."

"It was because the flight was full and thanks to the pilot who was my dad's friend, we were able to get squeezed in."

"That was a long flight. We were scared the plane might crash because were overloaded."

"You saw down below a landscape that inspired you. And you painted it later when you got home to Dagupan."

"We even wanted to go to Indonesia by a *banká* or *vinta* — those wild dreams — we were so adventurous."

"But tell me, that car, how did we meet those girls in that car?"

"I met one girl and she introduced us to another girl, and another, and another…"

"There were five girls all in all and just the two of us."

"Now everything's clear. All you need is a car."

"But somehow I was bored. Five days there. I was really bored."

## 6

The movement was too much for words. No one could really say what he felt. There were so many things but then, no one could speak them out. I've grown fat. Another 90 minutes and I'll eat again.

Noises everywhere. But there were those who kept quiet. This place is not conducive to studying. At this point in time, nothing is conducive to studying. Personalism. No one understands this made-up word. It begins and ends with travelling. There is only this travelling back and forth, to and fro, secret places, forever's nothingness. There are so many things to do, so many places to go to, a lot of things to say, and stories repeat themselves over and over but in different ways. Redundant but creative. Life is beginning to sound like a pinching eccentric machine with answers everyday. Answers that don't change life. Answers that don't care about life.

Is there real freedom in this world? No, I don't think so. Everyone is a slave of someone. We try to be free but it's futile. We need to be slaves. We need to be told what to do. If not, we won't know what to do. Is freedom boredom? It is if we don't know what to do. As slaves, we can say no when we're told to do something. That's freedom, freedom to get into trouble.

"You're not really bored. You just don't know what you're doing."
"How can I know what I'm doing? Do I even know myself?"

## 7

There must be some sense in what is being done. There is a lot of persecution going on and there is a lot of silence about it. For example, philosophy persecutes the philosopher when the problem of being or *etre* is presented. "To be or not to be", says Shakespeare. "Cogito ergo sum", says Descartes. What mind-boggling persecution!

For me, the word "being" is nonsensical. It is profoundly nonsensical. It is negative. Doubly negative. It is like a landscape that's there in your mind and disappears when another image comes. It is a man alone surrounded by people talking around him but his mind strays far away. He is absorbed in a cure for humanity's cancer, the cancer of being human.

Where was that day? That day. That day was in a basket of Easter eggs with chocolate inside. A game of indifference. A quiet swimming pool. Rich, cultured but disillusioned women. Is boredom only for the rich?

## 8

When one finds the answer to all, he doesn't become God. He only thinks he has the answer to all questions and mysteries, and this doesn't mean he becomes God. His answers may be wrong.

But the philosopher is always searching for an answer. He wants to know more. He is not happy with the simple life. He wants his life to be complex. When he loses his simplicity, he breaks away from life. He kills the simple life and moves on to live a complex life. There is no turning back.

A new life unknown to him opens up. A new hope, a new despair. A new future, a new past. A past now crowned with complexity, and a future now ridden with fear and anxiety. No more are the simple things of life — the purity and the innocence. He now feels awkward as he cannot turn back to the simple limitations of life. The remembrance of picking eggs in the farm of his childhood is no longer a lasting but rather, a temporary happiness, because now he broods into the complexities of picking eggs and asks questions like "How many eggs did I pick?" and "Why did I pick them?", etc.

He broods, but then, feels a temporary happiness because by some mysterious hand of fate, he passes his philosophy exams and treats himself to a vacation. He goes on vacation to Malaga and falls in love but quickly falls out of love.

He finds himself writing again. A plethora of words floods his expressions as he quietly writes and describes his characters who are waiting in the wings to be born. He would include every detail of his life in his characters, the weak points, the strong points. But he is distracted by studies, by scholarly research, and now, cannot write creatively. Only two sentences were written before he had the writers' block: "Man is related to the plant. The basis of this relation is an old clumsy typewriter."

## 9

I rise when the sun rises. I rise when there is silence. No turbulent nights. Light, darkness. Another dream: the revelation of imagined life, a search for truth, life. The sun always stays up. The sun never moves in Neverland. Or Nirvana. Or Eutopia. The lights stay bright. Blackness disappears. No more written complex poetry. Only spoken words. Simple spoken words. True freedom. Eternity. No redundancies. Freedom to imagine your own reality and others' realities. No painful realities. Only happy concrete realities, such as a kiss of love, or a happy get together. The reality of those who crave constancy. The reality of realizing the desire to express oneself without limitations. The reality of true hope in the future, like orange and blue colors of a painting.

## 10

Windy and chilly day a funny face a closing of ears, a vague groping into something tangible but yet untouched

white flaked soap suds love and forget a million times said the road zigzagged into my mind and every time every every time my eyes were opened to a new country something had to end the newness something lacking something dragging letters written to sons a language experiment describing faculties that start and end start and end unscientifically something to run away from vacuum touching groping hands

unfiltered friendship withering in spring where now friends close friends knowledge pit falling learning touching indescribable something words cannot express not express nice neat package with the label he is this and nothing more….

Fills remorse intoxicates numbness feel falling down the pit of knowledge…

I record memories of humiliation, power, innocence, a cowardly slap in the face and I am frightened to read words as they appear recalling past events with hidden thoughts. I wonder now what I thought when I gathered apples among many other apples and then feeling lost in a jungle of trees. Immediately I went home. The sun was cool, my thoughts were vague, I run and I saw negroes calling other negroes. Then the flood, après le deluge, the flood and the houses and everything ached. Silently I felt lacerated. I had grown, and I had lost the right to innocence. I had lost my childhood.

I remember Escolta. Escolta repeats itself to me many times. When I walked through her cobbled streets. Chinatown next to her. Those movie houses in Avenida Rizal: Ideal and others. They had balconies and lodges.

Escolta and her high class stores, Kairuz, remember? And the little bridge, leading to Pinpin in Chinatown, the office buildings along the cobbled street, friends I met, I walked with, I went to movies with. Many times I would be alone walking along Escolta and transforming myself into a thousand personalities and I'd feel a sudden rush of blood to my head and pains.

At times I would go to Luneta's seaside and stand alone watching Manila Bay. And the mountains of Bataan in the horizon where the sun set at six every evening. Loner. They called me loner.

I felt the surge of warm waters, sea waters, and a heavy presence of salt and vague infinity. Then dusk would come in orange flashes and streaks through twilight clouds.

In the summer I'd go from Baguio to Asin, from the cold of the mountains to the hot springs of Asin…those steep roads to Asin. I was with friends as we went down happily from the mountains through zigzag roads and as we descended, the heat would slowly creep up on us, a crawling heavy heat, and our ears would go deaf with the steep descent.

Then there was Ben from Pagsanjan. I was the godfather of his son. It was early morning of All Souls Day when we took that very early bus to Pagsanjan from Nichols through the Super Highway of Laguna.

The shadows of memories now move away, the shadows of my childhood, into obscurity.

The *santol* trees are still there. That old house is still there. It is now abandoned. Ghosts now live there. Ghost memories of San Juan where the mango trees were huge and shady like the *santol* trees. The *siniguela* tree still stands, and as a child I climbed that tree with its crooked branches and beside it, that rusty iron gate. There were happy memories in that huge San Juan house. The cemented stairs leading to the house are now mossy. I remember going with my cousin Tony hunting for *pugos* in the *talahib* nearby. I often asked questions and this bothered him because he didn't know the answers. He was five years older. Those happy summers.

## 11

"Ricardo, you have mentioned the movements to me. There is no escape from the allness of things. Please be aware that there is an evil spirit that may lead you to damnation. What would you gain enjoying all you have now and then after these short moments of bliss, you lose all?"

"But is there an afterlife that perhaps doesn't exist?"

"What if it does?"

"The mind must be clear about it."

"Can the mind seek answers from the world?"

"Free yourself of the mind. What do your instincts tell you?"

"There are just too many contraries. I can only speak of my reality, a reality of losing myself in order to receive the existence of another."

"Life and death are superficial propagandas. Life can be disillusioned. My instincts tell me of forebodings, a feeling of escaping from life."

The day ends. Another dialogue questioning eternity and life. Another chapter. Another fruitless step in life, life like the heat of a newborn day that surrenders to the coolness of a gloomy, cloudy night. I hear now the silence of of noise. I am sceptical of my senses as they perceive all falseness in the guise of trueness. No one knows but it disturbs me because I know but I don't understand.

## 12

Like humanity, everything drifts. These jetsam/flotsams drift attempting to communicate. But they cannot. They exist and yet, their words are sounds that mean nothing. The sound of the wind, the sound of snow falling, the sound of birds. The sounds of light. She lived and then she died. Christ died. The mass symbolizes this frustration. Only hearts remain. Deep inside me, something objective numbed me. It eats me up, corrupts me, like corrupt love, beautiful love that then rots, ground to pulp, over and over.

Symbols flicker. All peace as black butterflies fly to their death; then life radiates towards white.

The sky is brownish blue, a light sprinkled by a thousand twinkles. Here below is silence, a kind of silence that booms because of the numbness of this spring night announcing the advent of hot, summer days.

Tomorrow, today, yesterday — all projections of my conflicting existence.

Light showers darkness in a bright day. My mind's sea is infested by sharks, light-colored sharks that sight and laugh as they streak through the black night.

Today is yet again another transition, a non-existent transition of today's reality. My mind jumps again, a quiet train, a deep breath, a smile, a few tears, barbed wires lined together with New Year's firecrackers of my childhood joys, sentiments, uncertainty, mystery — a glass, a typewriter, a flight to transcendence, a voice in the past calling for some kind of happiness — good, alive, warm, devoid of pretense.

Yesterday, her eyes were green. Today they're blue. Yesterday her hair was blonde; today it's brown. I fly to Utopia. Utopia is love.

After all, heaven and hell are here on earth. What I am is a lost identity disparaged into anonymous personalities. I absorb other personalities because I hate myself for what I am, because I also love myself for what I am because love necessitates me.

Your name is a flower hushed in the din of a laughing past, a tearful past humming beautiful fluid tunes of idealism.

Here, in the dimness of my mind, I feel separated like the Pyrenees separating Spain from the rest of Europe, looking for dreams that come in colors at nights after cool days. Then life is anguish, an angst that repeats and bears down on your soul. It is a wheel that begins with life, turns, ends, turns again, wears out, and finally stops.

## 13

Passport: the hot sun moves my spirit. I feel impulsive again, like a poem. I look at myself in a mirror and find myself escaping from myself. In the sky I float fleeing with the hovering clouds. Restless I empty myself of a dream where two people dialogued. "The bus was empty and I was with you. I came with you. It was night and all of our youth was in that dark quiet night."

"There were sad moments because I felt your anguished shadow coming to me in so many forms."

"I'm blunt but I compensate with colors: blue, red, and green — painting themselves slowly with my life."

"Words beget words: versosimilitudes, afflictions, misunderstandings."

Now I smile. I smile because I remember those urine-smelling movie houses of my childhood followed by sudden gaps of sanctity: an acolyte ringing bells because Mass was about to start. Another gap: nothingness. Stairs of nothingness with symbolic fires towering towards transcendence. A going away into new towns, to breathe for a while a fresh newness. Sighs of make-believe in moving glasses where spirits of the dead approach systematically.

The day quickly ends. I feel a sudden gush of blood through my body corpuscling my system. I feel a certain strangeness. Speaking of confusion has become the answer to youth. Now I grasp a more expressive form of self meeting self in a synthesized dialogue.

## 14

Everything is shadowed and diffused into a millions things. I am idle. I converge pieces of things that hang out of my thoughts: truth, misery, freedom, concreteness, falseness, reality. Like pop art, they are jig-sawed into a pattern of questions and answers that seem senseless. I left this puzzle for a while and then touched God. In my hands, I hold God; I feel his existence. All of a sudden, I feel a surge of generosity. I want to give all that I have. But I have nothing. I smell truth impregnated by a dubious search for freedom. In truth, I see writers forming letters in the sun. The sun then sheds tears; it desires to die; it dies. The fire goes away. Then, sleepy moments. Vague moments. I am a God-inspired fool, careless of thought, believing blindly in a Supreme Being, and stupidly wanting to be a god so as to escape the obstinacies of life. Gods teach themselves selfishly then fly away into a world-less existence. They have no sex like angels. They turn from black to white like chameleons and do not express themselves in words as humans do, babelic humans who tragically express furious words with meaningless, menacing sentiments.

The day dies again. It began late today with European diets. Like an altercation of ideas that tragically commit themselves through communication. Again, I am diffused and indifferent to the lovelessness of this cold unpoetic day, this ungodly existence that permeates all over me.

Rhythm. I refuse to read, I only want to feel the lazy sun rhyming sun words of anguish because words come like love, all of a sudden, unexpected, impetuous, like my youth, unlimited like the skies and the universe, as I attempt to project myself from myself to myself synthesizing ego and superego.

Be like the sun — hot, impulsive, as it rises high, unkind to all, but as it sets, it becomes profound as truth is love and delight is freedom. As the sun changes moods, I also change, like werewolves who when the night descends howl for blood. Profoundness becomes the night and the writer starts his task of writing until the dawn shakes its shackles to the sun.

Gallantry is the mood for the day. No hint of sadness, or tears, or blurry memories. Gallantry and discretion are the motions of the day as look back these three years in search of fleeting identities—the one who escaped from linked hope, the yes-man of life, the no-man of oneness, the self-righteous, selfish, uncaring mischief to truth and falsity, to life and fame, to limited freedom, untrue freedom, liberty lost and misconstrued in solitude.

## 15

Desperation for a God who escapes me at nights when I awake to hear the humming of songs in my head as though someone were singing to me and reminding me of my sickly existence. The new day would open up a sad uselessness, a sad existence where I would ask myself in utter disgust what would become of me.

Can prayers answer a future of contentment and peace…?

And I would remember the prayers of the night before, offering my body and soul to someone, not wanting to freely decide, just desperately blinded and confused with that "someone" who would make all the decisions of my life, because I feel helpless, I can't decide, I can only depend now on someone who would make the decisions for me. Is it the heat that makes me helpless? Is it the end of Spring that tires me? I who am helpless. I who am useless. Utterly useless.

All the helplessness of the world cannot compare, cannot feel the sadness I feel. A certain gnawing inside me, a deep melancholy, an endless emptiness, as I feel the existence of this room too good, too real, too much…conservativeness still there…far away, is greatness far away?

Ambition's simplicity, restful and restless, tranquil and intranquility, marriage with meaninglessness. Lost, tired, tired of life, looking far away, utter disgust this morning, I cannot fly, but she thinks of her mother, she cannot give all.

The indifferent sun prays and looks far away, big with life, free to go to heaven because heaven is just there. I am still attached to life. I want to give it up, but where? When? Passive, empty feelings invade me…days of truth, end of the line. I was in khaki pants, those carpenters, the house was there, it was alone, and everyone was away. I was different from all of them.

I remember summer months. Summer was life. Now all forgotten. Just to live there. Just there with nothing else. I no longer like freedom. Now, alone, I speak. The speech is about myself surrendering because meaning is lost.

Everything would once again be me, its strangeness remains solid, as solid as water that pours questions that ask why and answer no. Simplicity to meaning.

Clarito, are you smiling at me now? Remember that Ateneo spirit. It's in you. The word "fight". Don't give up. Defeat doesn't exist. Don't make one or two failures put you down. Go on and live. Find yourself. Discover life. Redeem yourself. Suffer now but you'll reach the happiness you want.

The afternoon was hot except for some breezes in the shadows of Moncloa. Madrid entrances me again with her colourful people. Happy people, sensual women, their charisma converging into mine.

I decided not to give up. I now have an objective. Time doesn't matter. Just let things sink in first. Then, bite reality, grip it, dominate it. I decide my situation. I must taste bitterness and make it sweet. There is no such thing as fate or predestination. I decide what I want to be. No god will tell me what to do. I am free, absolutely free because I am human, and humans can do what they want to do.

Harden my personality. No senseless tenderness anymore. No more wimpiness. No senseless tenderness. Feel anguish without despair. No more idealism. Just the hard facts of life. No more dreaming of heaven and a comfortable home. Just a 50-peseta room with no hot water. No baths, no laundry. Just cheap food. No more rich boy stunts.

Everything now will be hard and tight. It must start now or it will never come to pass.

I must write with determination. No more castles in the air. Precise objective: work, pass each subject at university, study, focus on assignments, fill the emptiness and stupor with the hard facts of life. Then and only then will challenge be answered.

## 16

"It's a closed chapter", he continued. "That was my life then. I've lived enough. And so the chapter has finished."

"I should write a book and call it *Lost*. You think it's all right?"

"Yes, I guess so. Write it then."

The next morning I woke up and found myself perturbed by a black, restless dream. I woke up desperate and felt no hope but God. God could not put me down, I hoped. But that was not enough. We decide but God confirms. So I had to decide. But I still couldn't. I had robbed myself of freedom. I felt bitter about life and yet I had to go on living despite the nausea I felt. My indecision was due to a wretched groping for an unknown hope. I simply sighed "It is finished" and "That's life", and then felt sad disgust.

My hands are cold; my feet are sweating. I need to rest. But I must leave soon. Go to Ronda and discover my roots. Maybe I should study Arabic. But I'm not used to the university system in Europe. It's too free. No attendance taken. Only finals. So easy to stray away, to focus. Am I too old to learn? I guess not. I'm only 22.

In my youth, I have flashbacks which make me homesick. But it's more than homesickness; it's remorse for leaving home and coming to a foreign country. It's like a reversal of my soul, an entangled plight, and I'm here, no way out, I have a scholarship, and I can't shame myself and my parents by giving it up.

I'm going to Ceuta and buy a new typewriter. Then perhaps I'll be inspired to write more. Write abstractions. Write concrete objectives. Objectives, life goals, career goals. Shall I continue to be a writer? Or shall I just dream? Dream once in a while. No, enough of dreams. Convince yourself of hard facts. Reality. Just reality. The reality of the concrete. If I fail, I fail. But I'll go on. It's as simple as that. Decide for yourself. Nothing is predestined.

"Guy, you'll have to prove yourself."
"Why? I don't have to prove anything."
"At least hope. Be sure there's hope in all you do. Don't think of failures. Just move on through life. Have full confidence. Maybe that's the answer. Don't depend on fate. That's foolishness. Your fate is what you decide for yourself. I'm proud but I have to swallow my pride sometimes. Or many times. But I have the will to go on. Convince yourself; you can't do everything all at once. Do things one at a time. These words will dawn on you. There will be inconsistencies, but that's human nature. Or nonsensical things like predestination. They're all foolish, like that room, everyone talking all at the same time, doctors of philosophy, doctors of law, or what have you, but I'm better than all of them. I can look at them in the eye and tell them I had bitter experiences, more bitter than theirs. I have personal notes of my life but I'm ashamed to show them to you or publish them. "

He laughed. I saw his teeth with black around the corners. He smoked too much. He had not shaved for days. There were white hairs in his unshaven face mixed with tough black ones.

He continued: "Don't forget me. There will be times when you'll think of me. And I'll also think of you."

His sad eyes revealed a tortured soul. His voice quivered. His Visayan accent came out clearly like a bell.

``That seminary I went to was so quiet. I heard only bells. The bells are still clear in my mind. I could not stand the silence. I left after two weeks.'''

He took another cigarette from his pocket. "Another beer, please." He addressed the waiter then turned to me.
"Do you want anything?"
"No, it's all right." I replied.
"Oh, come on. Take something." He insisted.
"Well, okay. A glass of beer, please." I addressed the waiter.
He brought us two draft beers.

We left the bar after two more drafts. He continued talking about his spending money like water, giving hundred peseta tips to bellboys when he stayed at the Hilton Hotel of Madrid the first time he arrived from the Philippines. And now, he says, he walks the streets of Madrid a beggar, shoeless sometimes, eating beans in cheap restaurants, drinking draft beer from bar to bar.

We went to the feria of San Antonio where he befriended a priest who joined us for some beer in a little bar near his chapel. After that, Bing and I walked and played a few games. I won some sidra after putting a ring in one of the bottles. I tried to play other games and we ended up losing, and were given as consolation prizes a toy monkey and a plastic toy pistol. The pistol and the monkey. How symbolic.

I was dead drunk after the feria. I went back to the Colegio Mayor and Bing went his way, back to his crummy pension.

I felt nausea the next morning, and nostalgia at the same time. My face was pale; time was wild as it went back to my third year in high school when I fell into depths, depths I couldn't understand. I had thought my life had come to an end. It still haunts me like a black phantom that controlled that stage in my life. It hit me, for months, but when I got out of those lower depths, it was like getting out of a spell and I felt carefree and happy again.

I remember Baguio, at the Philippine Military Academy, the house where we lived…there was a new chapel being built for the cadets near our house on top of a hill. My dad was the Commandant of Cadets then. I felt a surge of happiness all of a sudden as I walked that street. I didn't even know why, but I felt happy as I stopped and stood there for a few seconds feeling the coolness of the breeze. It must have been a happy premonition to something that would happen. I was 15.

## 17

A problem to begin the day with. I wanted to write my Philosophy professor, but then, why not see him personally? I decided to do neither. Instead, I wrote:

"An engagement of life. Only the inspired and the follow-ups of all the sad and/or happy moments. The strangeness of wanting to meet an anguished newness to its full extent. The shallowness of time. The un-impulsiveness of finesse. A woman making love — an answer to sexual materialism? Books losing meaning, vileness of time, emotional surge to emotional brain loss, highest-sounding destiny of lives, friendship with God, blasphemy of contradictions, absurd love, remoteness, inspiration, challenge, terminologies of intelligence, drowsy streets of summer's Madrid, unjust words like pop sperms sprouting from flowers undiscovered…
Life injecting cursed symbols in abstract expressions of the universe,
Limited expressions
Inexperienced realities
Intelligence focused on aloneness,
solitary, brilliant and undiscovered;

sun shining, clouds, people,
self referenced in sad longitudes of existence;
friends begetting friends,
meaning begetting meaning,
limited bursts of unlimitedness
radicated in worsened spirits of the sublime
declining, like saturated sublimation
of Athenian materialism...
coolness of power, desires pictured in frames of the past,
questioned reiterations of afterthoughts,
rapture states and tranquility states
cowardice projected in days/realities of time
showering feelings of loss in anonymous groups
looking for more anonymity.
Losing is finding one's identity.
Society confronts the answer
Escape to all-ness
Art, yes, art is the answer
Art in fullness
Art in freedom and knowledge ...
"You have though, you have said, and suddenly,
you will feel love and rapture moving tears, tears of desire, tears
of longing, answering raptures as the softness of the day lingers and
when all is unravelled.
Fullness of feelings and the craziness of the world insane
to greatness, appearance attracts the lonely immune of hate, of
awkwardness, of anxiety, of freshness...
Words, words, words superiorise ideas within; transitions
transformed by life's borders, transformations of vulgarity into
discretions
Red as love
Redness of what is love
Can love exist?
Can love be intense?
Can love be meaningful?

Can love cherish desires of giving?
Inquisition to poverty and dread
Life's verbosity impregnated
Life with no obstacles, a utopia,
Words coining words
Life surges on
Love intensifies
Quenched desires
Piano keys
Green rain
Willow weep for me
Deciphering symbolic leaps of faith
Poetry: an answer to human angst?

## CONCLUSION

The novel within the novel ends; a poetic novel; a novel of dialogues, from lost friends, from dialogues of the mind, of self.

I have won and lost abstractness. The life of everything is dead. I live in eternity. Let me drift and lose myself in everything. Let me be lost with only a prayer of hope. In the darkness, an open window calls the night. Symbolically, my soul showers into nothingness. Poetry reins strong, and I feel hope groping mysteriously. Existence becomes redundant, like passing through green fields of pasture, pastured birth, ethereal existence, infinity's anguish.

There is no end to life. It passes on from life to life to life. Endlessly. The birds, the sky — they'll always be there. Disillusionment, profundity, dreams in black and white or colour, metaphysical madness, numbers that grow from six to nine to 293 expressing unfinished dreams, unfinished thoughts.

In this solitude, there is temporary happiness. I search for myself. I become nostalgic for home — Mayon Volcano sweeping in the sky; the flare of lights in Avenida Rizal; Trinidad Valley and all its strawberries and fresh vegetables; the university belt in Manila, Manila, the city of conflicts, a city of contrasts; Baguio, cold and reminiscent of my summers; the singkil of the south and the beautiful beach of Ipil in Surigao.

Fragile thoughts, fragile memories. Something meaningful when I lose myself in memories, when my soul captures the joy of profound remembrance...

**THE END**

# CHAPTER 4

# A SPANISH SUMMER

*Ronda: July 1966*

The bridge and the *tajo*, it's called. The old and the new Ronda, an old canyon, the *tajo*. The winds were strong; very deep precipice. The church bells breaking the silence of the wind. How *simpatico* is Ronda, old, sad, quiet, a town painted by old age. On the other side there's a hill. I belong in that hill because there I see unkempt life and fresh youth in revolt, life still full of zest, as open and as daring as this vigorous summer.

The day begins hot. I was going to the farm of my aunts. I had to walk again. I had no choice. Besides, I was bored staying the whole day in the house. For a little aching of the feet, I could at least temporarily release this boredom.

Last night, I didn't sleep well. It was a windy night. The wind bothered me. It made the balcony door of my room creak. The creaking disturbed me. But I didn't bother to stand up and close it. Probably I was lazy, or maybe I wanted to be disturbed. I wanted to be disturbed by the wind, the wind that would come in through my creaking balcony door. I like the wind; I've always liked the wind, I don't know why. Maybe it's because it's refreshing. That's why. It's refreshing. And I preferred to be disturbed by the creaking of the door instead of leaving it closed and feeling cooped up with no wind at all.

Yesterday I had nothing to do. So I went to Church to hear Mass. Then I sat on a bench in the park. It was a stone bench in front of the Church. I just sat there not knowing what to do. I felt like going to the edge of the park to see the precipice but I was tired looking at it. It looked the same, with the same little houses all the way down below. So I just sat on the bench looking at people passing by. When I got bored doing that, I stood up and looked at my watch. It was 9:15 pm, but the sun was still up. In Spain, supper is around 10 pm in the summer, and it's still afternoon. I started walking back to the house of my aunts and uncle.

They were old people and I felt silly being with them. Young people feel silly with old people. When I arrived, there was another old woman sitting with them in the living room. She was not really old; she was around forty, probably 46. She was bleached blonde and she had a hoarse voice. I don't know if it was naturally hoarse or not. Before she left, she told me to visit her. She lived in an old, huge house in front of the hotel where I was staying. My aunts didn't let me stay with them in their house because my uncle was sick. So I had to stay in the hotel during my visit in Ronda.

I never quite understood what my aunts were saying when they talked. It was the Andalusian accent. Sometimes I pretended I understood and just nodded as though I understood what they were saying. The only question I understood was "Where were you all day?"

I always had to prepare an answer when I arrived because I was sure they were going to ask me the same question. Sometimes, to avoid answering their questions, I just blabbered senselessly. Other times, I prepared an answer, but they wouldn't understand me. So I had to use gestures.

The most difficult to understand was my uncle. He mumbled when he talked. He always had to repeat what he was saying because I never understood him the first time. Sometimes he would get irritated after repeating his question to me three or four times.

That's old age, I thought to myself. They're waiting for death to come. They are cloistered in a house smelling of death. There is nothing but death here. Four aunts and one uncle, tired of life; the house, so spotlessly clean, kept clean by a ruddy-faced servant girl.

Life feels stagnant in Ronda. A passive place. A very conservative little town. Old. Very old.

*July 6*

I was sitting again at that stone bench in front of the church. I started feeling past sentiments. I had walked for a while, walked through the narrow, dusty streets of this old town. This was my grandfather's birthplace and I had seen the house where he was born. It was a large house with chandeliered rooms and a big kitchen and stairs leading from the patio to the rooms upstairs. I remembered Luna. Luna, La Union in the Ilocos region of the Philippines where my grandfather met my grandmother and eventually got married.

We went there every summer to attend the Holy Week rites. Dark churches, visita iglesia, the processions, the whimpering of old women in black singing *Mater dolorosa*. The summer would end and I would find myself back home in Nichols walking Sales street. It was called Andrews Street once, but they changed it to Sales. Just like Azcarraga in Manila. It's now Recto. When I was a boy walking these streets, I daydreamed and wished I were to grow up to be six feet tall.

But now, I think of the infinity of prayer and the hot winds of Ronda. It fills me with that feeling of old age that looks back at youth, as though now I were old looking back at the rocky beaches of Poro Point…we were all dark-skinned from the summer winds, hot tropical winds more humid than the dry wind I feel now. An old car, unwanted memories of my teenage years, Max's fried chicken, then the pouring monsoon rains of June that lasted till October, the cool quiet nights when the rains stopped momentarily. My aunts when I was a boy, they sang that song I now remember vaguely: "En la orilla de una mar, vivía…" I forget the lyrics now but the melody floats in my head. It lingers like the child in me still lingers, crystal clear like starry nights. I remember once taking a flashlight and pointing it at the black night hoping to see the night better, but the light never reached the black sky.

*July 7*

I remember my old colleague and friend Juaning. The maid-servant of my aunts reminded me of him. He would joke with our coded word "tar" only we both knew, and then he'd twitch nervously, bite his nails and not know what to do. He was like that. He was a good guy, but others thought he wasn't. What's good to one is bad to another.

Palali remembers me and its red soil, the hot days of Palali and its cool evenings. My aunt's house was on top of a hill. She used to have white leghorn chickens and I helped gather the eggs. The house is gone, and only memory spirits hover over Palali.

I feel the strong winds of Ronda blowing again, Spanish winds, strong hot winds of remembrance. I look back and see myself surrounded by relatives who took care of me. I was never alone in my childhood, unlike now, in this aloneness, as I imagine myself flying over the tajo like the birds below, flying with the tireless winds of Ronda, drifting back in time.

A fickled kind of heat, sometimes a terrible, irritating dry heat. In my hotel balcony, there's a flower pot smiling with her yellow, red, pink and white flowers. Baguio and my childhood: there was that white horse I rode. I was afraid because it was big and I was so small. My aunt always brought me horseback riding; then, she would play mahjong. She was kind. Everyday, she would give me a gift.

Words begin and end, chapters begin and end, short sentences, paragraphs, commas, like the tram in Madrid that stopped then went then paused. Madrid. I was there just last month. That was the time I met Bing. His brother had just died in the Congo fighting as a mercenary. Bing was bitter about his death. He loved his brother and his eyes were sad and tearful when he talked about him. We drank beer quietly in one of the bars in Madrid, then his sadness would go away momentarily and afterwards, he would talk again:

"Germany. I was there too. I learned to cook there and after that, I worked in a hotel. I was paid well."

I was looking at his eyes. They were sad. I had a brief flashback. I saw Arsenio walking with me looking for that restaurant in Madrid where Rizal used to hang out for coffee and drinks with the other ex-pat Filipinos. Rod was also in Madrid, but just left for the Philippines. We were in the same SAS flight from Manila. We met in the plane and we became close friends.

At the Colegio Mayor de Guadalupe, I started close friendships: Jose Guzman, the Spaniard from Galicia; Eugenio Dittborn, the painter from Chile; and the other Filipino students who were studying at the Instituto de Cultura Hispanica.

"Do you want another drink?" Bing brought me back from my flashbacks.
"I'm okay for now, Bing."

There was another silence. It was always silence between us and a few words. Another friend who rode the verbena with me, had tinto and aceitunas for aperitifs. He always gave the olives to me because he knew I liked olives. We walked around the feria and I played punch the bag and it registered 1000 kgs. I didn't believe it. I paid two pesetas to punch that bag. We laughed, naturally, and I was tipsy after all those drinks and those two bottles of sidra. After a few days, his brother from the Philippines came, and that was about the time I also left for Ronda.

It was funny but I didn't speak Spanish well, although sometimes I was lucid and spoke it fluently. At other times, I stammered. I was inconsistent. I don't know why. When I was with someone who didn't speak Spanish, I spoke it well. When I was with Bing, he always did the talking, or with Juaning, the same thing — I was the listener. Perhaps I was just not in the mood to talk. I spoke more English than Spanish.

I'm in my aunts' house in Ronda, with my old typewriter, in a little corner of the living room, typing, looking at my aunts with their incessant talk about relatives, where so and so is now, what he's doing, who's the cousin of who, who died recently, who gave birth, etc. Gossip, just plain gossip; old women's gossip. I was feeling more and more irritated.

Then their blonde friend came, smelling of face powder. I never got the chance to visit her. In four days, I'm leaving Ronda.

*July 11*

This is cousin Migueling's birthday. He's 25 today. I'm 23. Two years apart. My aunts are together praying the rosary, and in-between, giving orders to the maid:

"Dios te salve Maria...pero mira, digalo que...."
"Santa Maria Madre de Dios...y le he hecho encargo...el segundo misterio....Padre nuestro que estas en el cielo...."

"La mesa, preparalo....Dios te salve ...." And they mumble the prayers.

"Oye, ya esta preparada....Santisima Virgen..."

"Tienes que comprar eso para manana...Santa Maria...."

I feel it's time to go to another new place. Ceuta, Malaga, Cadiz...to feel the sun, to feel free with the sea, to look for happiness. Happiness is newness, where each day is new, each place is new and fresh. That's happiness for me. To be away from this irritating heat of Ronda's summer.

I feel drowsy now, half asleep as I half dream and see a rooftop, my childhood's rooftop and below I see myself. There I am in short pants and marching with those officers, friends of mine. I am smiling on my rooftop despite the heat of the day living crisp glowing fantasies of being carefree, no thoughts of life's miseries, merely the innocence and naivete of childhood...

*July 12*

The heat of Ronda has a certain smell to it. It tickles my feet. It talks to me. It laughs and looks for me in past dialogues...dialogues of the mind? Or dialogues from dreams or the remembered past....

"The day was a happy day. I told you that Albert was going abroad. And he did."

"You're humourless."

"Why?"

"You don't know how to open yourself up. You were always closed, closed to everything."

"I was closed because the table was round."

"What the hell has the table to do with being closed?"

"It's life. It's absurd. It's disconnected. It's distracting. It's destructing."

"Are you playing with words?"

"No, I just want to say what comes to mind. Right now, I think of youth and old age. Young people know that old people are silly, naïve, perhaps."

"Old people are sincere."

"But that's how it goes. The more sincere you are, the more absurd and silly you become. Sometimes they become eccentric, and they brand you. Old and eccentric. Eccentricity is defeat. As the saying goes, 'He was an eccentric old Spaniard who needed a woman. And he found her.' "

"Going back to Albert. He talks well. People didn't think he was Filipino...."

The dialogues now fade away as I walk the narrow, dusty streets of Ronda again, the houses whitewashed. As I walk, I remember four years ago, I went to a movie and I felt guilty because I cut classes. It was a rainy day and I didn't feel like going to class. I didn't feel like studying. I was indifferent to studies. And now I'm a scholar of the Spanish government. How absurd life is!

The streets of Ronda are the days that narrowly pass through and force themselves to go through narrow time. A few years back, I was in La Union, at Cresta Ola beach, the sweet and sad sands of Cresta Ola. I was in red and my lover was in black. She was happy and sad. I said to her, "You feel too much". Was it her youth? She said: "I'm just sentimental."

"I'll always think of you. I will. The days will go fast."

And after that, we rode away in my green Jeep.

Another page of broken memories. Of thoughts. Of dialogues. Of the memory of the Virgen de la Paz. Watered down remembrance of disillusionment, harshness and gentleness. Sky and sun dwindles in the maze of Andalusian fervor.

Afternoon has come. Climactic visages: the end of a day that has momentarily celebrated the importance of time. I superjudge the aqueduct of dreams lost and imaginary, the stupefying savageness of me, intoxicated with youthful memories, pale and mitigating.

A moment came, a religious experience, a mystic intention in the midst of restless youth, an error of truth, an element of stability, a meaningless journey of existence.

Time and youth, love and meaninglessness, death and the awakening from a dream, as though life were a twinkled memory, so short, so fleeting.

Revolt is no longer subtle; fire and ice mix, as in cold hate, and yet, there is the touch of kindness that leads to transcendence. Transcendence. Could that be the answer?

Youth, rebelling, conflicting, emotional battle cries repeated generation after generation—ever continuing conflict.

Last night, another dream. I saw myself talking but there were no sounds, no utterance. I shouted but the words only formed themselves in my mouth. I saw but could not hear myself. People were walking around me looking at me as I sought forgiveness from them, but they were unforgiving.

I was awakened by flies buzzing around me. One fly was crawling on my half-naked body. From the dream, I learned a lesson of humility.

*July 13*

Tomorrow I leave. The wind calls loud now. I feel indifferent; perhaps I'm bored again. Or perhaps because I feel out of place here. I'm a stranger here. I came to try to look back, to absorb the ghosts of my ancestors. And now it's time to go. The hope and hopelessness of what tomorrow might bring.

A few months ago, I was in Cuenca. Autumn in Cuenca. The lake was beginning to feel like a winter lake. A cold day. The zigzag roads and time flew again, fast, like blowing winds. The days then were stifled with confusion; my creativity was one of despair, as though falling into a black hole of depression, the despair of disillusioned youth. I did not understand that feeling. Goodness turned to bitterness. Questions like "Why are afternoons lazy?" or why one is born, why time erases wounds, why we believe in freedom that doesn't exist, why we hope.

My desire to seek new places is burning more than ever now, my desire to feel the happiness of newness, whistling Brubeck in the air, live life impulsively, be excited, rest from Madrid, travel, travel.

I am restless. I cannot stay too long in one place. I will have to go again because I want to get out of the routine of the same places, the same people, the same Colegio Mayor, the same university, the same classrooms. No more of that, I hope. Perhaps another university, another new dream.

Hot winds of Ronda, hot streets where old age treads. Where are your hot shores? Blow, winds, blow. The Mediterranean shores now call me, and that is my craving, the sea, the answer to my hope. No more spiritual turmoil; only the peaceful sea to calm my spirit....

....passing through another memory
the drifted memory timed on brinks
flung open like doors,
old women's chatters,
truth observed,
typewriter of olden times,
a dead Rondenan sun
steaming hot against life and death,
against itself,
against eyes that sadden

or dreams that are endless,
in newness never returning to oldness….

# CHAPTER 5

*Ceuta*

The night is foggy; the day ends with another sigh. The touch of the clouds, the mist of the sky, the oblivion, confusion, love…and the sea roars silently in the night carrying my words in her waves. Love songs play with the sea winds and the misty touch of the fog walks like a dream where a vague image calls from afar, from the sea, perhaps where a vague image calls, where the waves touch the shores silently. I go to the vague image in the dream to kiss it, to kiss it, to say goodbye to it, as it fades away, goes away with the whisper of the waves…will she come back again from the fog to walk with me?

The night turns to a moonlit night as the fog fades away. There is only the moon now and a slight mist in the sky. Some people walk the streets. A sign reads "Ateneo Ceuti". Green lights twinkle into yellow. Children play in the night under the white lights through the moving fog and home is where the lights are bright and where my dreams forsake me momentarily.

The name of that playground like all playgrounds where children play is called Glorietta. Children play here everyday — football and all sorts of games. I want so much to be like them, to be a child again as I see the children play. Flashback of my childhood with tia Luisa. She brings me to the barber for a haircut as she plays mahjong.

I left for Spain leaving so many unfinished things behind. All that is left for me to do now is to write, to write my memories, impulsively, perhaps, with feeling, with emotions as I look back at my childhood. I suffered too in my childhood. It was too secure. There was no freedom.

The sadness of a lost day. I had to go far away to write about orange skies lined against black mountains. Africa is in the distance.

Morning-filled day, soft and absurd;
Say "hello" to me, say sweet words
And record those days with time
As memory flows dreams
On restless rivers....

I decided to write my cousin, Migueling.

Querido Migueling,

How are you, man? I'm writing you again. I thought of you and all of a sudden, I find myself writing you. I need to write and remember, and you are a link to my memories. I'm grateful to you for so many things: for my childhood, for our walks together, and the trip to Dagupan, remember? The sea was beautiful...far, far away from Manila...

I stopped writing the letter. The sun was out and I wanted to go out and feel its warmth and wait for the sad slow days of time to pass. It's time to move on, I always tell myself. The sea is here again to bring back memories. The sun glows...where is Nenet? I see myself with you, laughing with you, recalling prayers, repenting over lost dreams. You dressed well, and then what happened? All of a sudden your life turned upside down. How cruel can life be!

I look up at the serene sky so blue so sad how sad it is to see a blue sky turn dark when night comes stars against black velvet like diamonds on black velvet cloth. How happy we were all once.

Rocky beaches here in Ceuta kissed by the sea love-making with the sky as the thirsty sun reaches for the sea. Palm trees on beaches sway with the wind as flowers in the park bloom as though spring were here. Time passes slowly here.

Soft-hearted pine trees reach for the sky swaying to and fro quietly' sad days passing; hot sun; fresh winds suffering the bitter anguish I now feel. Love comes so suddenly. Things that come too quickly can't be trusted. One must be patient.

There's a time to laugh, there's a time for love, there's a time to travel, there's a time to feel sad, there's a time to get together and feel happy, to feel bitter, to be unforgettable. Happy moments, caring for those happy moments, but they pass so quickly. Days of waiting are slow. Is that all we do? Wait? Wait to be happy? Wait for God? Wait for the days to go by?

No answer. Everything is now. Sad years, enchanting years, hope sometimes boosting my morale, then hope goes away, weakens me, helpless, a certain kind of hopelessness and tiredness I can't understand.

Then it's all over. These impulsive jumps from sad to happy, up and down, weak, then strong again, an unconscious inconsistency to life that makes me sick, sick of the past that moves to the present and then the unknown future, a past that haunts — the long walks, the sun, the football fields, the championship games, catching the yellow Halili bus or the red UBL.

I felt a winner then, and now the setbacks come, the hubris, the proud now down on his knees, frowning as the rocks in this beach frown on me.

The swift sinking of ships, the blurred days of time, moments up and away, brisk walks, breezes sway now women's hair, the touch of their soft fingers, a kiss, another touch, like words on fibreglass begetting more words.

Were we alone in Madrid? The neon-colored lights twinkled as I prayed harshly, meditating distractedly. I was alone and you came to fill my loneliness. The days were then terrible and tear-filled when you left. I then created characters in my mind who talked:

"He's dead and I'm alive. That's what makes me go on living." He sipped his beer. His bitterness swallowed him.

My throat felt the cold beer rush into it, then down towards my throat and into my stomach.

"There were so many people and so many bright lights."
"There is blackness in my thoughts. The bright days are over. I'm facing life now. I'm facing everything I ran away from. But I'm moving forward. I can do what others can do - look at the sky and hear people talk. I can feel the presence of life. So why can't I live?"

It's dawn. I whisper praying words. Solitude's pain glowing in the suddenness of time, the past, windowed and electrified, shakes the I don't know of things; solitude grasps indescribable shadows, shadows with no forms, gloom hovering over gloom.

And so it was: the memory of a present projecting into the past, a mellowness, an awakening, and an injection of a half-truth, of a half-moment, unfinished, philosophical, sad and happy.

Grope: I find a silent whisper groping; I catch happiness loving madness; a bitter mixture of both. Feel me, I exist. You do not.

The past suddenly clutters: I see Danny again, the fish pond, the games, the house. Danny's house was just in front of our house. When he left, another Danny came along, a Danny from Zamboanga. Friends of mine. Clotted my life. Was I happy? Yes; to go far, to forget, during mornings, contentment raptured with tranquility; life seduced by other lives; a telephone call. Long distance. There was no answer. There was a red car in the field. I came. I saw her. She was beautiful. But I had to leave her. Sunny days gloomed. Escape to subtle anguish, the very short months, the generosity — all I see now is myself faltering in the midst of eternity, dying one death at a time, dreaming of lost happiness, jumping back to a sad past, singing tunes of eternal life, a life mixed with other lives...then all of a sudden, mother would bring lunch to us, and we would eat all together, my brothers and I. I was in high school then, third year, I remember clearly. My father was in Baguio. He was then the Commandant of Cadets at the Academy there.

These thoughts and reminiscences scatter like the sea winds scatter dry beach sands; in these thoughts I see black on grey in the bitter awakening of myself to myself:

"Why do we have to live if after all we are going to die?"
"To be happier, I suppose."
"Is it true that a happy childhood brings sad adulthood?"
"Who says so?"
"I thought I was already a man. The car roared. I heard it clearly. It sounded like a noisy motor. I had awakened and the sky was cloudy. It was not a matter of being happy or sad. It was one of those awakenings. In my childhood, my soul was asleep. Now my soul has awakened. I forget all...all comes to all..."

"Did you know? Did you feel? Or maybe you saw that friend."

"That friend. I just wanted to see them laugh. I was tired. That girl came and brought me flowers. Rosemary. That was the name of that girl. People just go around crowding streets looking for love. But love came to me. So easily sometimes. I miss all of them but I can't be with them all at the same time. Only when I'm alone. Only then can I fantasize and be with them all at the same time. All I need is a quiet place where I can rest and write my memories, my impressions. Sometimes the turbulent past needs rest. I must give it a rest. Maybe the sea will make me happy. But the ugly sea is turbulent and sorrowful. It calls and roars and spumes, and then becomes cold. It withers cold suffering like I suffer. Lonely and disturbed."

"You're too emotional."

"Eso es lo que me has dicho."

"You have to conform. Don't be yourself all the time."

"Y llorabas…la bocina…"

"I wrote a note that said Adios."

"Conform to life, with the times, times that rebel, times that feel empty with the conditions of the present. |All this comfort for nothing. All this. This temporary novelty."

The fields will die soon. It's time to shed tears again. The stars are impaled. Stare at the stars, they are just stars, far away, far away, emptiness, far away stars.

A new day again. A new challenge to go on existing. But I run away from this challenge. I just want to do nothing, delight in my comfort of eating three times a day and doing nothing in-between; no more restlessness, no more escapes towards futility.

"Some people just don't have common sense", you said.

I'm in the house of tio Vicente and his kind wife tia Remedios. Jose Mari, the eldest, is 10; Miguel, the second, is 8. They are my guides in Ceuta. Then there are the other 6 brothers and sisters. Pilar, Juanito, Remedios…I don't remember all their names now. A few passing days with my uncle, a pharmacist at the military base in Ceuta. Juanito my little cousin is here now, smiling at me.

"Senseless, yes, that's the word. That's the whole goddam thing about life. You learn life, you live it, then you go away."

That day, the sun was still and the moments were sad. There was that little girl flowing with innocence in that beach in Alicante. I was one of the first backpackers in those days. How melancholy I felt watching the little girl beaming with innocence because I had already lost all my innocence. Innocence fades, then dies slowly with the passing of time, with life maturing, with the months and the years.

My mother wrote that Tony is now married to a Chinese girl and living in Hong Kong. Victor meant many things to me. Before he left for Sweden, he said goodbye to me. It was the beginning of summer of 1966 in the Metro in Moncloa, at the Ciudad Universitaria. He said AMDG to me before he left. I smiled and said goodbye.

"Don't put all the eggs in one basket. You're not God. Just do things one at a time."

"Yes, it's oppression. I feel it when I do things all at the same time."

"The good news is you choose what you want to do. When the day ends, there are no more duties to perform. Inspiration might come. Don't depend so much on consideration. The world is full of those who have established contact with lost time, but they do not complain of their defeats. They go on and on struggling trying to find an answer to the endless search for humanity. Humanity, so much of humanity is still undiscovered."

"But happiness cannot really be found; happiness cannot really exist. I can only wait for time to pass. And pray, meanwhile."

"Don't depend so much on prayer. Depend on yourself."

"I'm still looking for myself."

"That's a nice way of sinning sympathy."

"I made friends with all of you because at one time I loved all of you. But I was always alone."

"Guy, you're lost. Don't think of love in terms o love."

"Even when I searched simplicity in life, the more it got complicated. I had to struggle, to make decisions, to think four times before making my move. Security, dependence, and other so-called benefits of the simple life."

"Time is not yet ripe. It appears useless. But next year will be another year."

I was watching these characters talk. The room was bright.

I simply didn't have the patience any more to write these dialogues. Sometimes there were dialogues with God which I couldn't write. Prayer dialogues in supplication forms. Prayer can be selfish sometimes. Yet what I prayed for were selfless things like humility and simplicity, generosity and faith. And hope.

Fr. Jimenez was a kind priest. I was an acolyte, and when I was older, he left for another parish. I don't know where he went. But one day, when I was in Cagayan, I thought I saw him. He was in a barber shop and at first, I wasn't sure. Then I knew it was him. I was happy to see him. I served his masses. He invited me to eat out many times. He used to tell me, even though I was just a boy, about his affairs with women. But I didn't understand at that time. He called me "Kid".

"Kid, that's how it is. I'm just human."

He still had the green Volkswagen which he brought to Cagayan from Manila. He was a chaplain in the Army camp there.

Danny from Zamboanga comes back to my thoughts. I hit him jokingly with my missal just for the hell of it. He was patient with me. He was another kind and understanding friend. I miss him. I wonder where he is now. The last I heard he was in Bukidnon.

Twenty years of flashback go through my mind: Migueling, my aunts, my parents, Nichols, cadre, the sari-sari store, the parking space, the bicycle is still there, strange, but it seems still waiting for me to claim it; the cards on the table, the brightly grey uniforms I wore for ROTC — we marched under the hot sun and we wore blue sashes that strided with the wind, hot tropical winds…

Cry, half-wind, cry and sink in depths of strength
Love in half-disillusioned instances
Intimacies of lost days.

That day, I ran across the field in twilight. I felt intimate with nature and life then and yet I wasn't conscious of it. In my childhood, I felt a kind of a happy discovery just going to my new home beside those warm fields called Pump Hill, open to the sky and the wind.

Eagles were still blue and the ground was happy to receive my awkward steps at play, fun-filled unconscious of everything around me, joyous, vague images calling me home, wanting me back. God was near, I felt, a God of joy saying "yes" to my empty words and I am swept back to captured remembrances of even earlier years, when I was five, and my teacher's name was Mrs. Red. And I remember napping in her classes.

Tony used to stay with us in Lipa during the summer. We went to hunt for magnet in planes that were lying in the junk yard of Fernando Air Base. We played with these magnets with nails. Child's play.

One day I was walking and smiling in front of our house and an older friend called Rene was also there. He was the leader of the boys because he was the eldest. We went to the fields. Migueling was there too. Migueling was smiling and he gave his harmonica to Juancho because Juancho cooked corn he stole from the corn fields and gave us some. They were burning the fields and Juancho cooked the corn there.

There was another neighbour, Sonny. Sonny and I played together. We had a driver, Marquez. He was nice, kind. He drove the jeep. I saw him years later in Poro Point. Migueling was with me. He didn't want to show his thin body. He played ukulele well. Migueling helped me in so many ways....

I'm exhausted. I need to rest now. The college days are over. There were a lot of ups and downs during my college years. I went from honor student, in one semester, to a failing student in another. All those activities — ROTC, Drama, Social Club, ACIL, etc.

I needed to rest from all that. Was it just two years ago? Then I taught for another year, and now I'm in Ceuta, this tiny part of Africa which Spain owns. Those turbulent outflows of life's past that jump back and make us sad and happy.

Migueling wanted to run away too. We used to play billiards at the Officers' Club in Nichols just to pass the time...I wrote in my diary:

"The day ended. It was dark. Twilight. The cold entered through the marrow of my bones. The soft dark twilight ended and disappeared again into the night, endless night, tiring me with its endlessness, me, helpless and angry biting my tongue unconsciously as though someone were thinking of me. I felt my cracked lips. It must have been the dry cold. I heard misty noises in the distance as though someone were calling me. I lit a cigarette, sat down and watched the smoke curling up, losing form, losing itself in the darkness.

The next day it was winter again. All the trees had lost their summer leaves. The day was gloomy. It was welcoming rain. And rain poured, cold, icy rain. I felt myself drifting with these strange seasons that shift so fast. At home, it only rained; and after the rain, it was always warm and dry. Here, the rain, then the greenness, then the cold, then the heat, passing so fast. The soft sadness of those passing days hovered over me; loneliness, as strong as the sea, even stronger than days that welcome rains, cold shores, strong seas, fervent days, weak days, like faltering, fretting words."

# CHAPTER 6

*Ceuta*

Those bright suns have been left behind. Misty memories sling to my insignificant existence. I don't know how to live anymore. I've lived those two years but there was nothing glorious about them. Nothing worthwhile. All useless. The life of a common man. Boring. Routine.

I felt bitter about those two useless years. About life. It returns. This bitterness. A useless struggle that doesn't fade away to this slow, dying day. Double your efforts. Get out of the inertia. Progress is futile but aim for it. How the years pass! How regrets pile up! Scratching blood from life. Oh, if I could tear the skin from off my body and let the blood flow endlessly to the ground! Oh, soft melting skies! Cold, cold sea, whisper, whimper like dying swans in the water, blue clean waters of life's lake where seas find no match to turbulence!

Now just this caged room, cage for birds, cage for dreams, a table, pictures, a rolled-up bed, a cup, the world on a map, a flower vase, a grey typewriter clicking black letters against white paper; a blue pail, blue pants, blue shirt; one year, no, almost a year; sun still bright and shining; lost dreams, lost clouds…

This morning when I awoke, there were clouds in my room. The clouds descended because the gods from Olympus walked here this

70

morning. But everyone was sleeping and the gods had a quiet feast by themselves. Then the clouds ascended again with the gods riding them, flying towards the sun as it rose in the horizon.

*July 19*

The clouds now fall towards the mountains. Fat and white clouds reminding me so much of Baguio. Clouds clutching those sleepy mountains towering over the deep blueness of the sea. I feel that fresh sea breeze. My thoughts are heavy.

*July 20*

Last night, I dreamt. I felt anguish. There was no fire. There was only a vague forgetfulness moving towards someone in faded colors. Then more people entered in the dream, more vague faces, and I felt that they had a blind kind of hope for me.

Truth is sad. Day's dawn. Bright skies experiment from my flighty thoughts to endless dreams that still do not exist. I try to meditate. I am paralyzed by my existence. An existence that hopes for brighter ventures and firmer aspirations. Can one smell truth? Can one gain anything from hardship? Flaunt despair! Secret meanings are hidden in empty words.

I had a haircut and my shirt was full of hair at the collar. Somebody put all the letters together. Was it Eugenio? Or was it another dream? Where's Valera? He brought me to Cavite once. He married twice. Many things cannot be accepted, like bigamy in a "civilized" society. Or revolutions.

What can I do with my style? I'm a scholar, am I not? Prayers. That word has been haunting me. People who sympathise with me. Nice neat package. A vague puzzle. Why, yes, of course. The prayer has been answered but in a different way. God replies in ways we don't understand. Many times I get excited and I run to catch the sky with my hands. Restless, like restless shores on the sea, like endless sighs, like smoke that flies up into eternity…up, up, up until it diffuses with nothingness.

It's all in the mind: you can't hide subtleness. The nail clipper is in your hands. Suddenly, the sea calls. No one forgives with tears. When ribbons are red, no one understands. Stagnant like Sta. Cruz Church. The last few days were short… Time was clear. All things had to come. They had to. I couldn't decide. Or if I did decide, my decision wasn't truly a decision. Somebody decided for me. Wonderful moments fade with the passing of time. Happiness fades. Like love. You can't complain. Life cannot be told what to do. Life controls you. Decisions are futile. You're living — you didn't decide that. You didn't decide that one day you'll live in this world. Life decided that for you.

*July 25*

"Please come back", the plea is still clear in my mind.
"No, I can't. Please understand why. I can't even help myself. How can I come back to you?"
"It doesn't matter. So long as you're back."

The plea resounded with the waves from these North African shores. The waves were strong and proud, winds blowing from the Gibraltar Strait. Poems cannot answer pleas. Poems are selfish. They are sad songs lamenting human existence, despair, and the wings of time. The echoes of the past resounded clearly through the night. Clear like the sea…

I whisper to let the winds of time carry my words in the years to come, but the whispers return when the sea is calm and sad. The echoes repeat in the calmness of the sea and the sadness is unbearable. Her words resounded in my memory:

"I didn't want to bother you but I thought of you. The separation is bitter. The solitude eats me all the time. You don't believe in God but I do. Perhaps someday you'll believe. I think God still sleeps in the souls of those who don't believe in Him. Maybe he'll awake one day and wake you from your sad slumber. I pray for you always, but my prayers seem useless because now I feel empty all the time. I've forgotten what love is all about; love doesn't seem to be there anymore. I've withered like flowers in late summer. But sometimes the sea gives life back to me. Many times I feel the sea flowing all over me and I've alive again. Maybe God is beginning to fall asleep in my soul."

The roses, they were growing on air, floating in some kind of nothingness, disappearing surrealistically in time. Time runs. It now runs so fast it's eating up my existence. My existence that's getting sickly as the seconds tick. I wanted to give whatever love I had, but I couldn't. I was sick, almost dead with this lingering something, something eternally sad, something that ate up all of me. I don't know what it was. *Saudade?* Something like that. Spanish sentimentalist that I am. I thought of happiness, so remote, but I hoped, I searched for lost smiles. Nothing. Only my shadow moving into dark eternity, vague against the light, yet absurdly resigned to my existence.

I thought of death and nothingness. But I was afraid to let the sea swallow me. I was also afraid to fell the pain of a bullet or a knife in my body. One has to be really brave to take one's life. I lacked this courage. I wish I were brave.

"I wish I were as brave as you. I miss your touch. I miss your smile. You made me brave once. When I was with you, I was brave. Little by little, my courage died. When I lost you, I also lost all of myself. I no longer know who I am. I'm really lost. I have to start believing in God again so I don't lose hope. I can only love you. Sometimes the past is too painful to look back to: a past of fury with no meaning. Now I've lost all that vigour and fire. I've been dragged towards indifference. God's been silent."

I looked far away and I thought I saw someone calling. I was almost sure it was her, and I ran towards her. But it wasn't her. I cried. I'm tired of running and looking for her. And I don't have the courage to face the future.

The past flashes back. It was a bright happy night. Yinyi sat beside me. She was lovely. There were two other girls. They sat at the backseat of the car. The car got stuck that night. Oil dripped all over, and my shirt was filled with oil. I liked Yinyi that night, but the night passed quickly away.

When I was a child, my older cousin Nenita took care of me. She was good to me. I also remember Doro. His foot. He had an infection. He called me "senorito". I remember everyone calling me senorito. I don't like it anymore. And then Saria. She was deaf-mute. And Marcela…all part of my childhood.

Then there was my classmate Arjan. I was afraid to go home because I took the jeep and took off for two days. The jeep broke down. I stayed over at his place.

It's time to sleep now. I hope I'll have a happy dream.

*July 26*

"Life is absurd because you make it absurd," Dittborn told me once. He was my friend, and he left for England, then Chile and I never saw him again. I met other friends but none as good a friend as Dittborn. We laughed a lot. Our laughter will resound again someday.

There's another friend I remember. I remember him only as Pal. I met him at a Novena in Baclaran. He was a wonderful friend. I miss him a lot.

The dream I had last night was colored yellow. Someone I knew but cannot remember appeared in that dream.

When I was in Grade Three, I had a teacher called Mr. Santos. The first day in school, my cousin Tony was in Grade Six, in the old Ateneo in Padre Faura. Those big acacia trees, the swimming pool, the airplane. And in the theatre, someone was killed. I can remember that smell of death that lingered — the smell of dry blood mixed with some kind of stuffed something, as though the theatre had never been aired.

The floods came and people walked with the water knee deep or even waist deep sometimes — brown, muddy water.

And then, during those days, children had to entertain their guests; and my mother always asked me to recite that speech that Carlos Romulo delivered at the UN during the Second World War, the one that went "We are here gathered to honor those Filipino and American soldiers, etc."

There was our leader Rolly. I really admired him. He liked me a lot and I liked him too. He was a great guy. Many didn't like him, but I did. My childhood memories. My throat aches now. Tears I don't want to shed as I remember all these.

There was Rod and Art. They were good to me. We wanted to go down to the beach because it was cold in Baguio.

The first time I went to Dagupan was a really happy event. I was with tita Adeling. She was a paseadora and she always took me with her when I was a child. With her around, you can always expect a good reception wherever we go. Dagupan was great. My cousin Boy took us around. He was a painter and I started painting because of him. He saw me off when I left for Spain in 1965. He wrote me once, and that was it.

Rafael was at the Philippine Military Academy and Migueling should have visited him. We were childhood friends.

They say you must be satisfied with what you are.

I walked and saw yellow lights reflected on a statue. I smiled. Once again, I was truly myself.

*July 28*

The night has passed again. I pick up a note Bing wrote when we were in Segovia written like an illiterate: "Edei beleveme I'am drunk but Iam not only a little bit happy and it reminds me of my brod Juaning". He thought of his brother who had died as a mercenary in the Congo. They were together in Segovia before he left for the Congo.

All of a sudden, a flashback of a dialogue with my lost love:

"I'll always think of you; I'll always hope that we'll be together again."
"We will. We'll love once again."

*July 29*

It's 2.40 pm. Lovely day. Life comes in parcels, happy, sad, like a parcel of morning then afternoon then night. Is the sky a symbol of desire, of love? Why does it have to be "truth and love" together?

Silence. Let me know what they know. I've been reduced to a dreamer: a very painful experiment when reality besieges and confuses you.

Ceuta disturbs me a lot. The sea makes me helpless. I feel heavy. I long to sleep for months like bears in hibernation and their almost endless dreams.

They told me to wait but I was impatient and restless to leave. And now it pains my soul...dreamless sleep, the sea...

That willow tree writes time, walks time, back-marching...I was marching in military uniform with my classmates during summer cadre, over dust, under the hot noon sun, with our canteens and rifles. The sun was hot but I was familiar with its heat. Summer was hot. The winds were hot. I realized what humility was that summer.

I went to the sea afterwards that summer. I enjoyed the salt water in my eyes. The words "truth and love" kept on repeating in my subconscious, I don't know why. Two inseparables. Like fresh and salt water.

*July 31*

I didn't know how to say goodbye and thank my uncle.

"Tío, pienso marcharme el viernes."
"Cuando quieras. Mi casa es tu hogar."

*August 1*

I needed to be alone by myself again. Dream alone. There's no choice. You can't dream with others. You must dream alone. And my dreams were always there beside me. Near my pillows.
*August 3*

Listen listlessly to the night that heralds a cold day as restless clouds turn from white to turbulent grey. Laugh a laugh of despair after a whispered windy night.

Yesterday, I saw the city from a mountaintop: the stillness of white-washed edifices scattered along rocky shores; half-misty mountains in the distance; and Gibraltar, "el peon", towering, a white chalky speck in its summit. Coming up, the road zigzags like the Kennon road of Baguio City, and from another angle, the African mountains to the south take shape like the sleeping woman of Manila Bay.

It is past seven in the evening and the sun is still warm. But at this time in Manila, by the Bay, no one would be able to see the silhouette of the sleeping woman with her long hair floating in the sea. At seven, hovers over Manila and only the lights in Luneta shine bright in the night. Ten years ago, when Roxas Boulevard was called Dewey, it was even darker, and only Bulakena restaurant stood out.

I looked farther away, to the west, to the Atlantic, an empty horizon, just the sea reaching into nothingness; only the sky in the distance. My uncle Vicente was kind to me. He took me with his small VW Beetle around town all the way to where there were small castles still standing on hills. That was the border, he said, between Ceuta and Morocco. "Morocco used to be Spanish once", he explained. From there we returned home.

*August 4*

Nostalgia again. I smell the ink of the freshly-delivered newspaper and I remember how excited I would be as a child when I picked up the Manila Times and hurriedly opened the movie pages. I liked movies, and this was because of my Aunt Luisa who would always take me along with her downtown with my cousin Angeling to watch the new movies showing at Avenida Rizal. I remember she always scolded Angeling, but never scolded me once in her life. There was my other aunt, the strict tia Lolita who was a different sort. She was more aggressive: whatever she says goes. But she was also very nice to me, for some reason or other. And I remember my cousin Pepit who looked like my mother somehow, I don't know why; the genes, I guess. All of them formed my childhood. They saw me grow, they saw me change. Tia Lolita's husband, tio Dionisio was also kind to me.

There was a time in San Juan when I felt so homesick because my parents were away somewhere. And tio Dionisio took me with him to watch a movie. I still remember the movie — an Audie Murphy movie. I was no longer sad and lonely. Years later, we played chess. He was a good chess player. I lost, of course.

I wish I could go back and repay the good things people have done to me. I guess by doing good things to others.

All those family reunions in San Juan. I was so ordinary, so simple, so innocent then. I've lost all that.

Tomorrow, the experiment will be over. Tomorrow, Ceuta will be behind me. It will be another reminiscence like Ronda. I will spend more days here in the south, close to the sea, misty days, sometimes sunny, as Spanish southern weather is, days of happiness, days of tearful remembrance, new days, new acquaintances, meeting more distant relatives.

Far away, in some distant shore, someone looks in the distance as I do, someone who remembers me, but time will tell; time that rhymes, withers and recreates. Have I given all of myself? Not yet. Wait for new dialogues, for a new hope, a new absurdity that may be waiting silently in the wings of lost futility.

# CHAPTER 7

*Cadiz*

*August 11*

Chide stars! Winds clamour in exodus. Black elementary songs of time sway timeless winds towards tranquility. Fly! Fly! Fly!

Time! Time! Time! Flight and Time. Oh, how time affects us all! Silent, passing time. Portions of glory, and the subconscious bridge to consciousness repeating itself — truth and love, truth and love, truth and love! Oh, how these words affect me as I waste away abstractly and losing touch of all reality!

Love, stars! Will someone up there ever know? Will someone ever care? Sin, sin, sin! Thrice shall I say this word. Unjustified sin resulting in humility, shame and sin again. In my tragic joy, I must, like a gypsy, wander carelessly.

*August 12*

A frightful dream last night. It felt so real. My heart beat furiously. And yet I don't remember anything. I'm in a room. This is a retreat home. Those who stayed here have written things around the room. Someone wrote: "Soy un pobre pecador de 26 años; si alguna vez lees estas mal trazadas líneas, te pido por Dios una oración por mí y por todos aquellos que han encontrado a Cristo." Another wrote: "Soy Mari Carmen Gómez y estoy contentísima aquí de haber estado aquí tan cerca de Cristo."

Not a very nice room but Christ seems to be here because the people who stayed here found Him. A retreat here in Cadiz where I found some happiness. I was lonely and in my solitude I sat down on a bench in the park beside the sea thinking and remembering so many people who touched my life, good people, bad people. I wanted to stay longer but I felt helpless. I felt I needed to leave again and find some place new.

The winds from the sea of Cadiz are not strong. The days bother me. A kind of anguished sadness, like losing the little happiness I felt earlier, invades me. Like you're about to catch something and you lose it, and all of a sudden, you're out of touch with life, and life becomes a kiss, a poisoned kiss, weariness, an agony.

Children are enraptured with their innocence as they play. I look at the sky and pray. Then a farewell to Cadiz, that historic city where sailors left to venture to the New World. I lost my rosary, the one I bought in Lourdes. The sands are white in Cadiz; the day, bright. The heat, the breeze, the remembrance of today, and the hope/despair of the happy/bitter days to come … crucifixes, smiles, rain hot sands. Cadiz will be remembered like Valencia, like Paris and the wet snow; escapes into memories; sun and cold; the bright dawning light; thoughts of the day; a cold wildness; southern fire; purgated judgments; more fire against fire; then the salty water of the sea and the white calmness of the beaches.

Puerto de Santa Maria — gone; that ferry, those Cuban seminarians, Andres and his Andalusian imitation of the gypsy song "saete" ….

"Yo soy un andaluz…naci en Jerez…"

The warm nights, the end of another day, the painful passing of another day in Cadiz, the sea is rouge again, the Mediterranean Sea that opens towards the Atlantic then towards horizons that end with the sky. More ships come in. The park is quiet with lovers holding hands; the churches whisper silent darkness. The azoteas whirl with hanging clothes. The moon mellows in emptiness.

The simple sea, the passing cars beside the sea, moments ticking away, awakened days, new days...it's five to twelve midnight. A rosary in my hand, peace, love, words against words, the nowness, the newness, emotional bells ringing. Two minutes to twelve. Christ in Heaven, lights closing, night passing away....

*Sevilla, August 13*

Sevilla. Hot. Very hot. A passionate heat. Guadalquivir: steaming. Pimps all around asking if I wanted a whore; a railroad station; a grey typewriter; an open park; birds singing dreams; day buzzes by; a town that gives the impression of passion; sensual, alive, Catholic and yet, pagan in many ways. Women who look half-oriental, dark-skinned but with European features. The day floods the mind with sensual love. Jerez: I was in Jerez just a few hours ago, tasting wine, the best of Spanish wines. Now, Sevilla: the palm trees are still there, the Moorish palm trees swaying with the hot winds. Then, Sevilla darkens towards night; Sevilla is still. The parks are green; the hot day ends. Sevilla is a grape vine, barren, lingering, fruitless.

I gave my guide 100 pesetas. He complained. Whores. Sevillan whores: fat, bosomy, ugly. I do not dare. I leave the brothel with a lame excuse.

Train back to Madrid. I sit with an atheist and a priest. A sleepless atheist and a sleeping priest. The atheist talks to me about Camus and Sartre, and his nightmares, one in particular — a tall man beside a short man holding hands.

I have to take a Greek exam in Madrid. Delays, delays. Spanish trains, always delayed. I was in Sevilla for just a few hours.

Six weeks I was away. Now back to Madrid. Six weeks of feeling sad, hot, lonely, helpless and tired.

# CHAPTER 8

*Madrid, August 20, 1966*

I would have those moments. Then God would catch me like J.D. Salinger's catcher in the rye and make me once again a day. The day comes with the absurdity of time. Cruelty seems like a wonderful reception. There are many and exciting moments, knowing sadness, tears…

I felt the heat of Madrid. A hungry day, answered prayers, someone waiting in disguise. Truth beckoning goodness: indifferent, don't wait for me. A day has passed: atheism — you borrowed the end of a tearful moment; soft spots cry once again lie never before. A simple style, a sad word, a happy cry; and then the deer comes running again.

Experimental attempts towards life; mysticism…we would be together, we would answer half-heard questions. Yes, you were often asked and you simply said "no". Remember all those people who repeated your same words? You said that the past will answer like no one ever answered before. You then were supposed to answer but you never answered.

I must go on writing and believing; I must go on studying the same verses of truth and inconsistency. Then and there will I encounter sad moments again, despair. To talk of loftiness; to talk of the child within; I would search deep and find utter loneliness in my search.

I open with a smile. Charming smile. Sincere, brave, preparing for a dialogue to discuss the passage of time — the past to the present to the future.

My emotions call sad awakenings; life's awakenings in time. Just wait. The waiting and the least expected will then happen. The love you looked for will be realized. People will seek joy and I might come like someone with that certain smile and then understand my fragile existence.

A monstrosity in disguise — Johnny, Bing, and all those people who transformed me into a love monster, love overflows like nothing does. Like God.

Always a duality; what you like and what you don't. If you heed a call, then there will be a lost prayer wandering in the night. Darkness will devour prayers and light once again will shine as though darkness never existed. I am the day and when the night closes in, when the day obscures to night, I am again alone in my dreams.

Books can no longer be read. One can't say "I've finished" because it's time to write and not to read. The time for reading has passed. But then, we have to go back and read again.

There must be other people I care for. There must have been people I loved once. Resurrect! Whimpers and sighs can't answer the end of a day. Diaries must be burned and lights distracted from thoughts. Questions like "Who was he?" and prayers prayed as though prayers were never prayed before. "Put on the lights!" screams my alter persona but instead, the lights were put out.

Marie was beautiful. She was blonde. She had a baby. She was Cuban. She was wonderful. She must have eaten light; that was why she was so beautiful and shining. Her husband called her *maja* because she was beautiful.

Culture is foreboding. I have to see the world, a world of houses made of wood and bricks, an advanced world and not Spain, the last of the frontiers, an extension of Africa and not a part of Europe.

*August 26*

They felt the numbness I felt. A hungry night. A black dream. My life reunites with other lives. Withered, weak, saddened by a fruitless desire to do what all people do: pray. My prayer resounds like tears resound, intense like the sun. Imagine how I care: lacteal ways towards darkness; morbid, guilty, guilty of innocence, fragile innocence.

Time drags like glue. A painful touch of existence coveting painless agonies of life, my life, like no other lives I've had before, like a new life, a new agony, an endless agony, on and on, until nothing claims nothing.

Wind blows against the night. Tune of trumpets in the quiet streets. Silent murmur of darkness looking for light.

The phone will ring any moment now. The Pavlov dogs are ready. Waiting aches. Nights drag. Once, the coolness of a year waiting idly for turbulent terminations. Bells chime: a relentless release from self into eternity.

Again, there is a walk along lucid streets, against the bright and hateful sun breaking all barriers to reach you and fire your coldness away. It is bright and glaring like eternal stares that don't glow unless one is alive and disturbed. Moments, time, love calling love, love that blooms, love that waits for eternity to begin again, love hungering for infinity's meaning and eternal pleasure, love seeking absoluteness, love in all its absurdity and temporality. The search keeps on beginning like desire touching poetry with dying sighs, sighs reflecting the breath of death.

Everyday, a challenging day, life, books, relax now, then back to work, time to think now, then back to writing, ageless memories of humanity recalling time and redundancy. Cycles beginning and ending, beginning menacingly and then sudden defeat, sudden plunges into nothingness. Or being.

Sky clutches other skies; skies clutch lives. "Kingdome come" blooms with torment. The white dreaming gowns of newlyweds; time for waiting.

The phone rings. I don't answer. Someone sleeps with tears in his eyes. Someone hates and yet the hate is full of love. Embarrassment. |Spanish: bitter, proud, anguished about existence. Moods change. Hot days, bright hateful sun of summer. Breezes of nights, winds that bring whispers from one side of the world to the other. "I love you" whispers the wind. Yes, the wind brings empty words to my ear. The winds bring an answer to the boredom of waiting for this life to go on from second to second, from moment to moment, waiting, everything in life is waiting for the ultimate destination: death.

"Yes, we'll be happy." There was hope in her youthful eyes. She smiled and I loved her smile. I said, "Maybe there was a falling star and when you saw that star, you wished our love." She smiled.

*August 28*

Heat, helpless, unused to; nothing, just nothing can be done with this Madrilenian heat pouring heat over heat, heat over you. Life is now stagnant in Madrid. Nobody wants to move because of the heat. I feel stagnant.

Lost search: youth is still there. I jump from the past, my childhood, to now, my youth, to then the future, my old age. But let youth live on, I remember Mr. A. telling me that. And I dread old age, sour days, motionless moments, stupidity of complaints, nothing will make an old man happy (of and undeserved age scorning the emptiness of life's routine).

Where are all those that come with the touch of a new day? Where are all those that feel the emptiness of escape? I don't find concurrence; I look for it; I then sadly go by; I find time again, goodness searches for opportunity...look for yourself first among the myriad of the others. Many look for others finding themselves in others. Wild openness, daytime touching, a day, a touch, a newborn day, a newborn touch ridding old days, old memories, dawn till twilight, then night filtering towered stars in naked blackness; thoughts upon thoughts; likes upon likes; fishing towering stars with baits of love, craving towering nights, the nucleus of torn ornaments, ornaments of misbehaviour, ornaments of the nuclei of search, search unfounded, search that will never be found.

Mornings of unslept nights. Hanging windows of briefs and panties hung on laundry strings. Unshaped windows curl soft ugliness against the darkness of a midnight. Cold begins next month marking a year of my Spanish existence. Wind slapping Fate to my face; wind charging its Fate electricity.

The night is cold with half-winter arrivals. The night remembers me with sung songs of the past — the nakedness, the night, denuded fantasies; the car, lost love, the future, my destiny — destiny is a prayer to the gods who carve one's fate accordingly, who do what one asks them to do. The gods are kind to those who ask them in sweet sincere prayers a fateful destiny of flowers and sweet water from rivers; of unmelancholic dreams and of undisturbed nights; of an impure soul that makes humanity human; and of life un-delineated from a sister's dream

I want to see you when agony turns to ecstasy; when dreams pass from illusion to reality. I want to see you soft with your hair against the sky, the poetic sky that reaches for blue simplicity. Then the dream will come; separation will be lost, lost in the swinging afterthought, like the song of a canary. (When tears fall, sorrow wanes; waning sorrow is a tear un-cried.)

*August 29*

Bing was there like lightning, unexpected. Those moments returned like the coming breezes of winter. Winter would freeze the day, winter that comes, leaves, and then returns. I was because her name was Elena. It could have been Eulalia. The important thing was existence; she was not there because Elena thought of me. And Eulalia went on loving me, like the sun that shadows, like the moon's heat, like the day Toledo returns with winter.

When lightning strikes, the dead will resurrect; insanity will twilight into sanity; dawn will turn existence into non-being. The day will end falsely; people one again; the days, difficult with favours to be done; sanity, a battle-cry (I said that once).

And he was insane, that was the catch and I was caught — he went insane because his brother died (I said that too). He should not have mentioned it but just the same, it was there. It would have been better if I hadn't seen him. The whole thing complicated itself once again. "Strangers in the night" was the popular song; it was pitiful; it smelled like iodine.

"Hasta manana, Bing."

"Hasta manana." His soft sad voice. Here was a bum. Here were tears, full of sadness. There were just people who cared; there were just skies, the night and the sadness of tears. The song hums on (and the days again ends in night...when can days ever end in days?)

Sharp, very sharp. And Ceuta was with the sea in Cadiz. Cadiz and the gaditanos. Another subtle love affair.

"I'm good", I said. The night was sleepless, the laughter resounded once again. The bitter life, life that comes in parcels. Loneliness is the medicine. I was there where the bright lights were. My heart was weeping far away. My love was performed. I had to grow more and love will more and more drown me. The vaiven of sadness and happiness, nostalgia and madness. A sigh calls, the answer waivers. Youth, vigorous, needs me and I must return where love is impure because humans are only human; where tears and the sun and the cold satisfy each other. Language is short of words; speech calls; news spreads; glories of justification, listen to nothingness: a tangible nothingness, no hurry, wait, write. The brother was sincere. I wait and the tides will call.

*August 31*

The have forgotten the call of the tides. I walked and I felt the subtle emptiness of the day, wonderful day with the sun; and yet I could not understand that dull feeling I felt, that certain redundancy to life, that certain cry, that certain thought, that certain longing. It was a bright street, a street that cried with the sun. The last of the suns of summer shines; afterwards, autumn and the rain; then winter with the winds and the cold. Five days and then a disappearance into nothingness. Room number five: five years will pass by; someone has to wait for me; youth, a satisfying day. No one knows the goodness and the sincerity that cannot belong to this world. The inconsistency and the absurdity of it all. The call of the tides is strong.

I was holding electricity in my hand. A quick embrace with the past. Put the brakes on: the degree, God, changing, the whole world, a disguise. I don't know, simplicity, no one tells me what to do. A smiling call, a happy resounding call; words, human words, only humans can say words, words that rise and fall into impurities, profanities, blasphemies because we are impure, profane, blasphemous human beings, human, as the rain and the sun and the wet streets and the many persevering days, the same, yet changing days that understand the foolhardiness of being human.

Rivers will dry with the touch of snow, the touch of coolness perseveres and the heat will forever vanish as the sun vanishes into an unknown hemisphere in mid-winter.

I am human and I fall, I falter as all humans fall and falter, "and punishment will come to those who sin". Forget sin! Struggle without shame! Goodness, truth, and struggle...struggle is stronger, existence is existence, yes, existence for existence: to end all and to be all. Happiness comes later.

*Undated*

The chandeliers were broken. There was only one light on; the rest were broken. There was the summer heat. There were women with passionate eyes. But that was all. I could only look at them and they would only look back, wanting to make love but not knowing how, where to begin, breaking the ice; not knowing how desire is expressed in a hot, passionate night like this.

The man in red was lying down waiting for a kitchen where he could use his hands once again in his culinary trade. But no one satisfied him. Neither did he desire work that offered little to a man who claimed to be a chief cook.

I looked in illusion waiting for an answer in a hopeful prayer, waiting for a land that might answer all the hardships that dragged me into uselessness. The song still lingers: someday, somewhere, somehow, a new place of living. Memories linger.

The harmonica played a tune, a tune from South America. There was hunger there also, in the look of a child, the struggle of life, the same struggle like the passing of time, the passing of lost innocence.

I suffered because I waited for a day that would bring back lost passion, lost desire, fulfilment. There were only cries of innocence that shook me and made me tremble with the anguish of knowing that one day I would come back with a lost remembrance that remembers; a remembrance that irritates; the hot passion that freezes and makes me feel the touch of a lost heaven.

The man in red saw me. He looked at me and stared deep into my soul: there was a silent understanding between us. I shouted at him, I embarrassed him and yet, he continued loving me with that sadness in his eyes, unshed tears in his eyes and a memory rooted deep in his soul: tears of life and death in his anguished soul.

My silence, crying in whispers, sighing, whimpering, weeping for more memories, for persons who formed my life, twisting, moulding, painting my lifeless personality into a blossoming existence, giving birth to a dormant personality long in slumber.

But they no longer exist: only real people now, laughing, crying, talking of life — only they exist now; only these now try to feel the surging emptiness of my soul, my superficial soul seeking depth and fulfilment; my soul, empty with superficial laughter and dialogues of the day; and then, the monologue with God that seeks no answer but the silent murmur of life, life-forms — people clothed well, pearled earrings, blonde hair swaying against the wind, the stillness of undiscovered virginity, sensual passion, these Spanish women who smile and then look away. I stare at them and they stare back but I shy away…

Indifference, indifference. And life trembles with this same monotony, the same tune to boredom, the same playground of repeated truth and life and society and people. Yes, people. People who form life's core, selfish people, selfless people, indulgent, useless, cross-eyed, angry, sad, happy…

Once there were trees that were people. God's breath blew on them and they turned to people. But they became selfish, materialistic, like worms that eat the dead flesh of humans. Last night, a lack of foresight, foresight lost because of lost grace, sin that blackens and blinds humans from truth, the discontented inconsistency of humanity.

I must go to Barcelona to find an outlet to my despair, to satiate the terrible anguish of my existence; maybe the days would be brighter there, maybe not. But there will be a new hope because there is a new place to see, to feel, to touch; there will be new people to talk to, new impulses, new faces, and new streets.

I'm tired of Madrid and the people of Madrid looking for lost utopias. This inner corruption of society eating away at everything to the bone: heat against passion, rendezvous with each dying day, a hot, very hot penetrating heat; anguish, despair, frightening frustrations, painful separation of love from love itself, and the final settling down into hate and evil and goodness and joy.

Lost grace that blackens souls from God: an evening that silently calls youth in the night, fallen youth, fallen despair, and a whistle in the night, a lonely whistle. When goodness loses touch with the past, a futile competition with the present, ensued resentment, flighty freedom, away from it all, yes, escape. Escape from it all, another escape, and another. Then there will be no exit. All exits will be closed. Only an empty room with no doors, no windows, and aloneness.

Frivolity is emptiness, a continuous emptiness that eats you up, eats you inside, and it doesn't stop there. There is no stop to this gnawing, even in death, death is too good and this gnawing loneliness just foes on and on, eternally, where there is no death. Is this hell?

How painful life is despite its joys! Material joys, so fleeting, how painful and yet one never learns; yet you go on senselessly doing all that is good, goodness that never learns, unseen goodness, only done but misunderstood. So no one does good because no one really understands the meaning of giving until it hurts, giving until your bones ache with pain. No one understands; not even me. Even I who know still close my eyes and refuse to see; for prayers are lonely words, empty monologues with oneself.

Tomorrow is Sunday. Tomorrow, another unfilled day for me. The buildings will be the same. The beautiful women of Madrid will still stare at me, and I will again look away. And the men of Madrid will go on looking for something they don't understand. Men want sex, they want love. And marriage is so far away so distant as the northern star but there is no running away from marriage. It will come. It will seem to be the end of the road. But there are so many women to love first, many beautiful women, and only one to marry. Is this unfair? Isn't man polygamous? Life is unfair, life suffers, like winds suffer in autumn and the cold of winter. Seasons are faltering words — they come as time comes lost like orphans looking for playgrounds with swings and green grass and a kiosk that sells ice cream. But there are only streetcars and noisy cars in Madrid; yes, there are ice cream kiosks, but very expensive ice cream, ice cream too expensive for children. Because life is an excruciating process: children will have lost their childhood illusions of looking for the pot of gold at the end of the rainbow.

*September 5*

The day ends quietly. Only its dregs remain. Dregs of emptiness. Dregs of realized nothingness in forces of colours against the lustful heat of Madrid. Now, life's approach must be through tinted glasses. (The Saints were also sinners.)

I remember that futile night. The night club was like all the other night clubs of Madrid: prostitutes and lovers exhibiting. The night was noisy with "ye-ye" music, the smell of lust from the subtle looks of the women around wanting to be picked up, and an air conditioner that didn't air condition at all. Perhaps because the basement club was filled up with too many people. Saturday, that's why. And it was a hot night in Madrid, as summer nights are here. People were staring at each other, but I was staring at nothing. I felt that certain angst I felt when I was in Ceuta, and that emptiness from Ronda. All these forces invaded me. I felt slashed by these feelings, bitten by them as though by serpents.

But all of a sudden, a sense of ennui overwhelmed me. I yawned. My moods were changing abruptly. Suddenly I laughed. Then, silence. Darkness. The roar of music, taxis with taxi girls outside at the Plaza de Espana. A night that travels with provincial smells.

It was the road to Portugal that we took: west. There were six of us. The Spaniard, a member of the band in that club, a friend of Inday. Then there was Tessie, Purita, and Manolo. We stopped in a small restaurant. We talked about gangs and trouble and other things like killings and so forth in the Philippines; then we had some bocadillos de jamon: dry hard bread and old hard ham, bitter coffee, anis, all in the early morning. There were Segovians in the other table, singing emotionally like Andalusians and drinking Jerez, shouting "ole". Even in early morning festivities don't stop in Spain. Every hour of the day is a fiesta.

Manolo was five years younger than I. We talked about the hukbalahaps and gangsters and problems in the Philippines. Revolution? I don't think Filipinos are rebellious, I said. They're not like Latin Americans where revolution is a way of life. Filipinos are quieter. More patient, less revolting. He agreed.

Juego de la oca: a slight upjump into another topic, a theme, an experimental movie made by a vanguard group of Spain. And we talked and talked. (Once again, the day quickly turned to night.)

*Undated*

Barrio of Moncloa. This is the barrio where I stay. It is really hot here in the summer. Madrid is always hot in the summer. The university colegio mayors are closed in the summer, and so I have to stay in a pension. I've already transferred twice because the patronas get in your nerves. Imagine, being charged for taking a bath. That's how it is in Madrid during summer.

This barrio is situated close to the Ciudad universitaria. It's hot because all the pensiones are stuck together. Sometimes Madrid is fickle in the summer. Madrid is in a meseta and that's why the weather gets fickled. All of Castilla, like Salamanca or Valladolid. But in winter, the cold is terrible. The cold bites in all of Castilla.

The pension where I'm now staying is run by an elderly Latin American woman from Salvador. She's kind. Sometimes when there's no hot water in the bathroom, she gives me water she boils from the kitchen, unlike that asthmatic landlady in the last pension I stayed who charged me for hot showers.

My room has a nice terrace. Not bad for 50 pesetas a day. At any rate, the Colegio Mayor will open soon and I won't have any more problems. Even if the patronas are nice, you still feel uneasy because you have to sneak in quietly at nights if you come home late.

The sun was shining hot today. Funny how I now long for winter and the cold. Human nature. When it's hot, you want it cold, and vice versa. Never content.

The Salvadorenan woman was a grandmother. She had two grandchildren. As I saw them laugh and play, my memories took me back…

"Will we be together?" She looked at my left palm.
"Your life line curves and ends."
Do fortune tellers predict the future? You make plans, and life takes a curve. Like the meaninglessness of a hot summer day. The heat, like truth, only deeds talk. Then winter and the gloomy skies. (And life goes on with the fickle seasons of the year.)
A very senseless challenge: three years.

Manolo came looking for Ernie, but he was not in. We talk dreams, illusions. Too much love, no way of detecting cross-monologues with people, people who utter words, people who love, free spirits unleashed from materialism; selfless, civilized truth. Who are really civilized? Music: waltz beats, love-noise of music, the touch of a hand, the fervent experiment of love, lost, laughter, then tears.

No challenge. I desire the sea again despite the downtrodden feelings of Ceuta and Ronda, the loneliness of the sea, of the Tajo, uncertain destiny, this suffocating existence.

"We need to talk. We need to dialogue, to communicate, and the monologues with God."
"How about the god in you talking to the god in me?"
"Is it possible?"
"Anything is possible with God."

This night is neither silent nor dark. Heat intermingles with the fresh evening breezes in these last days of summer, days ending with the oncoming winds of autumn. Autumn that comes with yellow leaves, bright red leaves, lingering leaves from saddened trees. Nights swaying with warm, strong winds. Then, the willowing winter winds.

Snow awaiting. Days become shorter like lullabies dry against the moans of autumn rains.

*September 5*

Andy talked of so many things. He talked about the coming of the tides. I was restless afterwards and I did some yoga. Chicago was another chapter with Andy. Yesterday the sun was sober. I remember the Andalusian songs of early summer. Lovers' smiles as the benediction ceremony showed Christ as bread. I swallowed this bread while looking around for a man with a Jewish gown. He was nowhere in sight. I only saw people dressed in white shirts and pants as is the dress code of summer. Songs were sung incense smoke in the air — outside the fresh air of the night was happy because the world is happy tonight; the coolness comes softly.

Someone calls. A doubt in my mind. The cycle once again. Illusions once again. No real people in that uncertain future. Only disillusionment moving vaguely, fated by destiny. Destiny is the clue.

Days are passing fast now. I will sit again in classrooms and listen to philosophy lectures in Spanish. But I'll study it my way. My own unique way. I'll read books my way then write, observe, write again, learn my way, live my way. My way is not questioning life. Just accepting it calmly. Peacefully, despite its inconsistencies, because life is inconsistent. Defeatism, resignation — these are the solutions to life's inconsistencies. What else can be done?

Days will pass. Another year will pass. Writers like me will go on writing. Painters will go on growing their beards. People will continue drinking beer. Yet the world will seem silent with change.

Ceiling sounds in the night, inspiring sounds, like a child calling, or that distinct smell of a night that soars into eternity.

Spanish women were once beautiful with that restless disturbing kind of beauty, the whiteness of their Castilian skin, their light-coloured hair, their green eyes, and when my eyes touch theirs, I feel the mysteries of womanhood.

Now restless is gone. I feel rested. No more are restless words. God calms me as autumn approaches. That futile restlessness that once wracked my existence — my neck, my eyes, all of me. Dialogues cross my mind:

"Just do it. All of you depends on how you'd do it. People in your life — from childhood, then those awkward years, those women who found love in you — you had so much to offer."

"The trouble is you're too good. You exist too much to yourself that you forget yourself. You think of others but they don't think of you. That's what I always told you — that there are three kinds of people in this world: the maniacs, the perverts and the crazies. And you're crazy."

"People call me a fool. They say I'm stupid. Yes, even crazy. Never can they say that I didn't love. Nor that I'm bad. I love too much."

And love overflows....

That certain idleness, that certain mistake...the waiting and the painful agony once again. That unexplained order because all things have to come to an end as they did.

The sun begins its descent into the night. Twilight. Then another night, another day, tired, love, passion, strong...another country.... so many countries to see in Europe...hope/conflict/despair...another new conflict arising from the past, a narrated past jumping back and forth in dreams, hopes, dialogues, monologues, allness, intricacies, like JUEGO DE LA OCA, like a deluge (après moi, le deluge), a rush, like youth clinging to uncertainty, the uncertainty of forgiveness from God.

Explore scheduled time, a morrow of emptiness, that club called Pimpi with stunning waitresses waiting for smiles to initiate love-making, smiles that meant money and their living. The piropos flirting with attractive women, and outside my window, the piropo who gets slapped because of his insistency.

Around me, a green and yellow bed; straw chairs; lamplight; a blackboard of exercises; two flower portraits; a table dancing with originality; and of course, my typewriter beside my bottle of cognac, a Soberano Gonzalez-Byass.

I hitchhiked from Cadiz to Jerez, then Sevilla, a suffocating heat, those beautiful fountains, then the train ride from Sevilla with the atheist who searched for God and the absoluteness of individuality, and the priest...remembering them as the afternoon dies here in Madrid.

*September 7*

It was a disinterested signature. Words written before the signature expressing life in the past, the past that clings like a leech; and the future that stings with uncertain fire. The rest of the days are days preaching hypocrisies, fallacies, falsities, pretensions; days like bees that hive.

A novel is some kind of hope Hope like the innocence of infancy that bothers me; hope that comes like fire, fire with an unsteady flame flickering inconsistently; fire shifting clandestinely with the winds.

I want to write. I want to put my books away. A little child talks of freedom without knowing its meaning; freedom — wordless, fleeting...wait for the birth of a new idea; look for "possibilities", philosophers would say. I have to surrender my ideas in time because dreams are still dreams and thoughts are thoughts; because songs are still waiting to be sung in these 23 years and a half of my life, slowly passing away like tears dry and pass away to dry again, to say goodbye again, as it was seemingly a long time ago.

And then I reach home. Red is still red: neither friends nor lovers nor enemies; just a far-reaching out cry of love, of a despaired love, of a Virgin's birthday, of the hot winds of the day. The starting point of being human — when togetherness shifts to aloneness; when expression is solitude; when boredom reaches boredom. A weightless love affair.


*September 8*
*(No entry)*

*September 9*

The superficial wounds wind everlastingly like leaves bronzed against autumn oracles where prayers triumph with the winds, where sighs suspire, where poems only symbolize afterthoughts and dreams aspire for meaning and reality.

Dreams of a house with a blue tablecloth on the dining room table, a plastic existence, Greek letters of the glorious past, united in despair, yet conquering all, turning the tides into ashes foregone.

*September 10*

Ubiquitous whispers. A disturbed sleep. She sleeps on her side. She waits for the day that the blue prince will come along to take her with him to Fantasyland. She lives in a world of fantasy. But she waits.

Fate racks with life; fate brings back the dead and corrupts the living. Fate is destiny.

In the offing: grief, existence, ennui, illogicality, tedium. Seek an answer. Even the anxiety one feels…that sudden grip called demise. The break that ends all. Life ending bloodless, silent like ubiquitous whispers.

The new day, another blistering day coming to terms with the sun — a day of new loves, new-fangled straightforwardness, a daylight illuminating the evening's transparency, a sudden rush for words and then, absolute stillness. Meaningless, it seems. And you seek out exactness as days dwindle into twilights. You rest. There is that silent anguish of a lost day; then another silent anguish of another new day that will be perpetually lost as time sweeps by. And then eternity? Shall we be clinging to eternal branches? Eternal roots suspended in eternal space?

*September 11: Calle Donoso Cortes*

He walked with his eyes closed on a tightrope that was beginning to break. It breaks. He falls. God ex machine appears and saves him. But he dies. How can I feel the bothering heat of a summer night in September? How can I believe myself? How can I have proof of my faltering nature?

THERE WERE WORDS….

"Dear Toting, you're late. You should be here by now. I'm inside a bar full of people. I feel suffocated. I can't get out. I'm alone. People go by. Sera possible? Indeed it is."

"These Spaniards. They're all drunkards…son todos sin veguenzas y caras de dinero; la mayor'ia se pasa mas en el bar que en el despacho

LOVE, TRAVELS AND OTHER MEMOIRS OF A FILIPINO WRITER

y despues dicen que son muy cansados pero estan mas tiempo en en el bar y asi es Espana, que vergüenza! Desde luego, los mismos espanoles lo admiten."

"All they do is go to bars, drink beer and chat senselessly for three hours. They sit down, play dice. They are a public nuisance and top it all, they talk so loud that it makes your nerves tremble and for four pesetas, they ask lemon and other things just making the barman busy for nothing. |After they play their dice game come two hours of stupid gossip. Then comes lunch, and afterwards, siesta time. And the whole thing repeats itself day after day."

Nightmares. Afraid to close your eyes and fall into another nightmarish dream? Sleep is quiet but black. Black with remorse. Reality is full of colours. Damned cycle of existence! Days pass quickly.

You hear trumpets blow wild against distant horizons. You see figures wobble in the dark. And you walk an evening that is forgettable because it is an evening of apathy, of non-commitment. You go on walking along calle Donoso and you forget that this walk is meaningless. It's just a walk with no place to go. You just want to walk and feel lost, forgotten, timeless, uncomplicated, unattached.

Black dreams that gobble you overpoweringly, dreams that appear endless in their blackness — black that haunts with all the morbidity of screams emanating from nights of thunder and lightning, typhoons, mosquitoes and cicadas; the *aswang* and *kapre* and the frightful ghost stories of a childhood buried in the past; of demons and miracles and the fires of hell...

Now, only silence remains. The noises of the past are far away. Only a silence that awaits no one.

You remember Switzerland — the snow, the whiteness of the Alps in the distance, last winter. The remembered smell of snow enters your lungs. You remember your childhood in Kansas. You remember papers thrown about. There was a dried up hope, an unknown, unconscious something about that child who left with his parents and his sister aboard SS Wilson en route to San Francisco. Then that green "top down" Chevy my father bought, and that long drive to Leavenworth, Kansas.

Fifteen years later, with eyeglasses, he now departs with a sad smile for Europe aboard an airline with the letters SAS. He is on his way to Spain. The plane points to the sky like a big needle in oblique position. It seems to move in slow motion.

And months pass.

Do you remember the flies and the heat? Do you remember the winds and the not so barren plains of |Spain? You travelled and travelled. You saw the seas of Spain. You felt its seasons. You wanted something in Spain but Spain wandered with you, like a gypsy, away from the seas, towards the lands of La Mancha, the lands that called forth loneliness. Farmers were ploughing dry fields, lonely fields, lonely farmers waiting for the rains to parch their lips and their arid lands. Your eyed photographed these scenes and left them in memory. The pictures are getting vaguer because there are newer pictures in time. Time paints new pictures day be day, pictures that can be felt like the faces of the women you loved. Your mind is an attic, an attic of thoughts and memories. God too is in your mind even though he's worn out and almost forgotten. Adelaida was right. She said she saw two men in her nightmare. I told her they were God and I. But I was wrong. They were shadows of her mind. She was searching in vain. I told her I was searching more in vain.

"You were right. The surge would come strong. The surge is like a bee that stings and all of a sudden you swell and are infected. You feel that infection deep in your soul. Once I offered that infection to God and he didn't accept it."

"Why?"

"I don't know."

Then the dialogues dissipate into thin air and echo in memories.

"Your sorrow is the life you've had. I wish I could have been like you. People don't change. They are what they are from birth. I was born selfish and you were born selfless. I tried to change but I couldn't. It was impossible for me to change. I don't know why. I went to the deepest depths of depression asking God to change my selfish existence into a selfless one. But he refused just as he refused my offerings. He said I was born to be what I am: selfish, materialistic. You, you were born to be good and selfless. Heaven was made for you. For me, I don't know. Hell's mouth is ready to swallow me and burn me perpetually. But I go on hoping. Temptation is always there and I keep on falling. But I keep on asking the immaterial God to breathe grace into my soul so that I may be a little bit selfless, a little bit better so I could stand up once again and face life. Life disillusioned me with her bright lights and her selfishness. You never knew. You were too good to know. And I ran away many times because life forced me to run away. The ugliness of my being remains marked forever in my soul, an existence claiming death, life that patterns fate and destiny in all humans. Life is the ghost and the very shadow that silently moves within us. Our shadows do not frighten us, but they do others. Our shadows are the demons in us, the darkness in us. This is the infection that makes us sick; it is the bitter hopeless waiting for another day to pass, for the boredom that marks the senseless journey each one takes, an endless disillusionment, that certain emptiness that drives you into silence, a sick silence because there are demons that will torture you if you speak one word."
"What about prayer?"

"Prayer is a monologue. A soliloquy. You talk to yourself."
"They say prayer is talking to God."
"God doesn't exist."
"Why?"
"Because he is old-fashioned."
"What do you mean?"
"God, like people who believe in him, is outmoded. He was a tool used in olden times. Now he can no longer be used."
"You're not sincere with yourself."
"What is sincerity? Sincerity, like God, cannot exist. Sincerity, like God, is an ideal. An ideal does not exist, cannot exist. You talk of hope. That is another useless ideal that has no meaning. What exists is what we see now, what we say now, what we touch and taste. The other things are without meaning — values like goodness, faith, charity, etc. — all these are empty words that look for meaning in concrete things but unfortunately, they don't exist."
"Does it matter? I simply am myself existing; other existences that I perceive also exist. But words like love and God — yes I agree, empty words with no meaning."

The night is sweltering with that hot dry suffocating heat of Madrid. Imprisoned freedom, hot days, days gnawing painfully the insides of people, days burning their existence...prayers sympathize with the God who destines, the god who talks to other people on our behalf, the god who understands. This is the nature of hope.

Tonight I drag my body across lights then dark streets with other people walking in the heat. Earlier many had taken a bath in the waters of Puerta del Hierro; the others who didn't were used to the heat, the heat that helped their agony, their passion to love, to suffer. Lovers hand in hand teasing themselves in love. On the other side, just below the Arco del Triunfo, three men flirt at a woman, blonde, pretty, wearing a white dress. They seem to bother her. One of them just got slapped. Piropos they call these flirts here in Spain.

Far away I recall....

"It's as simple as that; and yet, the mind isn't that sharp."

"I just don't have order, that's why. I seem to want everything."

"Let's not go back to that. That was before. Now you have to change."

"You have to go on changing, transforming until you reach at least a little perfection."

"I just need a friend, a companion, that's all. Not someone who thinks of himself. Someone who cares and thinks of others; someone I can confide in. Just that."

The dogs now bark. The echoes resound in the big house. The silliness of a past, a sad, silly remembered past.

"I appreciate you. I really do."

No one can stop unsuspecting because life is that super-pitiful anguish that breeds poison. And we are victims, victims of soft voices, whispers that call names, your name, a reinforced existence of hoping and praying, of being bored by saints and spirits enjoying eternity and a god who rules. And then you wait again.

The days are perverted with a still, a very still kind of heat. The man in red is full of love; I, in brown, am full of uncertainty and indifference.

*September 21*

Another painful nostalgia: the rooster far away, the birds in mellow light singing their harsh morning whistles. (And Hernando, my roommate, snores.)

The day creeps slowly again. The autumn winds are still. The cold is preparing to descend.

Sin comes like God's moods. A letter will come, a letter with another whispering monologue. One year now; then two. And the monologues will go farther and farther into remoteness: the emptiness of a dead soul.

Smiling, love puffs in sighs. The streets smell of cooked olive oil; all around, there are sensual women — their lips, eyes, the imaginary touch of their soft hands, the intense warmth of their presence in these streets where I walk. Now, Spanish lovers holding love in the fixed search in their eyes, in their smiles; their embrace and the subtle touch of their bodies; the quietness in the surging palpitation of their hearts; the woman, with that expectant intensity of her *noviazgo*; and the man, with that certain inflating desire to kiss her breasts and the mysterious pubis that marriage will entitle him to. Marriage, the key to sexual freedom.

Nearby, a married woman; her husband is away. But her nights are not lonely because she has a lover.

Love searches for itself; love searches in the wilderness of time only to experiment the taste of life's curiosity.

The morning sadness of a day. I was just envious of the innocence of Andres, that's why.

The night is cold. It's the autumn announcing its arrival. I try to return where peace is; peace in the silence of the night and in the painful awakening of another disturbed day; peace, war, the sweet embrace of sad and happy; the sweet melancholy charms of afterthoughts, the irritation of having a thought of weakness. If she had a little more of that courage. And no one knows what might have become of me. And yet, it would not have been possible. It just could not happen. Things just happen, like the intensity of God. Maybe a simple sincere smile would do; or perhaps a desperate clutching of fists towards heaven.

No one can tell; no one will know. From spirit to matter. That jump, that subtle jump, those bothering moments of limitation. I did not say goodbye. How can God be with her? God wants to but she refuses. Remember Rita? Like the one in Baclaran. There God says: EL MAJESTAD ESTA AQUI. TE LLAMA. A call to me because I'm a sinner and I want him in me to purify me.

She had many inconsistencies. But I loved her. And I overlooked her faults because I loved her. And then I went away.

A farce; another day, another growing up, perpetually growing.

*September 22*

Another night finishing another day. Another disturbed night, night that invites passion, night that searches passion. And passion is fulfilled; a bitter sadness follows, a remorse that comes like black against white. Unfinished days, unlashed times, malnutrition — I'm not eating enough; infinity and the passing of time; not very immediate; people, people I come in contact with; they become me. Then books, music…how that Spanish girl, daughter of a Spanish air force General? She was petite, a brunette, and pretty. She liked you but you preferred the green-eyed blonde, as you walked in front of the Air Force Ministry in Moncloa. "Ye-ye" music they call it; so backward. Spain is 10 years behind the modern world.

A unique shift to convention — time reverts. I observe, I, the observer, begin to write about this reversal of time; I continue narrating the ugliness, the nostalgia, the happiness of a repeated past, repeating like the married woman and her lover, the complicated uncrowned fires yet al, all in the mind, reality touching the fourth dimension of the mind.

Consequences like words that are only words, the struggle of words and thoughts, or the Jesuit priest who said " It is difficult to be bad because God loves you so much that he makes evil so remote although he permits it to happen." Is that the secret of love? True love?

Oh, how I tire of existence! Let others speak out! I want to be silent now like the stillness of an autumn wind that is preparing to invade Madrid. Unawakened children like death of unpalpitating hearts; the memory of blindness without needing to be blind; summer and the waiting winter.

I hear a call, an unheard call. See, touch songs, see the crooked lines, lines new and old, the old in the young, a conventional doubt, a unique suspicion.

Society of good people, can you contaminate the evil ones? The touch of love in spring, did you say? Only in words not in deeds. Only in intention. Never boredom because of sadness. The ups and downs of joy and sadness, a constant vaiven.

The blueness of time, the blueness of innocence, short phrases of today, of people, of the blue, of the sky, here to write a poem once again, a poem for you; then the same degree, the same people, they'll have to hope again, like a new day with whiffs of smoke on the streets, and yet, this is sunny Spain where streets and impressions talk of absurdity; yes, impressions — life, ecstasy, the feeling of unevenness, the streets, the cars, the moods, the people, the trams, another day, and another, waiting, just like Beckett waited for God, an awakening, and what about the hope for the motherland or fatherland?

Vague intimacies of innocence lost. A desperate jump in search of lost innocence. Of a lost childhood. I feel strange again. I am always different. Each day I assimilate a new personality. I see my face changing from day to day, my body metamorphosizes, but mostly, my character, an indescribable newness in me.

Evening will come again. Another day. Another night. Fast passing days. Spain is growing on me.

*Undated*

An attraction, times coming, times ending, scream tent preachers, fire and brimstone, tides, the rush, they always come to haunt me, time tides, they come again and again. Agony, these time tides. Long ago, the waves, the attraction to those sea waves, ebb tides forming spumes of love; memories created and recreated. Now the winds do not blow strong. Madrid — a hot windless afternoon; sun against the walls. (Nino en rojo. Antonio es el nino en rojo.)

*Undated*

Poems that feel affection for hope and the savage torments of life, inclining moments falling like outlets of saturating remorse. Incredible cruelties of innocence, innocence, innocence that comes sturdy in childhood. Then, the vicissitudes: a black cat, the blackness of a soul, the black soul of angst. The subtlety of the past, overture pains, joys of deeds against deeds. Afterwards, the smell of dead victims against life's deaths: no answer; just a fleeting torment, a putrefied existence. Life: brilliant shades of being.

*September 26*

Day arriving, thinking the night ended the world but my eyes opened to witness the brightness of another day in Madrid. Frightened hours, lonely with the days ahead of you, youthful days, moments fearful of time.

A free resistance. Hungering days are over. Madrid, clouded again. The hot, glaring Andalusian vacations, so hot, have passed with the cool autumn then the cold triumph of passing seasons from balmy to wintry.

Another vague image, a season when birds fly south, then the sadness of Spring when they return; the repelling cold love of winter, a different kind of affection.

The concrete commensuration of time; yet even this will pass to allow the abstractness of existence to come in. Perhaps the rough days of sad life passing then into happiness, then anguish, the anguish of afterthoughts, that existential anguish of days passing painfully into nights. Of the drunken happy hours to relieve the transitional pain to twilight. Like love flying away and never returning, only hope through beautiful thoughts, a sudden rush of hope that life is after all still beautiful because you can experiment and feel the way that others feel, others who have longed for happiness too, a happiness that in this material world we too can laugh, laugh at the many absurd and silly things of life, and this opens up new possibilities to hope and optimism, from sharp pains to ecstatic joy, from dullness to brightness, glory and vision. (De los triunfos a pesar de las derrotas inolvidables.)

*Undated*

The meaning of destiny. Life turns slowly, sadly to the meaning of inadequacy staring you straight in the eye. I now feel everything converging on me; this whole summer, the misery of it all, the loneliness in Sevilla, the touch of the sand in Cadiz, the heat of Ronda, the sea of Malaga, the fog in Ceuta…where are the characters of my novel? My aunts and uncles from Andalusia tying up relations with my exiled grandfather? I've failed. I'm like a child recalling dreams, undisciplined dreams of written whispers and scattered insights. It's excruciating repeating thoughts and feelings of bitterness, loneliness, visceral words I exploit because I live alone here, alienated, in an insignificant spot somewhere between Europe and Africa, somewhere in this space containing my existence projecting spaceless thoughts in search.

I do walk like a somnambulist escaping from existence, aching existence, escaping from words and phrases I write.

Another summer ends. A summer of words, of memories, of flights into nothingness.

A senseless summer, a vain search. I have not yet discovered my soul. Somehow, my soul still drifts somewhere I know not where.

# CHAPTER 9

*November 9, 2 a.m.*

Eight votes because there were eight years waiting for me. Suddenly I felt the tragic urge to write this inconspicuous entry because the bathroom faucet was on and I heard people talking in the adjoining room. I wasn't feeling sleepy but I had no urge whatsoever to get up. But I forced myself even if I didn't want to. I feel a disturbing pain which happened when I saw a movie entitled OSCAR, a film about a Hollywood Oscar winner. I don't know why but I was bothered by this movie.

The night/early morning is a bit cold. There is a crack of cold air entering through my balcony which five other colegiales share. Quite a huge balcony.

I'm thinking of going to Paris again in January. A special trip there organized by the Colegio Mayor. I also have plans of publishing my first book of poems.

That disgusting pain still bothers me, perhaps because of winter.

There are aspirations, future ventures I want to accomplish. All of a sudden, the lethargy of summer transforms itself into restless activities of winter. I want to do so much now — travel, publish, write plays, essays, travel to Russia, Germany and England; wild, restless ventures, reaching for the heights, releasing myself from imprisoned summer, towards limitless activities — sing, dance, express myself totally.

I now remember Vilma, my Puerto Rican classmate in History of Philosophy at the University of Madrid. She helped me in a lot of things. She typed and gave me a copy of my play correcting all the errors. I wonder where she is now. She even left me a chapter, no, not even that, the first page of the first chapter of a story or a novel she was writing. CLIMAX was the proposed title, but she stopped. She didn't bother to continue. I don't know why.

Today I received a letter from my sister. She sent me an outline of her foot. She wants me to buy her sandals. But where the hell can I buy sandals in winter?

I also thought of Agnes. I'll call her. Maybe next week. By next week, I'll have forgotten the reminders of this week. Last week, I did a crazy thing. I had the stark impulse to go to Malaga again. And I did. I left without telling anyone. Everyone looked for me and wondered where the hell I disappeared to.

*November 11*

PORTE GRATUITO TELEGRAMA CENTRALIDA SR DIRECTOR AV SENECA COL GUADALUPE 15/6 46025 MADRID MALAGA AD 67 6 1130 SU TELEGRAMA NUM 1006 MADRED DE DIOS 8 NO ENTREGADO DESTINARIO DESCONOCIDO

That was how the blue crumpled piece of paper read. I was supposed to receive that telegram in Malaga but I had already left for Madrid, and no one in Madre de Dios 8 knew who I was; so the telegram was returned. I crumpled it and threw it away.

I woke up undecided today. Undecided because I wasn't sure whether I wanted to go to the ambassador's party. I have to paint now and rest. It's here where I can rest and see blue snow piling in the peak of the Cordillera far away, blue like a painting against the sky. That soft misty snow way out there. And here, just the smell of burnt leaves floating in the afternoon. In the west, the bright Spanish sun settling lazily— a young sun, flaming, almost like a painting in red and a mixture of other extracts of red like purple, orange and yellow. A bright afternoon with autumn leaves, quite still on a windless day, except for a slight breeze or two moving silhouettes against a blue sky. Birds now nesting on rooftops preparing for the cold gloomy winter.

This university city where cars silently pass by and occasionally, trucks roar by climbing the not too steep Calle Seneca where breezes are fresh from northern winds and the sun warm in autumn afternoons; where songs, bird songs, are heard from autumn birds delightfully preparing their nests for winter, and when leaves fall swiftly now, falling silently to hibernate.

The shadow of my face is black against the sunlit wall. The afternoon now groans slowly, slowly dying as bitter winds now from the north blow in autumn's passage. My shadow now drifts to my room as the sun descends. It feels me staring at it in envy, envious of the warmth of my room. And yet I feel its limitedness. Must I suffer sitting in this cold limitless balcony in the company of nature — the sun, the sky, the mountains, the trees, the breezes blowing against yellow leaves and my hair — or shall I retreat to the warmth of my claustrophobic room? Yes, I must suffer here to witness the dying glare of the afternoon sun and the blue-green trees awaiting twilight.

The sun now sinks slowly and solidly in the horizon, a slow melancholy descent, as I too turn melancholy remembering painfully the cold winds that blew like these in my first autumn here in Madrid, a burning coldness glaring like autumn as the sun slowly died diffusing itself with the smell of burnt autumn leaves, a memory freezing the tips of my fingers with the cold, a creeping cold against this typing machine I'm pounding on as the afternoon fades with the misty vagueness of lost time.

*Barcelona, December 25*

Remembering the cold rainy streets a year ago… to say Feliz Navidad — a ticket, a woman in red, a blonde, a sympathetic blonde. There are all sorts. Barcelona laughs with me as Eugene Ionesco converts the world into a world of animals, of breathing and thinking animals. And I'll go on laughing. Am I inspired this Christmas day? Barcelona, the lights, Franz Kafka, Man and Woman, all dreams, coloured dreams, experiments of life.

The Latin Americans here seem all alike — they shout, they laugh — but tonight it's Christmas and they mustn't laugh and specks of reminiscences are lost, whitely and purely. An attachment on the wall of the guest room reads: "I loved you in those cold humid nights. I can paint them with my coloured tears — blue against green — and once again I look for meaning in those yellow shades, in blood-red dripping from the past, slowly fading where other colours are, flat in black, stationless, dry like brown blood yet red in essence, perpetually red with wounded pain, a bitter pain."

Voices that accompany black, solid strokes and scratches; sleepy and tired night; a cold, a cough, an answer to end pain. A paint brush that strokes black despair; and red again, now a dark red, the colour of dark blood, of a dark nostalgia, painful, past nostalgia. Undulating in blue, water colors in abstraction like red Chinese calligraphy forming and destroying like the paradox of painful joy because of its temporariness, a sudden jerk from love to hate, distantly near.

Aloneness, only aloneness in search of temporary alleviation. Was it Destiny again? The painful rush of doors — a change, a mere change only to find little, very little meaning to my life. And yet, the vagueness only widens the gap, the incompleteness, those very slow perceptions. I can only perceive part of the meaning through smiles and words, but I don't see the entire picture. Like memories, they disappear in time and are taken over by new memories that follow and replace old ones. Or personalities that change and yet claim to be human, human nature in its instability, human urges of human nature, human hopes, intentions, frustrations. True-to-life stories that appear like illusions on celluloid, then frustrations which once again disappear only to breathe again new life, then breathe away old life.

Those trees — the colours — black is lost as red pushes me on in my restlessness, remorse, passion…shades, shades of yellow, very yellow shades, the night and the yellow stars, a hard cough, poems that lose themselves and later rediscover themselves in God: the abstract blueness of my life; the drums, the fears, the inspiration, youth, novel events, a song, a French song, a wide avenue, or a guitar played by a woman wasting love, love on all colours, loving all without care, burning violet, rainbows of despair…

I wake up. This place reminds me of that haggard-looking pension in Calle San Bernardo where I stayed last summer, in Madrid — the smell of antiquity, an ugly table, a disgusting room. But I like the director of this colegio mayor. He's a kindly man. It is here where I need to escape from Madrid for a while. "Son muy cerradas las catalanas", the latinos would say, and they go on to talk about "las extranjeras en verano….el amor libre….como es aqui en Europa". They don't consider Spain part of Europe. "Es una entidad completamente diferente al resto de Europa".

I've read enough of Ionesco and Kafka. I met this skinny Peruvian student who asked me if I wanted to go with him to a whorehouse. He said it was 1500 pesetas. I told him I didn't have the money and said I'll pass.

I went instead to see a new movie, A Man and a Woman, an art film in black and white turning to colors. I liked the song. The story was sentimental. Sufferings of modern man. Zorba the Greek, Fellini — all these movies interested me with their absurdity and human suffering.

I met Luna, a Spanish student, from Melilla, a Spanish city somewhere in the coast of North Africa. She liked to sing — her hoarse, raspy voice typical among Andalusians. It's strange how she sang well in English. She sang negro songs from New Orleans, the blues. Her breasts heaved high against the guitar and I almost felt her close to me.

*December 26*

Barcelona and her festive lights in red and white, passion and purity. A sleepless night of colours and frustrated dreams. It was a tired night, a drunken night, silent communication as I wasn't one of the Latinos.

*December 27*

A bad day, wet, dirty, cloudy. Black and white dream last night. I heard my lover calling me. I saw her and then she vanished.

Dreams grow on you.

The Peruvian asked me to come with him. He said "let's go to this joint. It's not too expensive." So I went. It was 8 pm and all of a sudden a nausea invaded me and I decided not to go with him. But I said I'll wait for him in the anteroom while he's with his whore and then we could go for beer, somewhere in the Ramblas. The wall to the room was so thin that I could hear the whore singing "Yellow Submarine" as she was doing it with the Peruvian.

119

He got out of the room around 9 and we went to the beer house where he talked about politics since he was majoring in this field, about the rich getting richer, and the poor getting poorer, the same song sung in all third world countries. I told him about my summer in southern Spain and how I tried my luck hitchhiking from Cadiz, and I only got as far as Jerez, 30 kilometers away and I ended up taking the train back to Madrid. That was my first and last time hitchhiking, I told him.

Ramblas, smelling of funeral flowers, dark streets where whorehouses hide intrigues, muffled laughs, kisses that can be heard clearly in the night, the touch of woman feeling man.

*December 28*

*Dia de los inocentes.* This is the Spanish equivalent of April Fool's Day. I met a Japanese student who effusively apologized to me for what his father and those of his father's generation did during the war. I said it wasn't his fault and not to worry about it. He went on to talk about Zen Buddhism and taught me a sitting position in yoga. He showed me how to stand on my head. I tried and now my neck hurts. I guess it got stiff. I then left the colegio to look for the sea here in Barcelona. Luna invited me to go with her.

*December 29*

Tomorrow I return to Madrid. The night is cold. I hear drums. I see people. Faceless people. My anguish is the anguish of stars that twinkle and never lose themselves. Then I'll have new memories, brief memories of Barcelona where I came to rest but did I rest? I'm even more restless now.

*December 30*

I am in Tibidabo. My soul shouts from atop this mountain overlooking Barcelona and the Costa Brava. Here, near the skies, I have the urge to cry happily. The forces come. I am dragged into esoteric ecstasy. I swim in a flood of poems. I smile and feel a happy anguish envelope me. The forces let loose from me, forces that say adieu, of hope and a revelation of awareness.

*December 31*

In this train ride to Madrid, I don't know why all of a sudden I feel a heaviness in my soul as I stare at distant lights, green lights, white lights that open the night. Distant lights that smell of Madrid. It's 9 pm and I've been travelling for 12 hours.

I travelled longer last spring, during Holy Week, 22 hours from Valencia to Malaga in a 3rd class coach. There were five of us cramped on one long seat. What penance! Leaving 8 in the evening and arriving 6 the next evening. I've learned my lesson the hard way — not to travel any more by third class especially for long trips like this. I was a zombie when I arrived in Malaga. A talgo just passed by. That's a king of a turbo-jet train, the fastest train in Spain.

Rapido this Barcelona-Madrid train is called. But it's not rapido or express; it still stops in different places and never arrives on schedule. It stops again. I hope this is the last one before arriving in Madrid. But I don't see the yellow lights that tell me we're close to Madrid.

It's 9.15. I feel butterflies in my stomach. The conductor announces that the next stop is Madrid. I wonder how everyone is in Madrid. I wonder if I have letters. I hope I have lots. Dad and Mom. I always feel giddy whenever I go back to the Colegio after being away for more than a week, as though something bad was going to happen, as though feeling guilty for going away.

Gosh, am I nervous for no reason at all! All I can reminisce now is the snow in Kansas when I was 7. I remember learning how to read. I was in Grade 1. I felt nervous and tense. Where is the phone number of Agnes? I feel so at ease when I'm with Agnes. I go out with her and also Becky. I remember their visiting me at the Colegio and we'd go out.

There's this poster in front of me that reads "Burgos". I was focusing on it and I all of a sudden felt as though I were there in the plaza of the city. The picture looks so real, the street so vivid, a small castle in the distance. Shucks! Is this Zen Satori invading my mind?

Almost in Madrid. The last stop was Alcala de Henares. Another fast talgo just zoomed by. These tafas and teras and talgos go by like jets!

9.25 pm. It's suppertime in the colegio. Those first few days with Rudy in Madrid. All that homesickness and mixed feelings of wanting to go home…

Better start packing. A few more minutes. Then I'll be counting the minutes to midnight and eating the customary 12 grapes.

*January 29, 1967*

I slept well, and I felt an insipid happiness when I woke up. Something vapid was floating within me, something between happy and sad. I just felt it was there. Turn down happy invitations, concentrate on happy friendships, project absurd thoughts, jumping into nonchalant imagination…these filled my emptiness.

It isn't enough to be practical; the normal progress of life bequeaths shame and despair and the zip code is suicide. Now where in heaven's name did that come from? Another absurdity, like life. Freedom — is this an outmoded word?

No one heeds anyone's call anymore. Sentences rattle away ungrammatically, their meanings lost with the lack of communication, lack of reality, and finally, the world comes to an absurd vicious circle of who's who beating the hell out of verve, a steeple, high up to nowhere, a temporary inoculation of chance, the heedless call of God, litanies formed from old lips castrated by time like old structures crumbling by themselves — moderation, continence, tedium, the whole lot, every concrete reality of space and time, in space and time, floating to nowhere, and I am barely an ineffective, talkative little speck in this vast immense of evolution.

Why these vague interpretations, these melancholy escapes, these drifting pleasures that make me rattle words that are supposedly sensible and sincere and yet slowly swallowed by the forgetfulness of passing time? Is this a way of saying yes or a hesitant I don't know? Shy smiles, nervous laughs, consistencies and inconsistencies that take deep root in a human being…once again, that sudden flashback of nostalgia, that certain wistful repetition of youth in dreamlike states, in frustrated projections of an unknown future, of imaginations that tickle…

She was in blue, very pretty, very in a hurry. Is someone waiting for her? I smile. A false smile. Where is sincerity? It's lost in ethereal eternity where no one treads.

The wine made me feel sleepy. I wanted to recall a lost dream, a conversation that brings an atmosphere of temporary relief (oh, ennui!), words clotting memories easily forgotten — the Metro, the concert, Ruben Dario and his corny poem, another slight smile, the disco Stones, the subtle touch of her hand, her hand that lacked sensuality. Another night, another day, another search for moderation.

*February 5*

123

A letter. A dilemma. Studies. Shall I continue with philosophy and wrack my brains, or take it easy and study Spanish Literature? Do I lack the determination for this long ride of studies in philosophy? I'm at that indecisive stage… Rebellion, is that why? Or just being wishy-washy? A coward's rebellion of many personalities, of discontentment, of having to do one thing at a time…

The smell of my room was Carmen in disguise. Her eyes raged with that chestnut glow of Spanish sensuality; fire in her moist lips. The room was just an empty room. She just wanted to have fun, that's all. To live and be ignorant of love, to just let it flow without looking for any meaning behind relationships, to merely be emotional and impulsive because she tells me that love only complicates. A preposterous love affair.

The champagne was now getting warm. I kiss her but it is she who kisses me. I am tired all of a sudden. My groins ache. My lips now search hers…

The whole affair was senseless and empty. And yet I felt no pity, no affection, no love. I just felt embarrassed and prostituted. What is purity? The priests make a big fuss about the purity of your soul. Purity! Another coin word that flows meaninglessly. Why did it have sense once? My prayers, that's why. Prayers that were vulgar aspirations. Prayers which rotted because I drifted, I, the give and take loafer drifting. Pride, narcissism — they ate me up. I had no way of communicating any longer. I was tired and disturbed. Nothing more than a concussion of the mind against who I am. Now, even insects crawl all over my impassioned self to remind me of my decay and damnation.

Times when artists themselves interpret their work of art — yes, thirteen will drift in bad times.

The sound of voices increase in intensity, voices that describe my sins. And I only feel more emptiness as I watch the hard features of the day looking at me and answering sadly my calls.

There is a ghost that dulls my chest. I tremble, I light a cigarette, and it burns my face. My cheeks ache now with the cold; my eyes hurt with the smoke; now my stomach aches, a painful thud. And my hands are cold. 3.30 am. What the hell am I doing, up at this hour? I suddenly tremble and ask myself where my Jerusalem rosary is. Is it lost in black eternity, in the night, in the dawn, in this cold winter? I am afraid. I might see the ghost that haunts and makes me tremble. I hurriedly look for my existence. An anguished solitude. A still night. No, I'm merely looking for an excuse, an excuse for my existence. My tears flow with the rain, my warm salty tears against the cold, fresh rain. My rosary is definitely lost in eternity.

A metamorphosis. Tomorrow and tomorrow and tomorrow. Only an emptiness; the prayers have flown away, and I am dull and empty. Wintry winds. A pipe, my pipe waiting in that little dark corner waiting to be smoked. It calls me in its solitude. I hear the roar of early morning trucks. More painful wounds in my soul. And muscle pains. Wounds that might heal in time. I smoke and my stomach aches more. A dizziness, nausea. They observed you, Dittborn; they hated you. You were an animal to them. My mother, your mother…loneliness… Madre solo hay una.

Days where yonder clouds call vagueness and mistiness…

*Undated*

The phone rang. You were not there. What is this pain called love? The questions are stereotyped, and yet, this Saturday night, I kissed my past with a whisper. I have lost touch of time and of God. I only eat and sleep now. Five more months to eat and sleep. Then maybe time will rule; maybe Fate. I don't know where fate will lead me.

Forever, she said. What does forever mean? Saturday night hates me like this blind sun hates me; like an unkempt balcony, no, it can no longer be perfect. There are no more falling stars. Why should I be ugly? You came quite too late. I was already in love. All the answers were no. The results are now out: I, a scholar, a shadowy scholar.

The clouds have missed Siberia. A short remembrance, a locked door; my twisted self justifying its own selfless conflict. Or must selfless be selfish? Like clouds cooling down the sun. Where is this perfect state of affairs? Heaven? A failure. Life is a failure because it ends with death.

*May 21*

The day is…

Must I capture you with my originality? Perhaps. But I have to go. There will be other princesses.

Does it matter? I'll be free at last. There where I can establish myself. Butterfly, when are you going to bloom? Love is not all.

My time has not yet come. Happy days have not yet come. Spring is already here. And you're waiting. Are you waiting for me? Love stories don't just end happily. Love is tragic. Shall I repeat clichés? All right: True love is never smooth, love hurts, etc.

Well, I have to keep up to date. Other women? Just a matter of having friends. And prayers. Christian prayers. Can they do a lot? For a reckless life, for people like me who smile and never stop smiling, idiotic smiles, well, I won't be around anymore. I am surrounded by unexpected dreams, by friends who dominate me, whom I dominate… friends are, after all, sad dreams that pass.

Is it time again for youth to spring in Spring? I want to bloom but no one blooms with me. My friend Rapela died last year. Why did he die? Because God needed him to play the drums in heaven, and Rapela is playing in heaven when storms come, when thunders drum their booms all over earth.

She won't call me anymore. She won't. I don't want her to call me anymore because she does not understand my eternity. She does not understand...love? Perhaps my soul is dead; that's why I can't progress anymore.

I don't need manicures, or did you just want to touch my hands? Happiness, slight happiness, you don't have to know what love is.

When this afternoon is warm, when this secret day knows my state, when I feel human weakness, when day is done, again...it will pass, like I will pass, like I will know, like you will know, that friends are like prayers that repeat tragically in dialogues that mean nothing in Spring, in Spring, insignificant Spring...but who will know? No one will know. No one.

*Undated*

I write badly sometimes. The priest asked me if I was in love. I said no. I told him I'm tired of loving. But you can't help love, he said. It comes, it goes, and you miss the one you love. Time then begins to take its place. I was punished, severely punished with pauses, too many pauses in life.

Spanish red and yellow colors abuse me this Sunday. They talk: "Give yourself to me. I know you'll do it. Must I take you for granted? Must I? No answer. There are no more answers. Experiment with life. Go and fly somewhere. Then come back. Refresh yourself. Forgive. Forget. Leave it at that. Leave it at that."

"Consider judging yourself. "

"But I'm running from myself. How could it be possible?"

"Think."

"I go crazy thinking."

"God is insane He created you."

"I also create."

"God died for you."

"Baloney! Big joke!"

"For love. They say for love."

"Sentimental, like Readers' Digest, according to Marianita."

"I feel guilty. I blame myself. I feel this moment like other men who felt and wrote."

"Yellow and black. Big ass!"

"Admiration, where will it bring you? "

"To conformity, I suppose."

"Throw your weight around. Throw it. No one cares anyway. You make your own absurdity. No one understands profoundness."

"Is your mueca still there buffeting the seas? I'll return, perhaps."

"I guess you're too busy. Too busy. Just be alone. You don't need people. Don't depend on people. They reek of life. "

"I must see myself pale and calm experimenting with life."

"I know but I have to live."

"What does it matter?"

"But I have to live…to suffer. I want no one to call me and yet I need to talk to someone."

"They're human after all."

"I've been losing myself in glaring poetry."

"What does it matter now, spoiled tomato, what does it matter now?"

"I steal, I lie, I laugh, I drift. I care, do I? I feel bitter. Very bitter. Sad, very sad. Now, can it all matter?"

Compose the decomposed. This is the vitality of life. Loopholes. Actually, I don't care and yet I do. If he's alone, he must be confused.

Don't say "lousy", Hooker, Jerry Lewis Hooker used to say in my high school days.

Chance worked on me. I cannot rebel against chance. I'm religious, after all. I do not refuse to see, after all. Man: foolish, absurd, silly. You understand the silence of this day. Silence speaks stronger…

Absurd people. Absurdity is life's meaning. God is absurd, after all. He is absurd because he creates absurdity. Quid pro quo. Man, the monster, destroying creation, making metal, distinguish, creator, distinguish — create from nothing and make from something, the Jesuits taught me that. I smile, after all. And no one understands.

Alone, you must be alone. Alone, convinced of life, of old age, Spain, here and now, the hours flow, I feel absurd like your passing, temporary moments in this sojourn, time, pass, time, pass…

Make a big fuss. I am pale, like this cold, Spring is pale. When will my transformation take place? When my hair flows with the wind? When? When Spring is sad? When I am sad? When my childish dreams come back to me? Why be particular? I belong where rebels belong. Who can remember now the fire of this man? Hopeless individual! Incarnated by life itself! Fondo negro. Profoundness.

Write, write! Then tell me I belong to you. Not only for the first time but the second and third times. That face had hope. I whistled. You are never always happy, nor ever always sad. There are breaks in life called hopes.

# CHAPTER 10

*Montreal. December 24, 1967*

Because you don't want to belong; because you don't need this kind of existence. Then let's just say: help me, pride, again…love… is in the mind.

Volkswagen 1957 for sale. Broken glass window, unclean, doesn't run more than 2o mph; two flat tires, radio works sometimes.

What about that discotheque with wrecked cars? CRASH, it was appropriately called.

People with white makeup, people who blow up, people who dialogue or monologue and people who say Spanish words in pantomime.

But let's talk about you. Shall I call you friend, or love, or just… nothing? No, not yet. Let me first indulge myself in this greasy day; well, there is some frost in my window, and my brother just coughed and is now snoring again. I had gone to the sala earlier to try to sleep there but I couldn't because of the drip-drip sound from the kitchen faucet.

I don't know what to do. I'm not sleepy. I'll just take it easy and let things flow, let time pass, sleepless, until I feel sleepy.

The family is together again. How sweet! But for only two weeks. It's not yet time for midnight mass. What happened to the paintings? Lost? Stolen? I hear the Supremes being played in the living room, the voices of my brothers, all three are there; I hear my father's voice now. My sister's in her room; mom's in the kitchen preparing for our traditional nochebuena and the customary cena de medianoche. Muy ibero. And now I think I hear church bells; it's around 10 degrees Fahrenheit, and a couple or more hours ago, we were in a Chinese restaurant for dinner with really good food, but the waiter was a sin verguenza.

My first Christmas with my family after two years. And in Canada, what a coincidence. Or fate. Another mystery. Paris in 1965 was lonely; Barcelona in 1966 was noisy; now, I don't know whether to feel happy or not. I suppose I should. I'm with family again. And next year? Who knows?

Well, let's look at this room now. Small but comfortable with a closet lacking hangers; and yet I have a thousand in Edmonton. I have my brown bag, a crazy brown bag that slips in and out...an unconventional brown bag.

*December 25*

How many times must I say Merry Christmas? Perpetually, Christmas everyday, more Christmas cards. Remembered dialogues....

"I'm afraid because you're so like me."
"Love exists but it flies away."
"You still haven't loved. You don't know."
"Is love in the mind?"
"No, you don't decide love. You feel it. It's there or it isn't."

That was Vivien who dialogued with me. She was Muslim. Enough remembering Spain. Here's Canada. Christmas. The Belen is there in the living room.

I'm tick-tocking on this typewriter and I don't like to do it because my sister is in the next room and my parents in the other and I don't want to disturb them.

But the silence is lonely. But you can't be lonely. You're with family now. The pain of aloneness is gone. It's just in your mind. It's a hangover from two years of being alone. No, I'm not alone. I'm not sad.

Do you know that love isn't in the mind? Love's in the heart. Let it flow; don't stop it. It doesn't come in labels that say THIS IS LOVE; TAKE IT OR LEAVE IT. No, love is something there, in the heart, not in the soul; perhaps in the soul but the soul that feels, not the one that thinks or the soul of the mind; but rather the soul that feels sentimental, that wants, cares, desires, feels, touches...do you understand? You still care, don't you? I hope you're whispering yes.

*Undated*

That glass. Spanish? Reminiscent. And the church, yes, the chapel, and now the snow, the freezing snow and my flimsy fingers, a broken bulb and don't laugh...my rundown VW Beetle 1957. You're smiling again. Remember...turkey or chicken...was it? *Don't know.* Crucifixions juxtaposed on paintings. Paint. I must paint again. Back home...where are all my friends? Don't close the envelope. Here's another sigh that I'll slip into it. Here's to her, to him, to them, to smiles, to anguish, to existence...oh hell, to everything that is... profound, poetic. I must paint in red to be poetic like flickering lights on snow, truly, the cold is poetic because it inspires me to freeze and die poetically, morbidly, to sleep away and never awaken. Coincidence, for a change, meet me in no place at no time. Forget Tuck Shop...

intertwined, half-bitten fingernails. Just some place called no place which will meet you and me, and a no-time to smile, to stop our chance meeting in January or February. No, not the coffee machines. You'll have amnesia. Tea? Kisses? And embrace.

*Undated, 1.10 am*

Just two years ago around this time, I was typing, I was beginning to write my novel. I was pounding around this time on my typewriter, when the leaves were gone, snow, Berne, Swiss Berne, and now Montreal, Canadian Montreal, two full-filled years, since like many years ago, how strange! Only two years ago I began writing a sad novel, nostalgic, but now I've changed.

A dialogue:

"After Switzerland, you went to Lourdes. You prayed. Don't you pray any more?"

"In two years' time."

"Back to Spain?"

"Yes, I suppose."

"Spain. In Madrid. Spain, and Spain…oh, I don't know. I'm just indifferent now. I'm not in the mood to tell you everything."

"Yes, I suppose."

"Spain. In Madrid. I'm in the mood to tell you everything."

"Then don't. Let's talk about New Year."

"Yes, what's you New Year's resolution?"

"I'll be a good boy and finish my thesis."

"Hey, that's pretty good."

"It's your turn."

"I can't think of anything new."

"Don't plan."

"But that's the only way I can dream."

"I'm trying to recapture a thought. I can't remember it now."

"It has to do with pride, beautiful faces, love, passion, plot, they change me, yet I want you as you are."

"You're mocking me."
"You're pessimistic."

Enough of dialogues. Recount: Today I went to McGill University. I also wrote a letter to Yale and other Ivy League big shots. Last night I saw a film, *Valley of the Dolls*, and tonight I'll see Frank Sinatra in *Tony Rome*. Good day.

*December 29*
Drowsy, produce, the lights, dramatic roles, be bored, read books, forget about everything; enigmatic, phlegmatic, shit, bullshit, f...g shit! Isn't humanity disgusting and tragic? But there must be happiness too. Something unexpected must come to make you happy sometimes. Perhaps after unforeseen moments of tragedy. Something that seems experimental; maybe an effluvium of laughter. No, not Amsterdamish dry laughs but rather something warm and caressing. Don't expect it; it'll come in indescribable forms. And you'll cry happily. You'll know truth in lies. My lies, but if you can discern, you'll see that lies are truer than truths.

Be, be! I know and yet I don't want to know. Knowledge is so puny, so worthless; the more you know, the harder it is to live, the more complicated life becomes because we're human and therefore, worthless, nothing, a certain nothingness humans possess such as spontaneous dialogues that mean nothing, trivial, trite, dialogues about the weather and the snow in winter and the heat in summer; extemporaneous thoughts, sudden existential jerks, dim candles, parties for two...

Do you remember our party for two? You didn't like punch. And we made love. Must I remember? But the spell has been broken, Japanese doll, they called you Japanese doll, and I never did see you naked. It's all over now. Let's begin afresh. All over again. I wish I were happy. I will be...again...I hope.

*December 30*

Happy birthday to 24 years. What does this Canadian birthday signify? Nothing, really nothing. Insignificant. Birthdays don't mean anything anymore. Birthdays have passed to indifference, boredom… words that reek of absurdity's hangover.

At most absurdity is funny…a respite from boredom. At least it's meaningful. Meaninglessness is too tragic and it hurts of memories of the past.

There's always a smile in absurdity. Or a loud laugh. Another year. And another. Means so little. Today is my birthday. I will have been born tomorrow or next year. And existence…is sweet? Yes, sometimes. When people make you happy. And tragic when people make you…tragic.

Nada. Absolutamente nada. Really. Good morning. Wake up and tell me what you see outside. Snow, of course. I'm too lazy to even get up and see the same slush. Or maybe afraid that it wouldn't be snow anymore but some black, cold substance in its place. But I'm almost sure there's snow outside. Together with the…sun? And all sing "Happy Birthday!"

I don't know how to feel. Really I don't. Rita our maid…no one ever knows what goes through her mind. Everyone thinks she's stupid. But not me. I think her acting stupid is just a front. I think she's planning to murder all of us. She's planning a perfect murder to assassinate all of us. Poisoned food, perhaps? She doesn't pray with us, doesn't eat with us. She just doesn't care. She does things pretentiously enthusiastic, but you never know the reason behind her enthusiasm. You expect her to be loyal. Is she just pretending? She's resigned when you get mad at her for not doing things right. You tell her to call you senorito instead of senor, and she humbly accedes. She's obedient. But she's not stupid.

She's the central character in this house. This home made up of Adams family members, as mom calls it. Rita is the central character because she does everything: she washes, she cleans, she does the beds, and she practically runs the house. What would become of us without her? Dishes would be unwashed, beds unmade, and so forth. Terrible, isn't it? 11.10 am. Mother calls "Rita, Rita!". She answers: Wen, umayakon.

Mother orders: "Dalusam datoy".

She answers obediently: Wen mam.

Another thing about Rita: she's a linguist. She speaks English, Spanish, Tagalog and Ilocano. Let's see you beat that.

*December 31*
Montreal: Dorval airport. Dark glasses. They leave, they come, they disturb….people who come and go. 5.05 pm. The snow catches my eyes. It drapes, curtainlike, in the night, in green, red, and white against moving twinkling yellow of FOLLOW ME trucks blinking. Truly I cannot feel the monotony of life awakened by these yellow lights that twinkle restlessly, like my soul. Yellow lights that bother my existence. Waiter in white. Do you really wait? A funny-looking jet passes. Reflections in this glass bubbling superfluous thoughts. A headache cured by…St. Joseph's oil for the Oratorium? Yes, confession. It rimes with fornication.

"Flight 92 from Miami".

"See you in March."

Kill time. Flies in your stomach. She's waiting. Let her wait. If she isn't there, I'll get drunk by myself. And write about New Year. My thoughts and this typewriter will keep me company tonight. I'll be alone.

"Air Canada Jetliner for Toronto, Edmonton, Vancouver. Proceed to Gate 36."

Shall I say goodbye? No. Not just yet. Just a…oh, I don't know."

*Edmonton. January 3, 1968*

This pillow that is no longer a pillow but a naked whiteness that stares at me because you are not here. This white gaze is ghastly because it shares a non-commitment with me; it shares a loneliness — dry, like tears that have gone.

I felt hurt when she said I didn't love her. I told her that love did exist but that it didn't matter to me whether it did or it didn't. I told her that love was a word, a word that actually meant nothing; just empty and indifferent like the silence of snow against an afternoon sun. And it was senseless, the whole thing was senseless. I didn't understand why I felt bad once again, why this certain sensitivity inside of me burned like fire against ice, like a very cold windy night that loses itself in black shadows.

"It's not whether I love you or not. It's just that I'm happy when I'm with you."

And somehow, I miss her when she's not around.

"In some way I love you", she said.

"In what way?"

"I want you to be with me at nights; and when you're not here, I get very lonely."

And again the cold air harassed me; and I wanted her. The skies dimmed quickly leaving behind patches of sunlight shadowed against the grey leaves that hovered dreamlessly above me in lost flight.

*January 7*

"Are you bored?"
Silence.

"I just love asking questions and getting no answers", she continued.

Silence.

Dave Brubeck plays on the stereo. The morning touched cloudless streams of thoughts; thoughts that mattered in trivial ways; just whispered, frightened and confused thoughts that drifted in time. I don't know but I just simply huddled selflessly against time, against the dry images of the snow. When storms freeze my cheeks. Where the touch of warmth is like another temporary silence...

"No, I won't make love to you. I'm not a whore."
"Whore frost."
"Did you see the leaves?"
"What leaves?"
"The empty white leaves floating, hanging on empty trees."
"Yes. They were white when I awoke this morning. They were white as the leaves are green in Spring."
"I have to now, just know why."
"You're not being profound."
"Are you going back to Spain?"

Silence.

"You're so silent. You don't tell me what I want to know. And I love you. Are you bored with me?"

Silence.

*January 7*

This perfume that excites me, that makes me close my eyes because I cry, because I love you, because you love me, because I feel you close to me, despite the emptiness that surrounds me; the non-fulfilment, the desire, yes, when you were here with me only a few minutes ago. But now I can only feel and imagine your soft whisper, the smell of your hair, the subtle touch of your warm body.

Love, you were in red, and I accepted you once again.

*January 9*

High level place. Early morning, maybe 2 or 3 am.

"Pig!"
"Ass!"
She's despicable and now I feel a bitter loneliness, the loneliness of the cold, the memories that creep in from the past, piercing like the ticking of a clock.

"I want to make love to you tonight."
"No."
"Why not?"
"Go with a prostitute."
"It's cold outside. Besides, I might get sick."

The lights freeze outside with the whiteness of the night. Silence. There's the hum of the fridge and the silent weeping of my typewriter testifying against the night. Around me, green books, papers reading black meaningless words, a tea cup, a flower, red, withered because love had withered, a red candle signifying lost time, and another green prop which will gather dust by tomorrow.

"And the letters?"
"The novel…"
"I don't hate you. You're just too…I don't know how to put it."
"I fell."
"Twice. With me. You must hold me. And you don't,"
"I don't know how. Teach me."

"I'm confused."

The letters were written and I no longer cared for the uprising of time. I no longer cared for desolation. Things just came and swallowed me; things that no longer inspired, froze; irregardless of time and space and Spanish remembrances heeding clichés that I considered trite and useless.

Nothing. Just a painted dot. A letter. Bills. No smiles. Bus drivers who were once kind in the summer and suddenly in winter lose kindness and smiles and happiness. They now frown at the cold, they say "f...g shit" — they're rude. Even taxi drivers no longer smile because the nights are longer, darker and sadder.

Shudder. Hybernate. Mechanically shift your tears. "Kill off...!" No, don't...weep, lament, cry...the letters have been made. Central Market will still be there with the heat, with the jitneys, with the Quiapo buses that make heated noises agains the sun, the humid sun, tropical Manila, warm, hot, windy, dusty, happy, disgusting and youthful.

I awoke and I found my fingers looking for my face. My face had changed. I had grown a beard. I no longer recognized myself that morning as I stared back at myself. And my mirror image smiled, and in his smile, I saw discovered myself again — absurd and idiotic. Marbled loneliness! Transparent tears like the drip-drip of water, like blue typewriters that touch your fingers and decide what you must write. Or like numbers, square numbers, cold nine months of the year and green the other three. Then silence again. Silence
That skips sometimes, that plays madly with smiles, red lipsticked smiles, red lips that touched me in...ecstasy?

"Stranger, don't be too personal."
"Smile again and touch my face."
"Tomorrow. Perhaps."

Flying with the awkwardness of flights. I felt in that strange moment a chill, a chill for women who morbidly lose their virginity, a chill for homosexuals who smile at me, a chill for friends who lose friendship and meaning because their personalities change and they reveal their disgusting personalities; and at that precise moment, I felt all of a sudden to leave all of them behind, to feel free and restless from the bonds of snow and disgusting friends.

Time makes you lose the indifference. You look for kindness and tenderness and like sleep, you can't but see surrealism — canned skins, bitter hair, sour smiles, sweet kisses. No nonsensical concreteness, just dreams with no explanation on why they appear. Is this death's hole like a gaping black hole or putrid disgusting love?

I was not happy at all. I barely remembered the dream, but I wasn't happy when I woke up. It was another of those dreams where you lose touch of everything happy.

"You seemed to let go of me. I say tomorrow but then fate does not decide tomorrow. Apparently we can't decide. Ultimately, someone or something called Destiny decides. You alone understand because I felt your breasts, your soft breasts, and I felt guilty for holding you, for wanting you. I was free but I wanted to be possessed, to possess you. I wanted freedom and yet I was enslaved because of my desire for you. I just wanted you, and if I tried to forget you, I was going to be lonely again. Maybe our kisses will once again float from our souls and blur themselves in oblivion. Maybe the past will leave another scar from wounds unhealed. Maybe the nights will again whisper "fog" to me, like those night clouds descending on Burnham Park looking for you, searching for lost meaning, in time, in the ticking sounds of this earth, when eternity is sought, and when desires are so great they're never attained."

*Undated*

She called. To console me? Perhaps.
We talked. I cajoled her.
"You're funny. Goodnight. Sweet dreams."

When I woke up, it was too late to go to the Student Union Building to get a hamburger. It was 11.15 pm. I wasn't hungry anyway. So I get this Brazilian record given to me on my birthday and I go over to the room of my Egyptian friend. I didn't have a phonograph yet.

I felt like flying back home to Montreal. Instead, I went to the fridge and got myself a beer. Well, I'm not home so I might just as well wait for another couple of months, Spring break so I can go home again.

I open the window but it's too cold and shut it again. I don't see any flickering lights. Only the snow and cold, half-silent people half-laughing in the Common Lounge. I played the tape recorder since I had nothing else to do. I also tried to get drunk so I could go back to sleep. At least that's better than just sitting down and staring at nothing. I just don't seem to know what to do tonight. It's almost one and I don't feel like calling anyone at this hour. Slowly getting drunk with my beers? No, not really. It's been years since I really got drunk. Looks like I'm now immune, after Spain. A pity, really. Letting seconds tick away. There's nothing else to do at this time of night.

*Undated*

I guess I won't stop writing you. Remember Casa do Brasil at the Ciudad Universitaria? Remember the Spaniard who said he was in university for years? He called himself a professional student. I saw that Camus play "L'Etranger". I could have played the role better. I was still in Montreal when Hotel Bonaventure burned. Funny. You go there to forget me and I'm just downstairs watching a movie at Place Bonaventure.

You didn't convince me about love. Is it truly not possessive?

"My eyes turn green when I'm mad. They're bluish-green now."

You either like a person or you don't. How could it be possible? I mean, your eyes changing colour. I'm 115 pounds and you're heavier by one pound. Talk to me; tell me something, a story, something funny. Something ridiculous like "Snow turns black in the summer." Or "Is green really luminous?"

Ask me another question, a sophisticated one, for a change, like "Do your boots go clomp-clomp when it snows?"

Laugh, laugh. I like you when you laugh. You have a squeaky, sneaky way of laughing. Like a child. And you're biting your nails. Stop it! Do something like chew gum.

How long will these two years pass? I guess happiness doesn't really exist. Another vicious cycle of life? Perhaps, my lovely friend. You're so lovely. It's better to say maybe. It's a less precise answer.

*January 9*

Athabasca Hall, room 305. My room. I'm remembering the sea. No, I'm not really homesick. I'm just remembering. And when I return, I'll probably want to leave again. I'll be happy for a while but then I'll feel like leaving again. The light is dim, but my eyes don't hurt.

Am I hurt?

No. Neither do I feel bitter. I'll remember you. Always. I know it's going to hurt then. I don't want to leave you, but Fate has other plans. I'll go. Maybe come back? Will you take me back? Stop planning! We'll be together and we'll smile always and we'll always be happy.

Indifference, my fault. I lie. But people are born like you to always be honest and tell the truth. I don't know why I lie. Fear? Society? I have to lie. But you love me despite my faults. Funny this thing called love, isn't it? I guess I love you too. Don't feel hurt when I say I guess, as though I were tentative. Life's like that. A smile, a trickled tear, an actor, a disguise, conflict, and then happiness at the end. I like you, I suppose. I hate your guts, but I need you. Talk to me. Talent? Gee, sigh, class again tomorrow. You must read but your eyes hurt. The cold is afraid of my warmth. But fear always triumphs; and I'll lose again, like mechanical keys that close on me, suffocate me, and then I'll say "Hello, I love you. Goodbye."

You're not hurt, are you?

No, I'm not mean. I guess I'm just crazy. And I lack words to express myself. I'm not at ease. I stammer, trembling lips, afraid, but soft and wonderful.

Please, answer the phone.

I'm hurt.

Why? Because you're mean. "If you keep on saying that, I'll really be mean." We fell twice in the snow. Wonderful, isn't it? Snow entered our shoes. And you were nice.

Don't say "hurt" again, please.

It will sound like existence. Meaningless. Overused. Try new words like "grape, ribbon, green, red, white, snow." I'm not funny. Just senseless, I suppose. Have you ever seen red snow? No, not even in dreams.

"They're not love letters. Just a novel I'm beginning to grope into."

"Do you want me to love you? No? If not, leave! I'll hate you."

"You're so heartless."

"But you told me you'll just be sad, forget, then, consider me dead."

"Hate you."

Exams. Coming…

I guess I'm alone. How long will this loneliness last? Nine more months?

"I'm afraid to tell you who I am. Because if I do, you'll not want me anymore."

"Don't be silly. Are you hiding something?"

"Forms."

"What forms?"

"Ghosts inside me that haunt me."

Spain. I hate myself. And yet, for others, it didn't matter. They were dull, and I was sensitive. They were insensitive. What things will make us feel hurt? Little, insignificant things? What can hurt you, tell me? Or are you just made of stone? Invulnerable? Are you incriminating me? No. My students. Fifth floor. Science, medicine. To see people. To be sad. Silly? Profound? How can I have impressed you so? My nothingness? Changed. I've changed you and I don't want to. I want you the way you are.

Be gentle. I just wanted to tell you why I always smile. I smile because that's the only charm I have. Pale. Struggling, like chestnut hair. Or shit hair. Mysterious, whatever that is. Do you know why I never answered your questions? It's because I'm tired of saying I don't know and although I know why you ask and what you ask, I pretend not to listen and look far away. I pretend to think something miles away up in the air. It's not profound. I'm just a copycat. I just reflect repetitiously the ideas of others who have starred in life, so to speak.

I'm just a big phoney. Naïve, perhaps; not very intelligent, but at least I do have friends like you who appreciate me for what I am.

Please, let me tell you something else. Don't go away. I wish I can beg you but I don't feel like begging or pleading. I'm just too humble and poor to do that (in spirit). And pride is only for those who have clean souls (if they believe they have souls). I wish I can believe I don't have a soul so that I don't have to worry about heaven and hell. But I do have a soul and there is a heaven and hell. It makes me afraid sometimes to think of an afterlife. I sometimes wish I were a Hindu who believes in reincarnation. But of course, I most sincerely want to believe in life now, and nothing else.

Don't brand me as an existentialist or hippie; and please, smoke another cigarette. Get bored for just a few more seconds; no, a minute, just one more minute of your time. You see, your life is so exciting and mine, so boring. But anyhow, there won't be any meaning if we tried to change our personalities. Or exchanged lives. Yes, I know you disagree, I see you frowning and your eyes changing back to green. Your lips are twitching.

I beg your pardon? What is it you said? Oh yes, I do.

Are you leaving? All right, you do what you want. I won't stop you. But listen to me first. What I'll ask you now is trivial but it may have some importance in your life. Is the summer night beautiful? Are the committees filled?

I wish I could tell you my secret, but you're no longer here and I feel guilty because I'm talking to myself again. You see, once I used to be someone until something struck me. I've written and continue writing puzzles on sleeves and pale footsteps, knocking on doors, on windows, ravens that rap on window sills, dusty roads, the sun, the pain, the constant desire to leave, the austerity of disgust, the dangerous yet enchanting black ice.

*7.15 pm*

It's because in a few minutes you'll form part of me. And I'll be part of you. No, no tears. Tears are like the sea that first enchants you with her ebb tides and later make you feel sad and lonely because the sounds stop and happiness disbands.

I always think of Utopia. Maybe truly black snow. Or reversed sea, earth and skies; clouds when you need them; wings that will make you fly; coloured dreams, happy, of course. I always think of Utopia.

Let me give you now an example of "knowing the answers to life" (or to questions about life). This is just a *repaso*. You see, when I leave next year, I'll want to rest and then, I'll want to go to a new place. But again, when I stay long enough, to pursue things that are conventionally pursued, I'll feel guilty again.

What then must I do? Running away sometimes is not an escape, as psychedelics say. It just so happens that you enter into a dialogue and you get bored. You give up. You lose what is normally referred to as ....I don't what word to use. It's probably another overused word. "Conventional", that's the word. Let's search for other words. Tell me, is "universal" another overused word? What IS a word? My mind is getting old and silly and I'm only 24. Please tell me an absurd story.

"I'm not bored. I'm just waiting for an excuse."
"For what?"
"Jealousy."
"He wasn't jealous."
"I just talk too much."
"Sense?"
"What difference does it make if I talk sense or nonsense? ...and that girls are beautiful, and that you say ghost stories are frightening. Tell me, will you have to say again what simplicity means? No, don't give me any more answers. No more abstract dialogues. "But they were not abstract; they were just dim, like this dim light that confuses my state of thought."
"People say I don't think. Maybe they're right. I think it's possible; I think I like you a lot. But I'm obnoxious."

"Thanks for the consolation."

"I hope you'll be there. Do you think I'll get tired of you? Don't say I don't know, please! You're supposed to know the answers to life, remember?"

"Yes, but I don't know is an answer, a profound one at that. Don't you know?"

"Hmmm. Say something poetic, for a change."

*January 10*

And I felt happy. But now I'm sad again. I'm sad because happy days have passed and there are going to be more happy days but distinct ones, different kinds…maybe the happiness of the snow when I see everything white; maybe the happiness of loneliness, of looking back at those days when sacrifice had meaning.

I don't seem to care anymore about the people I once cared for. Maybe you're the exception, I don't know. Somehow you're profound, and that's why I can express my emptiness to you, because you understand. Others do, but they understand my emptiness in their own way.

Maybe I've decided to be indifferent to life. And that's why I'm empty. To be indifferent to love, to be waiting to be innocent again when I cannot anymore…the drifting period of youth, a period where there is the now and the tomorrow, and nothing else. No plans. Only the impulsiveness of this now. And God, who is all meaning, is now a silent prop floating in unexplained eternity.

A series of events blown together by whispers, meaningless words, monotonous, mechanical words that somehow move your being. And yet I'm still indifferent. Maybe I'm not, maybe I am. I've lost touch of the meaning of things, the meaning of love, values that were before warm and sensitive…they're gone, prostituted perhaps by the years

I've been away: almost four years, years impregnated with life, life that I never felt before, saw, and made love to.

And when I now say I love God or am indifferent to him, or care about him, I no longer know what I'm saying. I've truly lost meaning; and I don't care to grope for it anymore, as I used to once. I seem to just live instinctively now and I don't know whether to feel guilty or not. I'm just another stereotype waiting for time to pass, preparing for tomorrow's routine because I have to, trying to get some sleep if I can; if not, I stay up nights waiting, waiting perhaps for someone to tell me not to be lonely. And yet, it does not matter anymore if someone will call or not. The past that once was warm has now frozen, then melted, and somehow steamed into nothingness.

Nothingness, eternity, silence…realities I don't know the meanings of and yet, I play with them, maybe to escape a little from the boredom and indifference of human life.

The night will pass again. I'll sleep again, if I can, and perhaps awaken to another day.

# CHAPTER 11

*Edmonton, January 15*

Because I don't die anymore. I don't love anymore. To die? To live eternally? I rest. For what? To rot! Fidelity. Does it matter anymore? Something, I don't know what, rots me and makes of me a vicissitude, an eternal vicissitude, black with remorse. Slowly, like the shores of tears, like the night that cools itself into nothingness.

Mil demonios! Yes, to express this vagueness, this uncertainty, and lines that perpetually disturb the soul. And little by little, the past begins to molest me, paining me, crucifying me; and I surrender helplessly. Sleep? Damned sleep! Just skip these nights, just hibernate, false empty dialogues that don't communicate, that just stupefy and carry thoughts, numb thoughts, intranquility...damned Canadians! False, cold, indifferent. Nor do I desire this uncertainty. Joder! Now what? Falsities! And the smiles — they no longer ask. Silence. Nothingness. All right. The night was unable to talk to me, to tell me that you understand why this loveliness putrefies, why this whole goddam affair flows, like noise that floats through my ears and perplexes me. Or like this melancholy drowsiness that tries to console me asking, "What is it, damn you, what is it?" And indifferently, I answer by telling short stories about moods, and dialogues, and floating instances, when indifference and boredom...indifference and boredom...

Shut up!

What?
Shut up!
Thank you.

No, nothing bothers me. Just a phone call. Just this subtle irritation, this "coming with me", this bourgeoisie, or maybe this certain comedy about life and truth and…stories of love? Yes, Dindi, yes. Oh Dindi, Sinatra sings. Brazilian afterthought. One night, you told me why Corcovado had quiet nights, quiet stars, shining restlessly, eternally. I love you, do you doubt that? No. I know you don't. I just hope there will be an end to my yearning passion. And did you ask me why I was tired of the cold and white snow?

Yes, the black snow, the burned hands, the sit-in-telephone booth, the "artistic" dialogue, monologue and…the song.

And the bridge. You walked. With me. Silently. Because it was cold with all the snow around us. Because you thought of nothing else. But…but nothing.

"I didn't say I wanted to stay."
"Impossible, and when the past…was the past impossible?"
"I was shocked and confused."
"Ha!"

The right senses, the right words, the stomached smiles, the absurdity of tears, of religious tears, of poems that come out in red hate, and smile and bless, as if they were gods. Hell! Hell!

And what else? No, no! I should not. The tears are dry. And there is nothing else. Nakedness, perhaps. Were you naked? No, you weren't. You were just reciting a poem, a poem that conversed and converted you into a dialogue.

Shit! All shit! Traversals; conditions; roads; snow; and semi-colons. And how about the car? Don't rest now. Go on. Tell me what you feel. I feel rotten. I feel as though the world, the beautiful controversial roads of the world all lined up on top of Tuck Shop.

You're joking now.
Yes I am.
And you're lying.
I was born a liar. So, don't tell me that because I know.
And how about that room at the top?
A stereotype. A confused stereotype, like the red lava of a volcano that seeps into mouths of people who say words they don't understand, to all the hypocrites of the world who don't understand what they feel. In love with a married man! Ha! That's the silliest, stupidest thing I ever heard! You're not. It's all in that silly, stupid mind of yours!
Will you paint me that?
When I hear noises.
Toots of cars. And the night, never silent. Never.
All right. And the pages? Stop. Stop the dialogue. And think. Don't remember. Just sneeze. And think. For a while.
No it doesn't make sense to do so. It doesn't make sense to be surprised at the rates of letters; at the nonsensical absurdities of meanings; at the inspirations of many who cast shadows of doubt, who transcend and who don't ask why. Why the world is round. Why the world was flat once. Because the world was flat once. Many centuries ago.

And now you've lost the flowing touch of letters, of thoughts that excited you once, again, once, no, because once is a remembrance in commas, of tenacious dreams, of misunderstood creativity, and of a thesis called "Search". Sure, you must know because you've been silent and now, you've consumed your silence and formed words that have meaninglessly been put wallowly together to signify "thoughts".

As though you think.

I don't say I do.

But you do. Because you're not a pig, nor an ass, nor a cat, nor a dog; just a warm afternoon that strides softly into a rainstorm, into laughing faces of youth, of a swimming pool of the past, of that priest, or that commandment which makes you know the "what" instead of the "why" of things. I must make sense, you must understand. And March is still far away.

No, Pepe, no, man. You're not bored. What you need is a woman, like our friend, our Andalusian friend who said he made love to someone in Mexico.

Perhaps it's the cold.

Si, me quita todo apetito sexual.

And you laugh, and I laugh, and I become incongruent, like a cloudy day that announces unrelaxed, tense, emotional snow that turns blue at 4.38 in the afternoon.

Do you like that number?

No, I just have to go back to it.

And the red book calculates tears, tears dedicated to hell where fires are burned with scorched love, with love that cannot be love. Besides, does it matter?

Maybe when the strides are innocent, when you hope to see her in a place, in a time, in a direction — all unknown. And a happy coincidence is sometimes frightful. Extrasensual, extrasensory perception is the term.

Coined afterthoughts.

Purple, I see satin purple when I focus my demands on you, when I invite you to be free, not to enslave yourself with love, or passion, or anything warm. No, don't be warm. Just be cold and indifferent, like Canadian snow.

Do you really think so?

It's such a big place. I was there to forget you.

And I burned your hotel.

Don't whisper ghosts to my ear.

You needn't be afraid. They're dead…those ghosts.

And the living ones, they're the ones who'll haunt you. They'll paint the sky green and yellow, well, pick any color…how about black?

Of course not, that's a real color.

How about velvet?

No, that's not a color.

Well, what color do you want?

Green. I think green because you were in green and I saw you when you told me with a smile, a happy, profound smile, not empty at all. Emptiness only belongs to people who move softly to the left…I love…I…love…you….Does it mean anything?

The stupid old man walks with his smile and his cane. But he tells me in yellowed blackness that that is not all there is to it. Something is even better. . No, not writers. Not even an abstract noun like "desolation" or something like "Fundamentals of the Spanish Language". How abstract can you get!

I only have a poem, or maybe a short story to write to you about… the present, the now that encompasses the past, and a tomorrow that may be a frightening future. Damn it!

Sweet poem, tell me why I must end the night like a rotten tomato in the snow.

No more I'm sorry, just like the walk, the afternoon walk, no apologies for an asylum of margins.

No more trying to decipher the meaning of understanding. Just feel it.

And now, what have I learned to ache for? The zigzags of youth. Do you know how I feel? I must write now, not to impress people, and not saying "do, do, do" — if you want to get rid of me because you're bored with me, do it. Get out. Leave me. Don't say it. Do it.

I have to get used to my defects.

And all of them loved me.
Poetic, isn't it? Isn't love poetic?
And what about the hat from "El Cid"?
It doesn't make sense.
But it was beautiful.
Does it make sense?
Yes.
And no.
Well, then, what do you make of it?

The nocturnal surf, the quietness of the night, when I knew that the stars were telling me to whisper words to you which were somehow vague and unpoetic.

But how can I? My lips hurt from the snow. The cold, the bitter cold. Cracked lips.

And the hamburger? Yes, the drowsy shape of a hamburger that invites sleep after restless moments.

And innocent?
And innocent...

I.

...When the trees asked me why they were in chalked green blackboards, why there were faces drawn in them, why they were philosophical such as "the essence of trees is their being", or "A tree has both essence and existence." And trees can also weep because they too have tears inside their leaves, and when they thirst, they suck the earth of its juices from rains that fall and nurture poems, poems as poetic as the green indifference of trees...

And innocent. Yes, innocent and leafless in winter.

And they shed tears in autumn. To die for a while in winter. So that poems, sad poems can be created by people who search God in the

155

most meaningless verses possible. Yet they do not find what they're searching.

But they continue to search.

And search.

And Spring comes, friendships end, eyes turn willowy, and trees die once again, they die with their indifferent green, like the green of Spring that colors the earth.

Conspiracy of the season? Perhaps the change, the constant change of life, monotony, and the threads of eternity spinning like fire.

Sweet fire. Frightened fire. No, you're not afraid. You're neither lonely nor bored. You're just resting for a while from your tireless restlessness. And again, you'll relieve the sun of its daylight restlessness; at night when you watch the stars and sigh cold smoke, like a hand that loses life.

Trivial like an X mark.

My studies are not sweet enough to retain the bitterness of this cold against my cracked lips.

Slip away, perhaps slip away….

## II.

The wine spilled. The days give way to love. And the cold winter gathers loyalty. The night searches for that friend who flew away on wings of black and fat cats, or brown and friendly dogs that convert themselves into laughing, human hyenas.

Feet are cold. The house has no lights in Christmas and most of all, the pigeon comes back to bite my gloved hand, my inexpressive hand that beckons sunset.

Were you reflecting when you walked?

No, but I smiled.

Why?

Because you were silent.

III.

The torn pieces must be gathered together to collect dry moss in summer. Did you tell me how summer was?
Warm.
Like love?
What's love?
Love is a...feeling? No...you...

IV.

Don't be silly. The tides have changed. The seas have converted into mountains. The mountains, the seas, humans, animals, lions, men, cats, women; and the earth has dried from white and icy and wet snow, to the warm and blue sky of Africa. And Canada no longer belongs to white animals, but to black cannibals.
Did you say...?
Yes I said...
I beg your pardon?
Not at all.
You're so kind.
And cannibals say goodbye to tigers; tigers to cats; and the sky no longer changes its green, indifferent color. It remains smiling, looking up into the earth.

V.

And transparent eyes, like seven times seven, or two times two, or multiply me with the things you see around me and you'll see me floating happily, innocently in an eternity you will never have imagined I would be.

VI.

A cough.
Love.

VII.

Letters…Once there was a man who was afraid of death and so, he committed suicide; dialog 68; and the Montreal affair. Odeon? Yes, I miss Montreal. Do you?

The mountain wasn't high. I went up. And its softness dies sometimes with the relics of the mind: wind, snow, slit and forsaken desires. The car, a 68 Chevy. Toronto waits for me. But the thought of weeks turning to months only bores me more.
However, I'm not frightened. I'm just a bit indifferent. And melancholy. Miserable sighs. Suggestions? Yes. Do…
What?
Mention letters in your dreams.
Do…!
Spring. No, Fall. The leaves were yellow. The afternoon, poetic. The pictures, smiling. And the walk, trite, boring, affectatious, and sometimes, I recall, sickly.
Talk…!
And so the days when kisses resounded with jealousy. When you never cared and I tired easily of your touch. When age crept, not verily, but steadily. And not very much like the subtleness, no, the impulsiveness of buying a…Greek record? Obviously not. It was Americanized.
Emily.
Sentimental.
Never learn to love that way. Brings you misery.
Bing.
Swindle.
Ning.

Accident.

Banlag. Blonde albino. To hell with memories!

## VIII.

Jackets. Stories of dreams. And the ordinary bitterness of having to write simple words against the bearded sounds of a university. Against a steepled silence of pine trees that root deep into the freezing cold. And most of all, against the days of thoughts, of books that write untruths mixed in one, silly upright American bundle. Everything is propaganda.

Even Vietnam.

No opinions please. There are just too many comments. Another is bound to cause a hot shooting world war culminating in a nervous breakdown for this planet called Earth.

And the planeteers from other places?

Mystery.

And God?

Man-made mystery.

And gods?

They belong to dreams. Dreams. Yes, I can only offer dreams. One, there was a green dream. Two, a god who saw, who knew why there were children who grew poetically into orange or yellow adults. Sick. Maybe the sickness of life conferred upon the righteousness of love. Of virginity. Of a painting in yellow and black. Sick love. A dry tear that can never be dry again. And the steak was hard like a shoe's sole. And your laughs were resounding and half-hysterical. And you were pale; no, no longer half a tomato. No longer a bitterness. Just a sigh, a sigh that awaits a dream, many dreams, like sordid love affairs. Like the tension that touches squarely with your sighs. Yes, another poem, another night. Maybe a restful sleep tonight, or a paragraph that might end sincerely with quotation marks. Maybe a kind of happiness, a real and sincere happiness that is misunderstood. Or a silence that reflects the many possibilities of life. Jumping boards of life, yes, that's the expression, jumping into sweet oblivion, the nothingness of death, and the censored afterlife.

Who knows?

No one. Only the dead.

But they're dead.

They no longer exist; they're forgotten.

Or remembered.

Superstition? The dead coming back to life?

Possibly.

Afraid. A bit, I am, of the dead who haunt the living and defy them to spiritual duels.

Who wins?

The dead.

Don't mock me.

But I must. Because my paleness does not act anymore, nor is it silent and cold like today was silent and cold; and then this night, conscience, if I must have one, no, they're no longer the end-all of things.

You are nothing. Nothing. And I crave for something.

Within.

Explain to me the meaning of indifference.

Once I loved. Now I don't.

I'm indifferent. That's what it means.

But love?

Does it matter?

No. Only dedicated love. This love stops you from breathing. It stops you from thinking. It is considerate of oblivion. It does not care for death. It is life.

Then, are you happy?

Yes.

What is happiness?

Happiness is…just another feeling.

*Edmonton, January 22.*

I only wanted to call the attention of today. Today is a grey day. Snow, perhaps, in the clouds. Now I await a phone call. In 30 minutes, perhaps. The naked breasts of this wooden carving stare at me like eyeballs jumping out of their sockets. Her aesthetic pose contemplates my painting above her.

Last night was another poetic night. No, not really. It was just a playful night, an acting night. I was the actor, the director, and the entertained. Transcendental egoism.

But today, did not call my attention. It only remembered how other days scandalized me: female days that shriek in early dawn; male days bulldozing iced roads; and neutral days skyscraping the skies, not really the skies, but the clouds that float below the skies. How long will it take this day to end?

Forever seems to be the answer.

And the tenses?

Variety is the answer. I used to and now I am and afterwards I shall be. Truly, life is variety's spice. Just as though love were not truly smooth; and the best freedom is life.

Am I playing with words?

Expected inspiration?

Monologued strangeness…the mind is just a mass of mattered grey called brains.

A soft knock on the door. Shaving cream from Banff. "You can have it."

"Gracias."

"No hay de que."

"I'm hungry but I haven't changed yet." Phone call.

"In about a week?"

Process.

"Thank you."

Wait for a week. Happy? Not so. It isn't here yet.

Wonder a little. Oh yes, why don't you type the poem you did last night? Okay, here it is:

Cognate of silent delirium
Creeping
And brushing away
This being
Unstaring
Dwindling in
Snow-flaked debility
Of afterthoughts
Red, green,
Other colours juxtapose
Projecting Halo Shampoo
Johnson's baby powder
Gilette foamy
Yardley's solidified brillantine
Ban
And a damned Spanish book,
*De primitiva Africa española y Antigua épica,*
Damned these people who care and care not
Like flashlights that shine now
And waste their battered blue against the night!

Oh, smoke! Why are you harsh to my throat? Why was the drink somehow unrequited? Why are these words blooming like dewdrops, like silent noises from clocks tinkle, twinkle...and boots that rubber their way into snow, into the night that sights people who cross labyrinthine and ethereal hemispheres?

Oh, damn, damn, damn are these trees that that somewhat tell me that I'm not being what I am! I'll just throw away these damned things and whisper red cheers against black hats and fathom greatness, a certain desire, a careful metaphor, very, very soft poem willowing silently like the night willowing silently.

Drunken are these nights that make love affairs unconditional! Blasted song! Was I to whisper?

No, no, I think I must engage myself in this smoked existence. Ha! Must I laugh? Must I suffer? Intentionally? Putrid snow, uncaring, don't weep, don't repeat yourself, experiment, experiment on how I must say things tonight, when this microphone swings back and forth strangling my neck.

Must I again tell you about a reminisced desire? Or must I just tell you that tonight is another rotten night of putrid poems sighing and looking at life's illogicality. Is it really illogical? Or is my spirit juxtaposing realities against thoughts, ideals against materialism, and perfumed, dry bread spilled in snow play.

But it's that I hear voices trying to tinkle away those sounds from me.

I'm just a pointless existence drinking away my meaningless self against a deprecating night that isn't very cold anymore. There was a blizzard, but that blizzard isn't here anymore.

Just remember this night when you tore away memories unforgotten. Whisper again. It's a secret. Possibly not. It's more than a secret, something more internal, something more exasperating, something that breathes and yet it doesn't; something that slowly, slowly drops eternally into oblivion.

Must you have some more secrets tonight? This night doesn't have any secrets. It opens itself cold, cold like Canadian cities are cold, and Canadians are cold, or are they just simply reserved? Perhaps, perhaps.

Squeaking ping-pong ball that slowly reminds you of that day you played ping-pong, squeak, squeak, cold, cold water bathing me, the waterfall, must I remember? Why should I try to remember, tell me?

Because dialogues are no longer dialogues but monologues of life, of people who once again talk with themselves and talk against themselves, and murmur sweet dreams, and murmur sweet words, words gently spitter-sputtering in black letters that skip in this Olivetti typewriter.

Just trying to make progress with memories, but the important thing is now. Time to forget old memories.

Damn people making all that noise outside. People who hate peace and quiet. Can't they float into eternity like I do? That's the answer to living, to answering questions that hum and lazily blow away distorted.

Must we know? What's the point of knowing so much? Can't we just love? I remember what you told me. You said love was … lonely? No, that wasn't it…or that love was kind and yet, it floats away clandestinely when kindness goes away…was that it? Or people loved you because they wanted to make love to you?

Let's talk about secrets — intense, deceiving, ironical. Or just silence.

Ping-pong ball goes back and forth.

Something funny happened. My slippers hid under my chair and I was looking for them and I couldn't find them, and I was getting mad, and that's funny, getting mad because you can't find your slippers!

Another thing: I spilled water all over the place. "Flush, flush the magic dragon lived by the sea and dadadadada"…or how about that nice Brazilian song Dindi "Oh Dindi…like a river that flows…" I forget…and the other one "How insensitive I must have been etc. etc."

Sleep. I must sleep. I'm just too tired being profound and looking for answers to floating desires, pigeons floating away…is it possible that a woman could reject a man? Shouldn't it be the other away around?

These few particles of myself…no more new friends…this poem, this state ends, a state of mind, a condition of existence, pulling away from nothingness.

Day ends. Funny, but it does. Slowly. Like a miracle that ends and is forgotten and no longer believed. I now want to call the attention of another day. Today is a grey day snow perhaps in the clouds. And I await a phone call…

# CHAPTER 12

*Edmonton, January 31.*

"There are other people to blame. Don't blame yourself."

"I wrote him a note. I told him I was sick; that I was undergoing a spiritual crisis."

"What did he say?"

"Nothing."

It was cold. They woke him at 9. Somebody was calling for him. Nut he didn't bother. He went back to sleep. He felt sick and tired. He put on the Miles Davis record. It didn't help. He didn't feel like smoking. The day was cold. "Damned day!"

It was now 1.30. He wanted to die. And see God.

"How do you know he's there?"

"I know he's there. He's He's here right now. He isn't smiling. But I know he's here. Hiding invisibly here somewhere." He closed his eyes. A tear trickled. And he breathed silently. He held her hand tight. But he didn't see God. Yet somehow he was breathing somewhere near him.

That night he lay awake. It must have been the coffee. He imagined making love to her. Somehow he felt happy. He didn't want to feel happy but he had no control over happiness at this moment.

Feelings control people. And when they decide to leave them, they just go away and possess other people. Snow chopping away into infinite particles blowing and scattering over the plains of Alberta. He smiled. There was some kind of meaning in his smile. Immensity? No. Just a passing thought.

The phone rang. But it wasn't her. She must have taken sleeping pills. Or attended her two o'clock class. And taken coffee. At least, he loved her. Troubled minds like Baroja's black cloud over a red crater or…a snowed glove that mouths tipped darkness.

He felt like calling home, but he decided not to. The pain was still there; a penetrating pain. He could do yoga and stand on his head, but decided to just do nothing and be quiet. Like a thinking thought never to come back again. Never.

Where are the others? There was P. He was bald and witty.
"Como te va la vida?"
"Bien. Es decir, jodida pero aun andando."

He blushed after making this clever comment. He went on to say that he just came back from Mexico where he made love to a Mexican prostitute. He was there for a conference. Some thought he was nuts, but I found him funny.

"Circles" by Davis was playing. He thought of her again, drifting, suffering, smiling, while he was touching trumpeted eternity slowly dying in twilight or dawn.

"Why did you tell him that you were going through a spiritual crisis?'
"I thought of no other excuse."

The mermaid elephant painting looked sick. Like the yellow and black painting. But on that particular day, it made sense. It didn't feel sickening anymore. It started transforming, symbolizing.

The ashes were strewn on the rugged sofa . She smiles.

"Are you happy?" He asks.
"Yes."

*February 7*

Ray Charles, tinkling glass, "Jump?" To smile again. White-haired Vodka. On time, profound: God, call it ashtray, fat lady, reincarnation of ants and pigeons. It doesn't take courage. It takes only…faith.
Pause.
The man smokes and people are indifferent to him. Quit school? Pink brush, yellow and red. The stamps are still in the green book. Part of the blues. Sprite soda, in green transparency. You see? How can it be possible?
Continuity just like spontaneity; cannot reject, crazy? Smile, more profoundly. "O pato" from Joao Gilberto, that's it.
Don't call it prose-poem. Call it me. Or courage. Shakesperean "What's in a name?" Fontana de Oro. One a.m. now. And the Cuban didn't understand. He said she loved me. He didn't understand when he talked about suicide. No bullets: Italian hair-do. Flit, camp, fairy, or queen? Your choice. Paged edges — yellow and red, or a red face, a 19th century face — moustache, turn-of-the-century coat … and Perez Galdos.

Jones: muted jazz, blues.
The hippy called him bastard. And the Cuban felt ashamed. He said he needed earmuffs. Buy it in Army and Navy. Curtailed electricity. Long hair and a beard? Red pumps: pimples, perhaps. Rosy cheeks; the comedians. For love, for hate. More words creating puzzles, jigsaws from fog to airplane landings and finally, love again.

Love is that strong.

When I say "less happy", when I say I want to see God in a less blurred vagueness, reincarnating myself in hope, I meant I wanted to see a flickering eternity, not only in juxtaposed words, limited, but in something I hope I'll see.

Zorba: house, children, wife, marriage — the full catastrophe. What else does Kazantsakis say? "Women are such creatures. They give you all they've got." And finally, the classic "Books are the agony of men who can't answer questions".

An invaded sanctuary. Death: the door to fame. Conked car radio.

25 degrees below zero…no, the clouds warmed the temperature. Beautiful 9 degrees below.

Let's go. We'll be late.

The mist clears. I am not yet less happy. The poems keep on coming. The stories dwindle into doctoral dissertations. Dreams disturb themselves.

Greek beaches leave the scene temporarily — eschewed rocks, aged fires, I, the world…you're thinking too much again. What do you do? Feet, head, hands. Hell! Choose. Sneeze. Life, trouble, death, not, madness, or else, he'll not dare cut the rope and be free.

"Who called you?"

"C."

*Tuck Shop*

White flesh parading. Orange students. The askance of contemplations. Thoughts creating thoughts like cigarette smoke from tobacco fire culminating in diffused air.

Answers to being and nothingness, shaved contemplation of reflected selves, the hot noise of plates and proletariat food in Western, cowboy standards. The finishingness of these moments writing itself unconsciously.

I allow myself to be released consciously letting these fingers type words, fathomed words, consequence of ideas and thoughts.

The "shop" crowds itself more — more people, more noise, more sun, more unheard music. This is not a poet's inspiration. It is the reversal of progress, decaying into rottenness.

The waiting minutes are passing half-slowly. The trembling beats of my heart shake my fingers softly, tenderly. Rough atmosphere. There's always a "once in a while" of tenderness: no clarity, no specificness; just unrecognized and ignored people.

I see disguised biscuit-Judy munching a chocolate bar. No tenderness; just a warm, Spring Edmontonian sun beaming rays through microphoned voices dying in loudness.

And then the aloneness of being human once again.

I wait. Uniformity of faces asks me — why individuality? Why smile? Why not stay longer? No interviews please. Just say "Es una lastima". Finish off with mature, green endings as in Sartre's *Intimacy*.

There are others who swoon unmindful of wet eyes on my neck. There are those who escape, unseen, pretending. But for them, there is no rest: just unconscious poems, unpiped but smoked, in an afternoon of Spring.

Words. Because I write. I don't read anymore.

*1.15 pm. Another day*

The limo comes at 1.45. 30 minutes to pretend. To feel cold when it's warm. To say bright when it's dim. Profoundly and sincerely. Somehow it's still the 19th century in disguise.

Brainwashing can take place in your own mind by yourself. Imagine it is the 19th century: summarize or compare the French revolution, the bourgeoisie, the many discontented poor, while the aristocrats smile scornfully.

Wait: think. I just saw a Jewish nose pass by. Now, existentialism and situations and pretensions. Do they all mean the same? Life is in a way all that. In other words, false?
Like the theatre, like cowboy-speaking Albertans; better still, Edmontonians. It's my city now. It's named after me.

Stability isn't false at all' transition is false; movement, like theatre, is life. Everything changes. The end justifies the means. Progress, typically bourgeois. Red carpet in the living room. Lost aristocracy. Long time ago.

Words representing stability. Take for example three old women, half-dead, walking into a taxi, almost staggering. The taxi goes. I don't see them anymore. A little while ago, they were getting into a taxi. Now they no longer exist; and yet, they still exist in my mind. This is where the complication begins. When you're bored and have nothing else to do, the tendency is to complicate yourself with some trivial matter like existence.

The limousine has just come. Someone said "just in time". Actually, it came seven minutes early. I leave the lobby. Macdonald Hotel. I guess it's the only good hotel here. No, there's the Chateau Lacombe. Alienation. Synonym: pride. Love. Antonym: companionship. Words, synonyms, ideas. Red-dressed men don't impress me unless they're doormen of first-class hotels. (Catch the ice with your lips!)

The mind: "Danger: ice falling from roof". Red, yellow and black sign. No particulars, please. "Thank you. That'll be $1.75". An old man wears a green hat. A native Indian? The bus moves. I can't stop. But I decide to stop. Just affection.

*Airport*

The flight's delayed an hour. The airport seats are still purple. "At least, say goodbye", she told me. No, I now decide silence. I decided to write. Or call. And probably, I'll decide something different in Montreal. I may not even decide. Perhaps I'll just do things impulsively. Saturday. A dry, cloudy day. No one's here. At home, perhaps. I'm anxious to leave. Feel situated, brood, pout; the black evening dress, a stranger, music, candlelight. Atmosphere. Sophistication. Dumb? No, mood, so to speak. I may be the only passenger. A golden-haired baby. Music: Mathis, "It's not for me to say".

A grey poodle. A farmer laughs. Drift, philosophise, existence in my mind. How do you know if what are real are just figments of the imagination and not sensible reality? How can you tell if illusions and imagination like now as I fly through the skies are more real than this glass airport I see? Zen Buddhism says that the eyes deceive, and that real existence is intuition and imagination because they are more proximate to me, more subjective than the purple chair my body sits in, or this glass airport my eyes see now. What I intuit is closer, as it were, to me because it is I thinking; it is I, a reflection within myself.

I now recall the character Isidora in *La desheredada* of Galdos. She believed she was a Marquise because she was lost in her dreams, her illusions of becoming one. And there's the manicomio. Two, actually, one the place where psychiatrists send people to, and the other, where psychiatrists turn themselves in. You're with the crazies, you end up being like them.

Enough of that. Philosophizing brings you nowhere. I'm just bored stiff, that's why. Waiting for this hour to pass. Something to do before they announce the departure of my flight.

I was just so happy to leave and get out of Edmonton. I wanted to play with the children who threw snowballs at me, and to smile and run and laugh. I felt free. And I smiled again. I felt free smiling at the sun warming my face from the striding cold lazily blowing on my face.

*Undated*

He wasn't sad. His tears were flowing because his love affair ended. He didn't want to see her again.

"Somehow I love you even if you're leaving me."

He was silent. He didn't look at her. He just stared blankly at the ceiling. She sat down and touched his face. He hadn't shaved for two days. She took off his glasses and toyed with his ear. He thought of nothing. After a while, his tears flowed again. He wasn't looking at her but knew she was crying too.

"Is that your way of telling me to shut up?"

He didn't say anything.

"Are you once again in your profound and silent mood?"

The music played: Sinatra and Jobim singing "Girl from Ipanema". It was senseless. He grabbed his bag and left slowly. She didn't understand. But he knew. That's why he didn't want to see her again. He fell in love with someone else. She didn't know that.

The phone rang and her mother answered.

"Hi, love. Can I see you?"
"Okay. How about meeting at 11ᵗʰ street? In an hour?"
"Okay."

She was in red. A smile. A silent smile. She was lovely. The snow rebelled against the white silence of the afternoon. No breeze. White houses against the glaring blue of the sky.

"I left through the back door. I didn't want my mom to know."
"Has you flight stewardess friend arrived?"
"She's probably home now. My father fetched her at the airport."
"And your boy friend?" He teased her.
A cynical look in her face. "He doesn't like you." A giggle. He held her hand. It was cold. Silence. She smiled at him.
"Why are you smiling?"
"I'm trying to think what you're thinking."
"I'm thinking of a five-minute lecture when I meet my class."
"What about?"
"Ruben Dario, the Nicaraguan poet."
"Anything else?"
"Wine, women and song."
They both laughed.

"Listen, come on over. I'll introduce you. She used to be my brother's girl friend. She's funny and interesting. Quite talkative. She's from BC, from Nelson. My brother met her at that Catholic university there when he was a student. She's quite chubby now, but she's pretty."

"I hear you write in Spanish. Have you published anything?"
"Yes, a book of poems."
"I hear you also paint."
"Yes, in Spain. I had a couple of exhibitions."
"Interesting."
"How about you?"
"Just a glorified waitress in the skies."
"Will you hurry up with the tea?" That was N's father.
"Yes, yes, coming." That was N's mother.

"Anyway, let me tell you what happened in today's flight. Boy, was I pissed. Well you see, I fractured my leg once, and I still have a slight limp, so when I was serving coffee to this old guy, I spilled coffee because there was an air bump. I apologized, of course, and started wiping his pants. The guy gets really mad and says 'Will you tell that pilot to bail out?' And I tell him, 'I can't do that, sir. He's the pilot. If he does that, the plane'll crash'. And he gets even madder thinking I'm being sarcastic. Maybe I was being sarcastic, subconsciously. So he answers me back saying, 'Is that so? I didn't know.' Now that was sarcastic."

"Some people are just ingrates."

"Anyways, you get all sorts of passengers. There were six who proposed to me: four Greeks and two Americans. I guess Greeks like their women on the chubby side."

We all laughed.

"And there was this Italian guy. I guess they also like women on the fat side. This Italian said 'Hello' to me once in this restaurant. I said 'Hello' and he joined me in my table and we chit-chatted for a while and from no where, he asks, 'Can I be your manager?' And I ask, 'What do you mean?' and the SOB says, 'You're a whore, aren't you? How much do you charge?' What a jerk!"

We all laughed.

"What did you say?" asks N.

"I played along with this little game, and I blurted 'A hundred dollars'. And he says, 'Yes, that's how much you should charge.' Eventually, he knew I was fooling around and embarrassed, he excused himself and walked away."

"Boy, you're funny." N's father laughed in his quiet, conservative way.

"Of course, I was stupid enough to give my address during out chit-chat, and he suddenly appears the next day and brings a wedding ring!"

"You should have accepted," N. joked.

"I didn't even know the guy! What a jerk! Two years ago, I was a blonde. And I told this story to my mother and told her, 'I think I'll quit the airlines and just earn a hundred dollars a day. She was furious. And listen to this. The next day, someone tries to pick me up again…I think he was Arab, and the guy was so aggressive. He asks for my phone number and address, and after learning my lesson the hard way, I say 'Look it up in the directory', and he asks in his Arab accent, 'But what's your name?' and I answered, 'Look that up too in the phone book.' I end up with all kinds of jerks!"

"You look the type that attracts psychos," N. joked.

"I guess I attract weirdoes because I was a weirdo once. When I was in High School, I burned my hair. So I colored it all black, and I went to school with black socks, a black turtle-neck sweater, dark glasses, and long hair up to my waist."

"I thought you said you burned your hair," interjected N's dad.

"That's the funny thing. Only half of my hair was up to my waist. And once, I was told by my teacher to go to the washroom to take off my lipstick. I came back with no lipstick, but I painted my face white and put a lot of black lines highlighting my eyes. I looked like a ghost. That's enough about me. What kind of poems did you publish?"

"Love poems."

"Tea is served!"

The next day, when they had lunch at Tuck Shop, N. told him about how her brother just broke off with her without saying goodbye. He went to Montreal to work, and married a Scottish woman. She felt hurt especially when he sent her an invitation to his wedding. "I ended up being her friend."

"Remember when you helped me with my play? I gave you the script. You came with me to rehearsals and after the play, we had a party."

"It was just the two of us."

"They say the play was a success, but I kind of felt empty afterwards, and I just wanted to be with you."

*Undated*

"But I don't like the Cuban. He's just nice and funny when there are people around, but then he twitches and gets all nervous when he's alone with me."

"Well, I guess that's how people are when they're alone with you."

"What about me?"

"You're a loner. That's probably what attracted me to you. I always go for the underdog. But I guess it's more than that."

"What do you mean?"

"I like the way you write."

"All those depressing poems?"

"It's literature. You can really write literature."

"The taxi's coming."

*Undated*
"Hi. It's me again."
"Hi love. How are you?"
"Did I wake you?"
"No. What are you doing?"
"Sitting. Doing nothing. And you?"
"Nothing. I don't feel like smoking or eating."
"Not smoking, eh? That doesn't sound like you. I phoned earlier."
"I went to the store."
"Three rings, but your mom answered the phone after two rings."

*With simple smiles*
*Laughs*
*Poems*
*In the dark vagueness*
*Of passion's delirium*
*A slight, relaxed state*
*Yet at night*
*Haunting, reckless, careless*
*Night that ends*
*Day must begin...*

*February 12*

One of my students laughed hysterically. I laughed too. I don't know why. Probably it's because her laugh was contagious. I didn't know why she was laughing but I laughed with her just the same, without really knowing why I did. Maybe it was because I had my boots halfway on top of the table and I was slouching and unshaved, and smiling idiotically, reading the lesson, sounding bored. That's probably why she laughed.

The day was grey again; the air was cool. Refreshing after being cooped in a classroom. I dragged my feet. You have to drag your feet when you're wearing boots walking in the snow.

I thought of that student who laughed hysterically. She was good-looking. I think I had a crush on her at the beginning of the year. She came to class with this attractive-looking black and white dress and pretty black stockings. She liked to giggle a lot, but she looked pretty, giggling and blushing.

There were six students today. It's like that at this time of the year. Tomorrow I'm sure there'll be six different ones. I like it that way. More variety. I get nervous when they're all there, all 12 students. They remind me of a jury passing judgment on you: guilty of insanity and boredom.

My student R.L. read his summary today. I bet he didn't understand what he was talking about. Everyone was talking while he was reading. They were probably bored with his monotone. But that's how students are. They don't like to listen. They talk when they're supposed to listen. They probably knew he didn't understand what he was reading. I was bored myself. I wasn't listening to him.

Then I had to go to my graduate class and the teacher, Mrs. N. who was still half-sick from a flu, gave an anaemic introduction to Berceo's *Milagros*. There were a few interesting things, though, despite the fact that I kept on yawning. But I wasn't bored. In fact, when we started the discussion, I was getting excited about it. I was always fascinated by the miracles of Our Lady in Lourdes and Fatima, and this medieval Spanish Benedictine monk wrote about these miracles. I was excited but Mrs. N. looked half-sleepy and bored. She looked dead sometimes. She frightens me when she smiles vivaciously. I guess you shouldn't smile if you look half-dead. Anyway, when I was in the middle of my excited discussion, she stopped me and said it's 3.30, class dismissed. We started at 1.30. Apparently, that's how it is in classes. When things start heating up, it's time to go.

*February 13*

N. wasn't where the coffee machines were. C. wrote me and told me she hated me for I did to her. She said she pitied me because I was a loner and had no friends. She also said that she was my only friend and that I had lost her now.

I wanted to write her and thank her but I was afraid she might get hurt. I just don't like hurting other people's feelings.

Today, I had three students in class. I hope I have three different ones tomorrow. I told these three students I'd give a test tomorrow. I told them that so they wouldn't show up. I don't like seeing my students two days in a row. It's boring.

Going back to C. and her letter, she said that the friends I had lost said bad things about me. I felt like writing her and saying thank you but as I said, I don't like hurting people's feelings. She might take it the wrong way.

She continued on saying that if I were really a poet and an artist, I should have feelings. I wanted very strongly to write her, but I controlled myself. A thank you note was bad. She might get hurt. After all, she was good to me at one time.

The day is grey again. A little drizzle of snow. The cold is biting.

N. wasn't where the coffee machines were. I miss her.

*February 14*

I sat in my classroom with my feet on top of the table with my mukluk boots on waiting for my students. They got used to seeing me that way. G.G. came to class after being absent for two weeks. He said he had a hair growth in one of his eyes and he had a minor operation.

Three of those who came to class today were the same three who showed up yesterday.

I said Happy Valentine's to my class of four before I dismissed them. They grumbled because I gave a long assignment for tomorrow. R.L., my German student, asked me why I go too fast with the lessons. And I answered: "Because others ask me why I go too slow." Another student looked at me and grumbled again before leaving the classroom.

The chocolate bar machine in the basement was out of order. You needn't put coins to get your chocolate. I put two dimes and I got four chocolates. I phoned N.

"Hi love".

"Hi."

"Happy Valentine's. Why weren't you at the coffee machines yesterday and also today?"

"I didn't go to class. I feel sad."

"Why???"

"My mother read my fortune this morning."

"Your mother? Does she know how to read fortunes."

"She's Rumanian, you know. She learned how to read palms from a Gypsy."

"What did she say?"

"She said you were going to leave me."

"I don't intend to."

"It's not up to us."

"Who then?"

"Fate. Destiny. Call it what you want."

"What about free will?"

"There's that too, but what we want doesn't necessarily mean it's going to happen."

"But why?"

"No one can explain why things happen in life."

"Well, let's see what happens. Do you want to go out?"

"No, love, I'm sorry. I'm just too depressed. I'm just going to ruin your evening."

"Okay. I understand. See you tomorrow?"

"Okay."

"Bye."

"Bye."

It pained me when she hung up the phone. It pained me about fate and being resigned to it because you can't fight it. Things happen whether you like it or not. Some kind of the flow of life, the flow of time, of the past, present and future. As though things have to happen. But fate can be kind. A door closes and perhaps five doors open.

I got back to my room around six and went to sleep. I woke up at nine. I wasn't hungry; so I ate the four chocolate bars. I read a little. Then I did a little yoga. I do yoga when I'm bored. You have to do something when you're bored. At least to know you're alive. To "confirm your existence" according to Beckett in *Waiting for Godot*. I did some sketches, and afterwards, I got bored again. So I ate a sandwich. That wasn't boring because I realized I was hungry again. When you're bored, you forget you're hungry until you start eating.

*1.44 a.m. February 15.*

I can't sleep. I guess it's because I napped for three hours. I wonder what I can write now. Maybe about how I spent the past three days and nights teaching, reading, writing, sketching and being indifferently bored.

I look at my record book and make an imaginary scale in my mind of those who'll pass, who'll get good grades, and so forth. I always like doing that. But then, the people I want to fail all of a sudden come to class and pass their tests and I don't feel like failing them anymore. But someone has to fail.

*2.05 a.m.*

I guess I'll just close my eyes and try to sleep. Maybe I'll be able to sleep.

No, it's no use. I'll just close my eyes and maybe by 5 or 6 I'll be able to sleep. I'll concentrate hearing the hissing and knocking sound of the radiator, and maybe I'll be able to sleep. There's a humming outside. I wonder where it's from. It's like the sound of a factory far away.

Later, the other noises will come: garbage collectors, people passing in corridors to the bathroom, cars starting up. There isn't real silence around here. Only temporary silence — you're afraid someone will suddenly make noise. Many times from oneself — the croaking of the intestines, biting of nails, cracking of fingers, clicking of teeth — no one can really keep still and silent for a long time. Even the fakirs have to move a bit. Maybe the thump-thump of their hearts, their breathing — you can't help it.

I sneeze. My windows are open. There's a draft. I like drafts. They make me sneeze. I blow my nose. I don't like blowing my nose. But I have to.

The day is grey. The sun might shine a bit. But it will be grey. Winters are grey here. All that remains are these paintings around me.

But they'll all be gone, maybe in a garbage dump. A few thoughts; some feelings — emotions, affections, sadness and happiness, all fleeting in this university life, in this human life.

It's life, it's living, time goes on and we leave behind traces of ourselves, oftentimes in doubt, sometimes in certainty, smiles, frowns, profound, superficial. Most of all you leave behind people who care for you but time erases the good and the bad.

Tears — a human factor. Do animals cry? Is it only humans who cry? Death. Human, earthly death. No one escapes death. I don't want to think about it. I want to live a long life and die when I can no longer take care of myself.

Buildings are constructed only to be demolished. New coins turn to old coins, profound blackness turns to superficial light. Earmuffs. Boots. A yellow Valentine card from C. Her way of saying goodbye? Books selflessly smiling, reaching for thoughts beyond black verses, or black prose, or simply black words staring, attempting communication, meanings forming subtleties. They'll vanish too, like poems, memories, safeguarded metaphors in red and black. A basement painted in fluorescence for winter, not summer in this cold town/city with conventionally indifferent people challenging me with its cold fingers, shameful eyes/ice thinness/frigidity. At last I se myself in uncoloured dreams and wave lengths.

Once again, I hear university noises but now in a different, more desirable way: construction machines, sound of cementing new buildings, ploughing a city's vague existence.

*February 16*

Water tasting of chocolate; paper, half-crumpled; this afternoon, coffee with my students. Sun shines finally. Today, unlike other days, the day isn't grey. No need to write: enjoy the sun's rays. This is your inspiration. Pockets empty of inspiration; at one time, my soul was full of it.

A typewriter half covered with books, a lighter, empty check book, transistor radio, enveloped, a record jacket, black earmuffs, a Titus watch.

Record player insists on playing; tapes have stopped; map still uncovered because the month has passed; style — bypassed; blue pants, like blue summer, still hanging; and old, worn-out grey coat also hanging, used and abused in Spain and other travels.

No other day but this; practiced hemisphere of misunderstood days; juxtaposed themes with cold, changing temperatures from sun to grey to humidity.

A piece of wood on my bed. What's it doing there? Crooked hanger, a waste basket and a man who asked me why God smiled. I gave the enigmatic answer of the Spanish painter, El Greco: "Because down there, there are prophets."

3.12 p.m. Sinatra sings: "Each day is Valentine's Day." Followed by Astrud Gilberto's "Quiet walks by quiet streams." All poems with high saxophones, beats and guitars.

The day is bright.

Soft songs.

The phone rings in the corridor. I hope it's not for me. The phone rings for twenty people in 20 rooms in Athabasca Hall Men's Dorm.

I slept well last night. I had a dream. But I've forgotten it. I always forget my dreams when I wake up. I remember them vaguely when I wake up but then, as I try to remember more, they fade away.

I eat half a sandwich.

3.30 p.m. I have to get dressed for my coffee class. A continuous Lorcan odyssey: prosaic understatements, another enveloped strangeness, happiness in disguise, more colored understatements, more continuities, more strangers, Hudson Bay gloves with a hole mark, and then a blackout.

Five months have gone by here. I don't know if I like it here. Probably not. I met N. after my coffee class and we talked about God, Man, Greeks, Romans. And then, there was a moment when I closed my eyes, held her hand tightly, and prayed.

# CHAPTER 13

*Edmonton. March 6, 1968*

*Chiau.*

It'll be your fault if you don't remember. The Dave Brubeck concert, laundry, stained socks; car, still parked in Spring. These days have been fruitless. Temptations. Cede, weak creature! Some friends have amazed me and now, the stars take their revenge again. He smiles.

They asked about my car. I said it still runs.

Reading about the embellishing of society. My pajamas are ripped. Naked days. Sentimental past.

This is the time of year in Canada when it's neither winter nor spring. An intercourse of winter and spring. Even the birds are indecisive. Did they fly back north by mistake? I can't see the pigeons of Athabasca. I melt like the snow — sad, fragile. Dewdrops in snow? The Cameron library smells of humidity from the Saskatchewan river.

When summer comes, the smell of manure will be strong, like the smell of September last year when I got here for the first time. They called it Indian summer.

Eight months for this Albertan school year. I'm restless; there's no rest for dynamic souls; there's no peace for me — intranquility, restlessness.

"You're in one of your moods: restless, but lazy."

A guffaw. *Carcajada.*

"You're funny."

Shall I cynically say, "Am I sentimental to a generation to come?" "Comrades" in Jesuit clothes. South American writers hated the Jesuits. There are priests everywhere.

This typewriter is aging. The taste of Spanish wine is a remembrance. Every Sunday, a Spanish wine called "Casa" was served at the Colegio Mayor.

These days remind me of certain plights, certain friends, certain people who open themselves up. Albertan cowboys, for example.

Divorce nature from God. I age. Lost innocence of youth. In my youth I swam seas, not rivers. Rivers are muddy, seas, warm seas, touching warm days, the countryside, the nipa huts. Vibrancy, no longer innocence. The winding roads, my ears felt the presence of pressured air. No books, only words and provincial smiles from kind but temperamental aunts, aunts who were of native descent cross-bred with Spanish, aunts who took me in their arms during my infancy. I remember their stares, their smiles, and now I know too much. Lost innocence.

Lost innocence. Now, all doubts, doubts questioning and answering themselves in more doubts, more depth, more reflections, sometimes too depressing to fathom during sleepless nights; unanswered doubts, more thinking nights, restless emotions flowing within me. The past is past. Now is now. Not bitter, not depressing, but present and breathing. Nostalgia. The past. An ashed past remembered in the losing dawn of the future. Smile, resentments — no one waits for me.

Red, a sickly yellow, a white greenness of this painting I now wait to dry. Another flight into the abstract.

I'll wait for you. Tuck Shop. Chew gum. Chew the heavenly reality of Spring. I weaken in Spring, my legs tremble; this feeling of love is fleeting. I feel a certain nothingness that pushes my fingers to relate, to narrate the half-truths of the day.

These half-truths invade me and ask why I am what I am. They bother me. I'm a young, unsuspecting poet and artist, dreaming of beauty and trespassing the dungeons of life where beauty and lies co-exist; a life full of restless journeys; searching for stability in the midst of instability. Nights that bother me with their solitude. A phonograph I don't use anymore. A tight blackness, an inconsequential dialogue:

"Cohen, is he always like that?"
"Yes, I guess so."
"Why does Frank Sinatra get divorces so often?"

Es un asno. Una expression sorprendidad. Estoy aburrido. La cinta flaca.

At year's end, the examination will come. 50 per cent, 25 chapters. Some will pass, some will fail. Abur, a Galdosian expression.

Por que?
Nada es nada.

A glass that foretells your future.

Were you my friends once? It's silly. It matters a lot, and yet it doesn't. More juxtaposed boredom? The twisting of realities, the squeaking of steps. Don't rely on dreams.

The smell of bleach, unending stories, phone rings, no more knocks on my door. No one calls me anymore. Good! Solitude is a check-out of Creativity.

*March 8*
The sky is red tonight. In the distance, the red glow of night plays in my eyes. I open the windows. There's a chill that comes from outside. Someone criss-crosses the sunlight as he enters. Now, the sun is gone again with clouds. Have the letter arrived? The shelves are empty. When were heroes decided upon? When were sofas invented? When are the maids cleaning the washrooms? When will the unending university hums from construction machines end?

I make judgments, and I ask: "Am I justified to make them?" I answer "No". But I go on making judgments. Why do I say "bored" when I'm alone? Ensconce the "I don't knows". Discharged battery, like my soul. Chocolate ice cream in cones. A license to pollute minds. The respected bourgeoisie. Sartre says that he pities that "paralyzed survival called immortality". Take off, bird, take off!

Why ask so many questions? Just turn on the light, close the windows, change shoes, and decide. Or let time pass. Perhaps wonder/ wander a bit. But young as I am, smiles as I am, students that are mine, yet in the depths of dreams and shadows, red lights will shine to remind me of a red light that glittered in the black horizons of Canada.

Not white. Below freezing point in Spring. I should not do it. I can't hanker anymore. Sights will dim in prophecies; gold will manifest itself into independence. How do those golden clichés go? "Silence is golden; all that glitters isn't gold", etc. There is no use wondering/

wandering. There is too little time in this short life. Yo digo si. Yo digo que si.

Amphora blue pipe tobacco. Manuscripts, resuenos, daydreams in solitude, unseen letters, time felt, fleeting, fleeing, gods playing with wrath games.

Some kind of warmth still lingers.

*...I knew him the Indian but I refused to recognise him because I didn't like him the duty of poets the right of artists to deny unbearded ones when they are supposed to be bearded they are lost then creation is like that from nothingness to nothingness the class is silent verdant spring ha disgust below freezing point a bump a library bump foot powder results updated unpicked father make a hell of life out of this one twitch then smile the golden blonde likes dark-haired men the cowboy sat beside her no he was not a cowboy he just liked to wear cowboy boots ...*

I held her hand. I felt nothing. Two more blocks. White haired father comes and picks us up. Last night, I was asked about my father. I transformed myself once again into one of the bourgeoisie.

Was I entertained? Frankly, no. I felt bitter at dawn. Dawn, when I slept. It was four. I was still awake. I don't know what time I slept. I heard a knock on my door. I woke up. I don't know what time it is. Someone wanted to come in. (Maid? Week's bed sheets?) I didn't answer. I didn't want to be bothered. I pretended I was still asleep.

Pretend: the essence of life? Are we all pretending in life? There is no running away from pretension. Forgive me. I'm a pretender.

Friday night. Study. Disgusting. Not really. Indifference comes quickly. It cracks. There was no snow when I said that insanity is when you're leased and when you're freed. Then, lighters are used in the mediocrity of all, cigarettes lighted, neckties worn, and life released. Tell me, why is there no escape? Why is there only a middle ground to slavery? Half freedoms? Half intuitions! Depend on my generosity. Brilliant, clever.

Why silence?

I laugh. I laugh, alone. My laugh echoes back and forth in the empty mountains within me, empty rivers, empty being, of essence, of existential decay, of a nothingness enclosed by a body. My worst enemy. Because it drags, urinates, defecates, eats, sleeps, talks, and worst of all, turns still in an event called death, and in time, shifts into another happening called ash. What then?

*March 9*

Saturday night. Let my hands think by themselves. Are you "happy"? Two a.m. I don't remember much about being "happy". I sleep at 6 or 7 and pout at 2. The phone rings and someone invites me to Calgary. Hell, why not? Let's go to Calgary. Go through Red Deer. And people?

Atmosphere: shades, wine, the smell of incense, and someone you like talking to. Computing machines? The A's go vertically and horizontally, and the improvised stories: yes, my hands were cold because I was happy. A story about a father who blushes: improvised. A story about Herman? A story about the lemon fruit that never grew because the land wasn't fit for it? Improvised or invented? Heard about it. Not plagiarised. Just a set of ideas: drift, inflexible, no limitation. Reality is limitation; dreams are illusions: *en un manicomio galdosiano.*

Computers: summarize. Goodbye. Why? Bored? No. I'm glad I met you. You're funny, crazy. Interesting. I'll probably see you at the library. No? Tomorrow perhaps?

The bathroom had a smell of paint. They'd just painted it white. At least I don't have to smell the chlorinated water coming from the showers. It smells of acid, and I imagine myself burning as I bathe, acid hot water coming down towards me.

Last night, I don't remember what time I slept. I went to bed around 2 a.m. but couldn't sleep. So I went down to the lounge to read the papers. My favourite pages are the Comics and the Ads section. There was an ad that read: "Farmer wants to correspond with a widow between 30 and 40; outings, dance, sports". I also like to look at the car ads. I have an old car and I dream of having a new car.

*March 10*
The washroom today had a smell of a dog that had just taken a bath. "It is winter again", the Doctor of Science commented. "Yes," I answered in my mediocre way, trying to make polite conversation. "Thanks a lot. Good night", I said as I closed the door of his car.

True enough, winter comes back with its bitter cold. My back aches. I feel partially paralysed by this weather. Words thrown back at me; weekend has passed. Surprise, laughs, an airport that chokes with lemon tea, a ten cent coin in the telephone slot. My car Greta was slow today. Smeared lipstick. No snowfall. Cold, though. Looking back at Christmas 3 months ago — Santa Claus laughing "Ho, ho, ho!" I hum a Christmas carol: "White Christmas". Exit: East. The mirror reflects. You laugh. I understand.

Lady's man, man's lady. And now these walls talk to me once again. Loneliness. Temporary.

She said the Vermouth was diluted. Cowboy grins. Pleasantly bored with Volkswagen music. The pool was hot. The day, cold. And the sundae, too much. You can't keep still. You have to go, go where you want to go. It's more fun. The foot, on the heater. The telephone:

the Turks are still there. Your boyfriend gave you a box of candies. Finally, fish and turkey. There was Neruda, of course, and the tearing down of walls. Just one wall, actually. The paintings are still there. No profoundness, now. Just a snowflaked, light day, passing.


*March 14*

Do you believe in fortunes?
Yes.
But they're not true.
That's why I believe in them.
I hate Edmonton.Why?
It's a growing city.
Shelley creates beauty.
I create beauty.
Yes.
Tonight was a wonderful night.
Presumptuous?
No. Premonitions. Don't get shocked.
I'm resigned. Destiny, you know.
We have another month of togetherness.
Then maybe more in Montreal.
I love you more.
I like you more.
You, premonitious you!
Even if I ate with my fingers
Impatient for the food to come.
Even if you nudged me to taste the wine.
Even if I stared in boredom at the burning barbecue.
Or bony spareribs.
All in all, tonight was wonderful:
The movie, waiting for the bus,
The cold, the passing headaches.
You in red, most of all.
Each day is Valentine's day, someone sang.

# CHAPTER 14

*Montreal. March 28, 1968*

It is at this time that I begin to write about the divisions of my life; about the curved awareness of truth; about radios that play in English and French. A rainy day in Montreal. Ten or more degrees above freezing. Not bad for a northern city this time of the year.

Stories begin to ache me.

I just ate some chicharon (piggies, as they call it here), dipping it in vinegar and garlic, and a glass of Cointreau. And now I smell of vinegary garlic. There is no routine in my life. There is only continuity — a touch of the "how" in the midst of this cloudy day, tender humidity, marrowing cold here at Ville la Fleche. This is where I live. I try not to be bored. I digress, I read, now I see; now I feel a slight tummy ache. Reality is truth, and truth disillusions. The house is typically bourgeois. Inside this home is a very Catholic family; in front of me is a medieval narrative poem about Alexander the Great which I have to prepare for my graduate class when I go back to Edmonton. Are there silent rebels in the house? Yes, I suppose. My youngest brothers. Non-conformists, in their own way. Too young to be independent.

Conjecture about myself: I'm always the exception to the rule, someone who can't help being "me", an actor, a human creator of words, a jack of all trades, an opportunist bitter about being part of the bourgeoisie, in the midst of an anonymous outsized city, writing — everyone writes, anyway. But the significant thing is the mystery of it all.

There's another thing to consider — the hunchbacked future. Khayyam's "Let's forget tomorrow for tomorrow may never come", but when it does come, what happens to security and the instinct for survival? To care about tomorrow or to care not? Two people: no solitude. But solitude is the happiness of a writer. And painters. All artists. Complete deviation from the world.

The twitching of stomachs, the miracles of the non-creative, the desire for a foggy day, the inconsistency of asking and not getting an answer. Except for an I don't know. Or perhaps the sad/happy mystic revelation — a smile, a happy happiness, and then pencils and papers interface. Today, a typewriter and linen paper sold at Macdonald Hotel, Edmonton, the oil capital of Canada.

Enough of cloudiness. Something written, something like a stereotype for avid readers of clichés. Just one trend of thought, some words, juxtaposed ideas, the hippies — the generation that follows the beatniks. No intelligent conversation. Just remember the absent-minded professor, or the flight stewardess who announces that passengers should leave by the back door when the plane is still in flight.

5 p.m. Almost foggy. I feel like throwing up. This unaccustomed stomach. Everything is so arranged, so seemingly perfect where wholeness is no longer whole. No meaning to it. Can I pretend to swallow my pride? Can I act as though I'm enslaved and inferior, and convince myself that I cannot really be humble? All of us are like Dr. Jekyll and Mr. Hyde. Two solitudes within. Schizo, call it what you want.

Broken diet. Bored. Overwhelming silence. Except for some James Bond music on the radio. Prepositions, propositions, the idiocy of the English language. Or of any language at that.

Slippers. A teacher goes to his class with his slippers because of a growing toe-nail. He shocks students with his beard and slippers. I did that. Three years ago. I left after teaching only a term. Things are too slow and artificially efficient, efficiency over things that don't need efficiency. Only happens in rich provinces like Alberta. What a waste!

The rest of the world are poor and grey, and all fountain pens and cars are blue, and mid-term examinations are formalities. Peace, peace, no quarrels please.
Planned.
A quiet place to say "something stupid like I love you", care of Sinatra.

Sartre's *No Exit* where shadows are blue, a pale blue, a somewhat greenish blue, a blue that doesn't whimper, sick, loyal, stable, sweet. A crucifix. A temporarily dead Christ. A rejected prophet, but now an invitation for psychedelics.

The wall is pale grey. There is no basement smell here, like the one I smelled the first night I was here. The flavour that now balances in my nostrils is a bitter kind of humidity. A flavour that meditates, that thinks it reflects and enters intuitive depths but actually resides only in a phoney-like cluster of prearranged things.

I'm now dazzled by a nauseous kind of existence. Something's stuck in my throat. Part of my heart? Part of my lungs? No, it's a flame that investigates the meaning of months, of days, of shortened, interrupted interludes, of mapled whiskey, and most of all, worst of all, a pipe-smoking poet retracing the useless travels that clot the blue veins of his past.

Retrace the puked past. Don't cross your legs. Make way to the numbness in your bones. Wait for the day to say 100% humidity, and let the enslaved thoughts, ideas of the here and now clutch deep in your soul, a soul that remembers prayers but refuses to remember. A soul that is blackened by enslaved freedom: there is no escape. This is a kind of freedom that lessens judgments, releasing thoughts, a freedom to smile and awaken insignificance. Not even ennui can triumph. It is silent with the moving, mechanically moving fingers of inspired fate. The supernatural beings have left. They're not gods. I can't even think or imagine what they are. Right now, I feel I'm only what I am: is there anything else beyond being?

A soul-searching atmosphere reduced to mumbled prayers. I listen to the night, mumbling prayers to the rain. Someone has made, out of nothing, a being that refuses to conform to the humidity of the days, to the abstraction of the years, to nights and days, and to repeated absurdities.

Decisionless: falseness inherent in our nature as it is for walls that listen, speak and shudder, sometimes sweat, sometimes think, sometimes grow old in their inanimation. Humility=humiliation. The mind, a makeshift of devices in time and space. Brainwashing to conform: this is the purpose of education. Result=students do exactly the opposite. Conformity is limitation. Vagueness+Concreteness=Idiocy. Life's quest? The nose that smells and the mind that visualizes.

Mistakes are rebellions against repentance: repentance comes in many forms. Papers falling. Fixing of beds by a maid in blue. Disturbance of silence. The mind/the soul/the intellect confronted by buildings that have grey hair. I am mistaken, and this is amorality. Repeat conflicts. Limit fingers and forearms. Chew, whisper clandestinely, regret. Why do we build scaffolds? Someone complains:" He charged me more this year than last year." The Economics of price and wage changes. Inflation.

The mind lives in a different world embodied in solitude. Chance, pick chance. Unwavering influence, abounding friendship, sympathy claims, understanding specks of truth. Love? An abstraction of the mind. I believe. I forget. I write. Vagueness gets vaguer, redundancy more redundant, irony more ironical. Things are more than what they are.

Defend. Judge. Trying out love with the concurrence of oblivion. Shadows abound. Unknown forces. Telepathic wavering. Defending freedom with the tools of slavery. The third eye. The creator. Forgotten thoughts. Revelation that youth is futile. Is there real truth in Zen Buddhism? Who can justify the Church's doctrine that there is no salvation outside of it? What about yoga and the beads? The releasing of the spirit — a new breed of freedom — spirit that denies reality.

Voluntary insights of take-care-kits. Studious. Philosophically impressed by reversals. There is no escape. Estudioso como dice el Sr. X, asi es.

Creativity in the continuum of things. The groping mind. World-weariness, sulk, contrast words heard and read. They never remain forgotten in lugubrious nights and revered days because words flow, yes, truly flow as they are written and are then forgotten for the time being but as they are heard, they are remembered again in the realms of fancy when we sigh, when we get down to the nitty-gritty, a conscious visage, a poetic painting, an obscure intellectualism.

Funny how things are what they are, how life really is! Not heart-rending, not apathetic, not ambiguous. Just funny, the funniness of vanguardian purgation turning ingenuity to inventiveness. Can we follow systems? Is it too late? Is it too early? Is there magnitude in solitude? Is there understanding in shifting? Shifting of sleep in high bed. Shifting and love-making in painted rooms.

We always want to say "We will be happy". False hopes. Hopes that sadness will lead to happiness. Solitude to companionship. Profundity to artificiality.

Nights will return with the fresh novelty of thoughts, mysticism, transcendence. When I was ten, they asked me what I wanted to be. I said I wanted to be an engineer because my spinster aunt wanted me to be an engineer. When I was fifteen, they asked me what I wanted to be. I said I wanted to be a soldier because my father was a soldier. When I was twenty, they asked me what I wanted to be. I said I wanted to be an economist because I was studying Economics. When I will be 25, they'll ask me what I'll want to be, and I'll say I want to be a philosopher because I'll decide to ask why. When I'll be thirty, they'll ask what I'll want to be and I'll say a Spanish teacher because I studied in Spain. When I'll be 35...

And I'll answer: everything. I want to be everything. But now I see that everything is nothing. There is no exit to nothingness. My mind controls me. My intellectual instincts have created a new being, a lazy being, yes, laziness, the fruit of too much wondering, too much thought, too much of everything. The result: nothing.

We are all actors. The world is a stage. We act. The weak actors are booed at silently. The good actors receive the glory, a momentary glory. Then they are reduced to something worse than the silent boos of the audience. The nothingness, the emptiness, the vacuum that an actor feels after a night of triumph. This nothingness, this emptiness is what Shakespeare said: "Life is a walking shadow; a poor player that struts and frets his hour on the stage and then is heard no more... an idiot full of sound and fury signifying nothing."

*March 23. Ville la Fleche.*

The night ends. The day runs. Take it the way you want to. Open days where visitors stay permanently. Uncompared reality, experimental thesis, traditional lifestyle. Romance languages originated from the very traditional attitude of an I-don't-know. Smell the kitchen sink or the Chesterfield sofa smelling of cigarette smoke. Hear the refrigerator hum. See the chequered green on the walls. Friday today. No Catholic obligation today. Lonely Friday night as I sit here in the kitchen. An everyday inconsistency of the now projecting into the past: forgotten Spain. Not really. Just hidden somewhere in my mind, in cobwebbed corners.

Lights shines only when there are artificial oranges and purples. Artists' delight. Café des artistes downtown. Limited generosity, self, increasing in conformity to limited and set ideas, even individuality which is an exception to the rule. There is no silence in individuality. There is only annoyance. Seclusion, aggravation overstated. The pine trees are gone. Uprooted love, skulking in sentimental journeys of the past, an insight into aging men who remain sentimental.

The days are foggy; the nights, even foggier. The taste of French aperitifs. The bells no longer ring. Four days ago, the sun was shining bright. But now, it's a foggy, rainy day, like the night I arrived. Rest and prepare for another day losing itself in night. And then to be with you again, happily. Just you. Never mind nothingness and despair.

Inevitability. Fearlessness. An ironic smile of rebellious resignation. A cowardly indifference of escape. Let the hours pass silently; let the minutes and seconds drift; let this meaningless self be terminated. It's 12.35. My sister calls me for lunch.

*Edmonton, April 1.*

I'm happy but I can't explain this happiness. It's a happiness because I'm here with you again, my love. Because we'll be happy together, in summer, in the quietness of university streets, in the warmth of days to come, and the coolness of summer nights. We'll walk hand in hand. Indeed, we'll be happy together. Please, let destiny be kind.

But there is something foreboding about this happiness. It may not last, as most things don't last here in this "mortal coil". Oh, it's so vague this life.

Another new month. Repetitious I love you's. Lower than freezing point last night. Confusion conquers the minds of the young. University students who become anonymous.

Calmness of truths. Disinterested reality. Abundance of illusionary truth. Conceited pride in sinful egoism. Windy structures of contemptful postures. Genial attempts at communication. The shifting channels of life: laughable. Justice remembered. Spain, reminisced: discotheques colored red, the oblivion of passing time, and the meaningless conjectures of trivial dialogues.

The necessity of directions. Comfortless and unseated songs: the hippies have rambled through society's images. Remember that lucidity is another reflected synthesis. The night has passed; happiness is passing, too; and now, there's only the future to reflect about.

Writers don't starve; their Indian spirits are content; they transcend physical reality and reach metaphysical heights in illusioned insanity, in forms genially packed into timed postponements. The glow of timeless Spring is locked in my soul.

*Undated*

Another writers' night. Lines of thought: adolescence, youth, sacrilege. Everything and nothing matters. Life is incongruous, anyhow. Meanings behind dictated truths: the past, remote and immediate. Past passing, present passing, future unknown. Nothing crystallizes. Horror movies come and go. Thoughts and decisions within 12 hours. Thoughts are no longer thoughts. Thoughts evolve into prostituted ideas, like cigarettes or binges, or certain idiosyncrasies.

All a temporary delight. Or a momentary melancholy. Unforgettable ventures. Dare the afternoon sun to set in the summer! Pauses are divinized. Matters replicate themselves. Don't mention boredom. That's getting sacrilegious!

Less contrasting stuff — perhaps bitter and ironic. Munificent premonitions distract this writer. Names abhorred. Save every penny for our Montreal spurge. Fifty dollars every three days. Of all places, in Edmonton, to support the towing business, the police department, the government of Alberta, the richest province of Canada!

TV: the Invaders and their pinkies that protrude; and Dean Martin sings "Return to me". And Greta, my VW, stammers, poor thing. It skidded in snow once. This time it almost rolls.

Last night, the Indian conversed with me and asked himself why he was studying Geophysics. He was in a philosophical mood — all his whys: why live, why be born, why die…a lot of philosophical fuss, and after an hour answering these questions, the end result: I don't know. I advised him to get a girlfriend. That might solve his philosophical anguish.

Pretend to be magnetic. Don't smoke. Sing "Laura", "Fools Rush In", "You Give Your Hand To Me", "Oh, Lonesome Me", "Buckaroo", etc. The writer writes: Church prostitution, amor libre, sociedad, amor bueno, Arcipreste de Hita, Sweet Georgia Brown. And you call that talent! Obviously. Prove it! You'll never see twenty-three this month. A birthday gift. A gift for my mother. A gift for my girlfriend. The stars are blue tonight. Friendly arguments. Scream, laugh. All my fault. Interest me. No need to exercise my eccentricities. Truth is fixed. Everytime time the cold comes I'll smile. Snow falls for a moment, then offensive jokes, a little thank you note, and then another touchy visit to passing time.

I decide to be small; I decide to be big. Humility? Nah! Of course not! Be! Or forget comfort. Forget about the whole affair. Each moment etcetera. The discotheque must be colored red: the mixture of sympathy and love. Shoot it out! The writer has finally reached himself; times are tinged; just kiss, then practice typing, and apply for a ground stewardess job, no air pockets; farmers, temperature steady tomorrow.

Subtle impressions. Ask, don't forget to ask. Steady. Stand by. Quote. God is angry. Now the toys rebel again: God's toys. The actor walks out many times. Limitation is like a door. It opens; it closes. Just that. Like a night limited by thoughts of 48 degrees Fahrenheit. A swim, a Chinese restaurant. Nails clipped, not bitten. Songs sung, not howled. You read. You're the reader, I'm the writer. The parking space is empty; the X section disappears. The Hungarian janitor, formerly a university professor in his country, has four black and white TV sets and one colored, and has a 1962 car with 19,000 miles, earns $400 a month, is disgusted with Hungary, the Russians and country girls who are nosy busybodies.

Writers' stomachs are garbage disposal and poets have half-smiles. The eyes of Leonard Cohen are like mine: elegiac. Tonight is a complete night because it's replete in idiocy, insipidness, rice, noodles, shrimps, a week's snow, sun and wind.

A subtle letter about psychological difficulties, about taking off for Montreal on May 11, about writing a thesis outline. It's a Canadian night: Chinese, Indians, Jews, Ukrainians, Albertan cowboys, philosophizing Indians, conceited Latin Americans. Irregular thoughts are no longer thoughts; rather, ideas based on emotion.

Presidents elected in a democracy are called accidental presidents. They're there by chance. No need to comment further about politics. Communism? No comment. Statistics lie. Politicians lie. Economists always predict wrongly. Don't pause: pauses are poison. You're in blue, as always with your "saco" and muffler, dark glasses and your usual idiotic, conceited half-smile.

Necessity is vicious and sadistic, like cold-blooded whispering Englishmen. Tom Jones on the radio. It's damp today; Spring, you know, professing its formal entry. Yes, the vicious circle of convention, of years of teaching and still not knowing the essence of things. Just words transmuted from one language to another, and then, vague poems, more movies, more far-away sighs, rapports, communication of thoughts…after all, we're all just actors in this stage of life, theatrical puppets manipulated in a world of humans.

Symbols treading the unknown, the mind's unknown, dialogues between mind and mind, the conscious and the unconscious. Subconscious dreams: my classmates pop up once in a while, and then heroes of the 19th and 20th centuries appear in a variety of makes and settings.

The variety that makes a man love a woman and vice versa; or the desire to continuously write in a Spanish morning: 2 A.M. Symbols aren't abstract at all. They are concrete generalities. They are projections of individuals: I the sea, you the sky. Indoctrinated abstractions, didactic, pompous.

Swimmers drink water mixed with chlorine as they swim on one side. They swim back on the other side. You say he doesn't like anyone? Not even himself? But isn't that human? Who dares say it's not human? Sober, be sober. Humanity, think of yourself; be egotistic the way you really are.

Reflect: folk rituals and other jumps of inspiration. Reflect on mad scientists. But who's afraid of madness? Digress. Agree. Don't ask. Don't deny. Does it matter? Obviously not. Nothing matters. That's why writers write nothing or talk about nothing. It's all a show, for entertainment purposes. That's the message, the eternal message, the

"I don't know" message, the eternal blackness of nothingness after death, the natural fears, the instinct to survive, to conform to society, to stand on top of eternal symbols, to have distinct and nasty hours of reflection. After all, the junction point is the conflict of vicissitudes, the intertwining, seemingly non-ending moments of each day, of seconds that appear and disappear, drifting in the tide of clichés, time, nights, days passing, slowly, fast, sometimes, many times, dreadful words, tragic plays, comic spontaneity, absurdity, laughter, hurrying seconds, crummy rooms, boredom, adaptation, friends, lost and gained, escapes and more escapes, extremes of knowledge, appreciation and suggestions. They don't matter. Optimism, like pessimism is just another word, another false hope, another consolation in this state of human affairs.

Conform to the standards of life, to morality set up by hooligans who bite back and get back at generations, revengeful of the younger generation and ungrateful to the older generation. Some things are not what they appear to be. Rebellions fall in the same pit of insignificance. Winchester Cathedral, are you falling too? Madrid: that's that. *Se acabo*. Piccadilly, Stones, Beatles singing Winchester Cathedral…are you breaking me down?

Yes, this night I dedicate to myself…trials…the night never beckons because beckoning nights are reserved only for French Dracula movies which end with "Fine". Fine, indeed. This is just tonight, a night of elongated canine teeth, foggy castles, good and bad creatures. No one believes anyone now. Even songs deceive; months of reflection and continuity; yes, life changes; and maybe, the snow has changed me; it has not made me an atheist; it has made me an imitator, a thinker whose freedom moves by itself and plays, like God plays, with consoling words like love and prolonged anti-masochism, anti-agony, and anti-sadism. That is why we are not really who we are. We don't even know what we want in life, or what to be sincere about, or satirical, or honest, or ironic. These don't make us what we are, not even with kindness or regret or the Catholic virtues of love, faith and hope.

Pause. Sentences end. They begin again. And end. And begin. Grumble, complain, pretend to be sincere. It doesn't matter. Life is absurd. And so, be what you want to be. I have not decided yet. Perhaps my decision will be indecision. That is somehow also a decision. It will be the perhaps of the be-all and end-all; that certain drifting, the ever-creating sensation of novelty.

Perhaps I'll conform. But this decision will be just a front. I'll still be the same rebellious non-conformist, a mad and confused writer who begins and ends, who wants to symbolize ethereal sensations, noise, sleepiness, everything in life, everything, even hope, like indirect autobiographies of poetic and non-poetic reflections, universal repetitions of the history of mankind, new faces but the same deeds, considerations, repeated conformity, people again, more people, more limitations, distances, reflections, more gods, blasphemous portrayals, usurpers like Lucifer.

Even philosophers will not understand the absurd mystery called life projected unto death, moving and moved by the mind and its dark corners — the unknown, never external because everything is here in psychological conflicts; these angsts of the spirit portrayed by unmentioned souls reflected over and over again by doubts, screams, and by more dialogues.

Ordered humanity: does your order have meaning? Can it possibly have meaning? The unknown: the object of the afterlife, the universal conjecture, this infinity, this debateable, mysterious absoluteness. Are you my friend even when musical instruments are torn apart? Even when years are added to your youth? Even these words mean nothing. I don't know why I write when I know how senseless everything is.

# CHAPTER 15

*Toronto, June 1969*

Even God might now ask why. Why these words are patterned with other words. Why my thoughts outgrow other things, other realities, poems and people, most of all, creations, ideas of the mind, like little squirrels that move fast, reflexively, in the rain.

And there may be younger people who bother me, bother my thoughts, disturb the rain, and my poems, and the cold that is wet in summer. I cannot stand cruelty, nor the passing of forced words; unremembered friends who haunt me, faceless, at night; in my dreams; in the colored everglades of my imagination. Stones that remind me of the warmth of lost poetry; lost in the wilderness of timeless space. Another one of those flashbacks. A little smile, a chat, a walk, a little dull time in my life, when they ask me to pursue my future win an airless whip that slashes winds, slowly, unenduringly, flowing and tired, with nothing but noiseless footsteps.

My ring has fallen off. Words reflecting spiritual pangs, pains that gnaw your insides, tortured, flighty. My passport picture: light specks in my eyes, that certain calmness in my face, a dignified and penetrating look.

The night now runs through the dark disguised with unwritten words. Time treads along. Time/Timeless. Now it's not. Days are counted. The first night comes, then the second, then the third, and so on.

It couldn't have been that long. Just a few years ago. Is my creativity going? It died with God. Just a few years ago.

There are moments when He lives, resurrected in me, slight spiritual sparks, light from within. Was that happiness? What then is happiness? The mysterious unknown, undisciplined sparks of memory?

I cannot surrender yet despite this vacuum of little unforsaken things — freed yet enslaved like earth to rain, pride and hate. I can no longer dwell with insights; even these have gone away; selected friends in the give-all of newness, rhyming loneliness, broken incompatibilities, stunned regrets, too late; tears reveal sentiments; and everyday, I just wait.

Hope was once beautiful. I saw experience in age, and yet, things come, blindless things, even in my fury, or in recalled sadness, other things spring up. Drama, Poetry: just plain interruptions, passing stages that express my years, when I pass from what I see and hear towards something I do not know about; and I whisper, unconvinced of myself; I look back and see that my life is a printed error in a poem, a poem seeking embellishment, and purity...even purity is now stained with thoughts of only me.

A few more quiet places; inquiries on life; praises for youth. Then...wondering repeatedly what the secret to happiness is. Love? It can't be. Money? No, people are miserable with money. I don't know. I really don't know. Maybe through the years ahead I'll find an answer to happiness.

In my poems, I've searched; in my scattered thoughts, projecting dispersed words, I've searched, and I couldn't find answers. I play with words like anguish and meaning and meaninglessness, to find, to mature, to go deeper, to say "you're right", or "you're wrong", and many times I not my head to say "yes", then I look vaguely at objects that are obscure in their colors.

My eyes are dimming slowly. I say "and yet" because once I laughed but I was never happy in my laughter. Or perhaps I was. I don't remember. I'm told to look into people's eyes, into their souls, people themselves, maybe little details that reveal what they are… still, I can't get over myself yet. I still feel unhappiness, disturbed dreams, people who ask and I attempt to answer by saying what I feel. I can't reveal what I don't have; I give all that I have.

I must return to the ridiculous clichés I learned in life, hearing people say the same old things, appearing phoney, trying to be nice, and having insights into what will be. Even death is a disguise.

My beliefs slip away; they become anonymous. I cannot mix life with what I do, but I must; it's part of me to express my life in what I do.

I go on thinking. I'm human, that's why. But I now find words difficult to express my soul. Words don't flow easily anymore the way they used to. I force them now. I've lost touch with what I was. But as time flies, we need to lose touch with the past, with what we were. We change constantly. I change. I've changed. There is no returning to what I was. A new self will be born. New selves keep on being born. Not flowing anymore; something more difficult that the flow, something that catches the concrete, the more understandable, the simpler things of life, things that strike me in different ways. No more clouds, hopes, fascinations — only the what-is-to-be-done, the now, the slow, more calculating, relaxed way of doing things.

Something more organized. Looking back once in a while and organizing the past into chapters, polishing the flightiness of very early youth. Or just forgetting.

Uneasy silence. Thoughts jump. Things blurred. A disease of the mind. A poetic word, or just plain simplicity.

People still live the way people have always lived: in little grammatical cubes, synthesized, organized. The years have made me indifferent — people, things. It's not me that has changed me; it's other things, I've outgrown them, and in their place, other more unhappy things are replaced. I guess I'll just have to half-smile the way I always do, and pretend to shrug the whole thing off.

Composed letters like blonde hair in the dusk. People I must dream about, stories that betray the evenness of things. No, and yet I must… I must learn to distinguish how things are, how shall and yet how precise things are.

Preciseness, perhaps…that's the answer. Like empty pauses of machines that throb like dark roads. Dark cruel words of this place at 610 35 Charles Street West. Allowances. Make allowances; give time a chance to shower spitefulness, a little somethingness, a little necessity…maybe misgivings? I don't like these colors in my new painting: they strangle my heart; I don't like these hands that clutch, creep and paint on this canvas. Weakly, I struggle, a struggle of hands, of hearts, of illusions, hoping these colors will reverberate…feel the moment. Unconsciously.

You do remember those days. But why remember? I hate remembering. Live for the moment. It isn't time to remember. Don't recall. Let time wake by itself, wait for time and dawn to break out, hear the cars pass, the ambulances singing their morbid tunes. Sharper, sharper…inspiration comes in strange and half-attached strings, from words to paint…white pearls…let me go away to misjudge, carry, observe how you frown with hatred and disgust.

There is now the sound of the swift slushing of water, colored water that falls on itself, beginning and ending. I decide undecidedly; I ask and answer…undecidedly. I pursue. I begin again covering things of the past. A perfect record of things, a make-up way of doing things. Suddenly, a desire, a prolonged and angry desire.

A few more words. A few more meanings, repeating themselves, beginning anew.

Selflessness? I've forgotten its meaning.

A light laughter? At least feel it in the air. Don't return and don't forget. But…where else can I go?

Maybe nowhere. Just stay in one place and don't go anywhere else. Listen to the ticking of time. Just do the little everyday things that you must learn, that you must do.

This questioning dialogue of self. This search for someone who doesn't care. Sometimes it's irritating. Sometimes people are irritating. They ask and you don't want to answer. Sometimes there are answers — answers of hate and anguish. Respite, unfavored, undecided, unwanted. Where else can you belong?

It's time to age. Just age. Don't think too far ahead. Just do what is to be done now.

Just lines, pearls of words, of scattered memories and thoughts, or just plain letters that speak silently.

I cannot have last entries in this diary. The winds no longer excite me. I feel that everything now is pointless, like a poet's life. I don't feel love anymore. There are only vulgar people who come to your house to disturb you, to make you hate more the vulgarity of things.

No more love; that's what matters. I feel that I have to return to my world of illusion; to hear the voices of my lost friends. I hope I hear them again. Perhaps when I do, I won't care as much as I used to, and when that happens, my thoughts will lose all intensity. I feel at this moment that life is futile. I've often thought of suicide but I'm afraid to die. I'm afraid of the how of dying. I lack the courage to kill myself. I lack the courage to face the afterlife.

Twilight nears. A Toronto twilight. It passes softly. It might have been better if it passed noisily, heavily, like winter's darkness. Three months and there will be another place to go to, another newness. That's how it'll always be. The world returns as it revolves. I have to return too. No more of fatherlands; no more of that romantic search for my identity. It no longer matters. I'll just write and live; know a little bit more of the history of man's cruelty to man, the cruelty of writers who have come and go.

A dream I must return to. Perhaps that'll be my salvation, a vague dream, in a few years, a few more thoughts on tastelessness, little details like a green table with red and black streaks; or a white balloon pointing to nowhere.

It repeats. Again. Considerably. Painstakingly. Like the choking darkness of this twilight cold, a windless Spring twilight. Like words that choke me; letters that struggle by themselves; red letters that stare over and over, again and again…lost agony, lost anguish. Neither anguish nor painful thoughts; neither spiritual struggles nor careless desires. Just a painless Spring. A Toronto Spring. A twilight that flickers out slowly.

When dark comes.

Dark has come. Intrepid dark, like cumbersome madness. To destroy even the pure, even the vulgar things of life. There can no longer be ends nor beginnings. The blackness of Spring is short, very short, and I'll dream, like my thoughts that thrive on cheese and bread and a glass of water.

Inspired by the oblivion of days. Days that wither, like the withering sun, hidden in the dark recesses of the other side, like self and its other sides.

When Spring ends, I too will end. I too will end these words, words, letters, a composite of goodbyes, untortured, creating, justifying. A shadow, an ugly shadow of imperfection.

No one else; no one else, make love, be silly, be perverse, hate each other's guts, no more poetry, just simple dialogues, dialogues of self, Toronto, idolization bourgeoisie, the purple noises of Yonge street, Bloor and Bay all together with police motorcycles clogging around, sirens from police cars and ambulances, trucks passing, simply and terribly noisy, Belleville, the quietness of Belleville, and I feel obtuse; remember Toronto, you'll keep on going back to it so many times, simple and ugly Toronto, its rains…I remember the rain the first day I arrived. Dull professors, a relief that I'm finally leaving, bringing banners with me…what month was it? Stutter, stutter, dot, dot…hellish, unwanted, strange, a few years, just a few more years… two, maybe three, to learn a bit of everything, ten thousand or more things to learn, t be industrialized, to proceed towards heights of untaught splendour…friends, yes, friends, a licensed way of saying how untrue friends are, not even loneliness, undisciplined mind, five more minutes, tell me to stop, no, not necessarily; unconsciously I'll stop, simply, truly, new places but the same things, same limited vocabulary, same kinds of people. When will I tire? Never! I'll never tire. Others might still think that I'm a piece of truth, a piece of love, like a piece of cake to be eaten madly at.

Slowly, I finish; slowly I'll die again, into dreams; what then will I dream of?

Insufferable people, very precisely that; nightmarish; undecided; I hear and from what I hear, I learn to revile. But I do see, but I do see and I learn and I detest, and I wish for always, for lines to come, verses that might mean something I cannot speak about now, something impossible, something between the lines, or words...I again really don't know but it's there, openly hidden, think of them, it was there, it was there, really it was, and then it went away, just simply went away...

The seconds have almost ended. It's 3 a.m. It's time to stop. To stop writing. Almost, like shadowed greens, unfamiliar names, but happy, truly happy...

# BOWLING GREEN CHRONICLES (1972)

*To my remembered friends Trausti, Benno, Larry, Ron, etc. if you're not yet dead from debauchery*

# FOREWORD

Why publish insights, poetic and otherwise, after more than 30 years? Perhaps it's the sentimental in me, the nostalgic, and I look at myself almost 40 years ago and I remember vaguely the friends I mention in these chronicles...Trausti and Stryggvi from Iceland, and Benno Signitzer from Austria, and others like Ron Hines who had just come back from the Vietnam War, an ex-marine wounded in battle, his right leg disabled.

I also vaguely remember the topics I was so familiar with: authors like Proust and Jung, Kierkegaard and Nietzsche, Joyce and Brecht... they all are a blur to me now. What I remember is that my writing style and my ideas were influenced by them.

**Bowling Green: 1972 Chronicles** is what it says it is— chronicles of writings when I was a graduate student in Bowling Green. Many of them originally written on napkins in the bars of Bowling Green with my friends Trausti, Benno, Larry, etc. Their names constantly appear. The chronicles reflect what we thought of anything under the sun: politics, society, studies, life, death, philosophy and so forth and so on. They are written in various ways, poetic, prose, thesis, anti-thesis, and other experimental forms we were creating as we went along. We did group writing in the form of group poetry where we would alternate writing verses, or alternate taking turns being a moderator in a debate...I chronicled all these.

The first two chapters of **Chronicles** is **Flow of Experience** 1 and 2 originally written in 3 parts, in 3 days, and on a continuous roll of paper sheets. I must have picked up left-over teletype paper from somewhere and wrote on this. I don't know where the original is now. I only remember a good friend of mine, Mercy, in San Francisco painstakingly photocopying these sheets. And this is what I have now: the photocopy which I've edited and reproduced in Word here.

My Bowling Green Chronicles may appear strange, funny, silly, meaningless, and obviously absurd, but I find them memorable, sentimentally nostalgically part of me, of what I was, how I thought, 20 years ago in Bowling Green.

# CHAPTER I

# FLOW OF EXPERIENCE I

the results are futile, and my love for Christ is intense, he finds the way, and in my depression

i find existential anguish,

not the same flow of experience of kant but that of joyce, the same lucky or joe of samuel beckett,

and I transcend looking forward to the happiness of rejection and the glory of god in the highest in psalms and the our fathers who reduce the words into meaningless knots and ping pong balls like friends in summer and spring and the ugly fat girl i loved and aggravating jay and charming paula and my friend chris and the other irish chris who decides about the antioch club rules and keys into wurzelian terms because the flowing esflumen is christ in this retrospection of epic flowing of music and context and mike panowsky or coporny or corny slobs and slavs and geology lessons which go on and on according to the antarctic regions of an imitation of beckett and hope and pessimism

this dynamic flow of existence, because i am poor but i love christ intensely but i am a secret agent christian, the silence of silence and embarrassing moments with the dialogue of friends and electric computers and more friends who disappear in yogurt fashion, someone threw it in the sink and washed my glass i have a cold and i am sick of thirst and this cold irritates me, but it is not a revolutionary cold, it is a common absurd call of the cold and rain and sun in bowling green, and the cold will pass to more colds and flu hongkong and otherwise

the inadequacy of poems that reject the kindness of human love; we perceive the unnamable, the unattached rhythm of reality in order to eschew the material from ensconced illusion. Life takes new forms of reality: the reality of dreams, of the heat in summer, of projected flights towards hope and despair although tragicomic real and paradoxical, heaven-hell dichotomy...

it reverberates with time and unexplained instances of few eye drops, created by viewers of triumph, of more anguish/happy results of this flow of esflumen;

Hesse was right in his mysticism; there are answers, and there are negations which come as if by chance, in philosophical outbreaks of words and music and faces which come and go in less than a split of a hair second... so it goes on and chance is chance, the commitment to a god, perhaps a bureaucratic god who owns all of heaven and hell, disguising himself as an old man, a loving comical father, and we his children, committed to him and his eldest son, Christ, el buen senor, our saviour who died for our sins, another bureaucratic lord and master, the kind of another world, a heavenly king and we are caught aghast in this putrid heaven/hell situation unaccustomed and Confused by life's segmentations, a ph.d. to philosophize and imitate the flow of experience of volumes of thoughts written and rewritten, repeated in circular fashions of cynicism and continuity...

transcending discontinuity to follow the archetypes of beckett who followed proust and jung who followed freud, and proust who followed descartes, and in this subconscious junk, fellini thrives with putrefied fantasies, explosions of ping-pong slams, of the reiteration of life and death, like my friend the east indian reddy's theory and search for god and for chance and scholarships and jobs: they all come like death when you least expect it.

and we go on planning like ants, ants who build and rebuild, burn down the ashes and after the ashes, ask whether builders are construed in other uncreative fashions, the patterns repeat themselves, words are excreted, minds are delved in personal fashions of the fifties with artie shaw and the sixties with sonny rollins and dave brubeck, and i remember my good buddy jess diaz who introduced me to jazz and frank sinatra, and after all this, everything repeats again, over and over, in original and unoriginal, primitive and scholarly waves of thoughts, interpretations and zeroisms

excretion is used as an example in human communication classes to analyze silence and obscenity, can anyone learn? can anyone withdraw from empirical studies? perhaps the disgust is still there, the bureaucracy, the capitalist issues are defended, as more heat waves are born and reborn into magic, into having to read more into nature and other misconceptions of time and ping-pong games.

I cannot be disgusted, i have entered a minimal point in nirvana, a point of awareness, a little light that is light and not heavy like alcohol which burns the stomach and makes one heavy,

the nirvanic light is almost christian, bahai perhaps, completely unatheistic, hating to use the much abused term inspiration and hope and the flow escapes me and i become trivial and trite and suddenly it returns to envision the mysticism of the seventies, the individual prophets from buchner's danton's death and well-made plays are again investigates in beowulf fashions and epic styles, like the unending, boring strives of bertolt brecht, the history of philosophy is the history of ideas which are naive and profound, which repeat themselves endlessly to express the consummate hope and anguish of mankind and in my nirvanic state, in this minimal state of mysticism and awareness, i reduce and deduce the redundance of words, the bourgeoisie, the elitists, where is education? in chuck steaks, chop suey and ice cold tea with lemon juice and for dessert, red watermelon and nectarine juices of summer fruits.

all in all, I summarize, beckettianwise, in order to synthesize, hegelianwise, this poem, this flow of experience that can neither dream nor type itself without this unmoved aristotelian mover inspiring me to say i am a jesus freak, a radical, but not a revolutionary, to talk of love taboos, to talk of the anguish and repetition of mankind, to say commitment in rebellious fashion because of my intellectuality, the intellectuality that does not reverse itself in quotes and misquotes from the avant-garde, the avant-garde that isn't avant-garde but back-garde,
fading away, refusing to stay blocked in history, moving away into other things, into playwrights who write farces of humanity, animal fables like aesop, and other such expressionistic forms of tragi-comedy.

there is a warmth of inclusion, there is a stoppage to madness because in this dire hope there is an amount of letters and prophecies, and yet in big letters they proclaim and shout:

**JESUS IS COMING! THE LORD OF LORDS, THE SAVIOUR OF SAVIOURS!**

and i weep because i am sentimental, because i piss in the rain as i cry, as tears converge in all of humanity, as the flowers and grass receive my warm piss, because i am sentimental,
because christ is here and he is descending from his throne in search of us, he came for us, he came for me, like repetitious jesus music, repeating the beautiful outcry of christianity and i pause to refresh...

i am not a committed agnostic, am christian, christian and insane, proclaim it to the world that the question has been answered in faith, a blind faith that is light and religion and intensity and i am reduced only by bodily instincts that must transcend and reach perpetual spirituality...

i resume: i confess that i am happy when i meditate into nirvana, whispering jesus as many as a thousand times until i am at peace, j.d. salinger called him the fat lady. i had an ugly, fat lady once. was she christ? christ is in other people: black, white, yellow, brown, deciphered with tongues hanging out —but people— like fellini 13 and a half, the experimental film i produced and called farolan 9 and a half, my imitation of fellini's 8 and a half...

i continue my synthesis: i have ended negativity, i have transcended positivity, i am now in a state of material words expressing the flow of stories and mindless junk in subconscious gas that synthesizes a future unplanned life, fearful, anxious, apprehensive, looking for new people, regarding the past,
a return to mother earth's womb, and earth becomes life, and life turns to animal, and animal to man, and we devour each other, it begins, it ends, it stops, it flows from microcosm to macrocosm, from cosmos to sub-cosmos, the universe within us, bodies and anti-bodies, the red versus the white blood corpuscles, and within us, the corpuscles reflect Kant's metaphysical logic and categories of the mind, categories of brain cells, and we survive in darwinian fashion, evolving from within to without, all based on my philosophical treatise that will be published in Reykjavik in the year 2005 **Experimental Poetics: The Philosophy of Aesthetics written within the endless trends of the backroads of my mind and other miscellaneous treatise on words**

follow Einstein's theory of relativity repudiating my futuristic theory based on alvin toffler who is said to have died of malaria in the philippines as he was hunting for a futuristic mosquito in Surigao near the Mindanao deep. My conclusions will be: the flow of experience written by God and

experimented by men was a dubious factor because if God were a stagehand, then man would be the director which further proves that from a theatrically and metaphorically unjustified point of view, words will have been created by stage hands and that directors only repeat them in predestined fashion. Furthermore, reality behind systematized monitoring as in the Wellesian Theory of 1984 begins to prove the fact that the Bible was inspired by a stagehand (God) and that Lucifer was created in bad faith.

Sartre contradicts this scholarly point of view on the ground that Signitzer studied Broadcasting in Bowling Green State University and that his Ph.D. from Salzburg, Austria was therefore a hoax. It is further

Written in dubious terms, the treatise concludes with the very enterprising word: **fart!**

i didn't want to go anyway to that damned graduation only because mothers cared and the day was nice, the clock radio rang, but i was in bed, at ten, i didn't feel like shaving or getting up, the warm summer breeze coming in through my room, as my dreams of sex, fantasies and utter frustrations were not wont to take place; i've lost all aggressiveness, i am sick of games, i want to be celibate…

there is an alcoholic blueberry yogurt that awaits the unconscious springs of duty, the return of urine, and the expression of an awaiting moment of nonchalance.

I do not despair this summer, i only smell the manure from the fields and await the money that flows in like flowless dreams.

The picture chris gave me is drawn against the wall; edsel did mine, as i look back in anguished nostalgia my youthful days in Madrid, and now the pimps are gone, and i am alone looking for myself, gone are those happy days with tony fernandez and the gang at the colegio madrid de guadalupe with louie the policeman and rudy eltanal, now looking for myself, looking for the initiates of hope, looking forward to the summers of 73 and 74, and the word of god sticks to my mid, and i always deviate and return to my instincts, that constant dichotomy of spirituality and materiality, and wherever the flow of experience takes me, and now i fruitlessly tilt the pinball machine, i crookedly slouch in howard's bar where the university scumbags hang out, those bearded dregs look at me and recognize my subtlety…perhaps in california i will recognize the stardom of officiality, the calls from within, the subtleness of thoughts, the simple yet naive voices of the instincts; the satanic cults are an experience that must be tempted upon children of god as the devils cower, and the spirits meditate upon good and evil, especially good, the all-transcending mysticism of **ohm** where we only attempt to visualize and release ourselves from the sacramental aims of catholicism and merely protrude the anguished forms of reality, and plead forgiveness, from god himself, from the fundamentalist point of view without end.

amen, amen, praise the lord they clamour and i find my soul besieged and tempted to join this rufusian pentecostalism but i am subdued by my luciferian intellect, and i cry out, creator, is the game over?

my arms ache from tilting the pinball machine. the midnight special was kim's black crab against the nostalgic and spoiled intellects of blacks singing and sweating as the comedy routines intellectually masturbated themselves, using brother ron's terms, and yet he limps in despair the same way the karate expert wallows in polio. why all this? why marijuana blended with scotch? only to presume that the sadness of despair is paradoxical, it blows hot like summer winds and cold like winter winds and rains in spring, and changes weather clandestinely.

225

It is the hope of this writer that my typist will call and immediately give back my dissertation. oh, the longing to leave and yet, the laziness, because god will care for us yet we must conform to his goodness and style of life: no sex, drink, grass—they are all the devil's ruin, the body's ruin, death to spirituality, and yet must i always be caught in this dilemma? no, because subconsciously, i have consciously received the lord, and in my reception, the flowingness of life becomes patterned and positively predestined.

IN OBSERVANCE OF PEOPLE diane was not cool, ordinary and dumb, the bearded fellow was tempted along his way, back to sameness, while diane was a jesus freak, but good, and in the interim, i watched, observed, but pretending not to know, because i knew too much about human affairs, too keen and oriental, perhaps, about life and its misgivings, the birth of spring, and the people who merely exchanged words calmly.

A certain quietude about people, maybe silence, but i will never be silent, i am always aloof, always noisy in my aloofness, it is the acting part, i am alienated from all of reality, and daydreaming as a loner by myself;

all this becomes only human and overcooked like filipino chop suey; i am overcome by the fact that the fan blows hot wind into my soul, and in the derision of attempting to circumvent myself, i am placated by patience, by a certain desire to be quiet like parisi, to do and not to say, and these are the quiet, good ones, and not the show greeks with their loud-mouthed women who are bad in bed, but the ugly, fat quiet ones who say "come follow me" and we are lost in bliss.

but it cannot repeat itself; history never repeats itself in particular moments; only in archetypal generalities; we are subdued by a certain philosophy that radicalizes virginity, mysticism and evangelism; the fact is that christ taught loneliness as in hinduism/buddhism but said at the same time "go and preach to all nations", and this certain contradictory dichotomy exists now in religions; we are supposed to do both if we can, as i can, not simultaneously, but attempting to fulfil every command, but if one can only evangelize that's that; my evangelism is a quiet one, i do not force, i only speak, and angelical music resounds in the background, like movies and broadway shows. But to add it all up, there are no conclusions to my beliefs; they flow continuously from birth to death and another rebirth, because we are immortal, even if we return to dust our minds think in the dust, we become dust particles that blow with the wind, the thinking wind, disappearing yet inanimate that we are we thing we float with the dust with our thoughts into the atoms of other minds in gravitational pull landing on small people who blow my mind with writers of science fiction who presuppose that life is not this life, this immediacy but a belief in a continual rebirth, a continuous flow of experience, an immortality that supersedes from one planet to another,

and all is faith coming from the lord in the highest, the aristotelian unmoved mover who has created the first spark that triggered off evolution and guides my hand in propagandizing his existence, as i write and love and express not in charismatic tongues but in written words, in literature that will be published one day in the form of an epic poem, modern and otherwise, a poem that is an existential plea to all future men that existentialism is in, eclecticism is in and out, and out and in because we express like fellini, the latin, half-latin that i am, in dubious thoughts, in oriental misgivings, like drumbeats that resound of primitivism, and yet in our poetic gestures, we are revolutionary, we seek the engagement of peopled poems, and peopled people, and structured flowingness of unstructured reality and others who may come along our way, personal, otherwise, or Freudian... we must continue to digest the realities, both mediate and immediate that come along our way, circumstantial justification for existence is a hysterical delirium, and typographical errors cannot be justified in this boring search for god, ants in dust are immortal, that you were dust and that you will be dust, the continuous flow of repetition and long-winded philosophical treatises and life-death-rebirth-reincarnation-resurrection cycles which have been the dilemmas of man forever and ever. AMEN

...

the detached bloopers and music men become unconditional in agatha christie gifts and other hairy experiences, grades and ratings are all political in nature, hesitant and yet, deciphered by all the railings of humanity, because my profession is that of poet and not teacher, guzman was right, he is still remembered despite bobby and the rest...

the music man is on, robert preston is on, singing knickerbocks, and in this state of voluptuousness, I decide I must be irresponsible aghast and against the forms that reproduce the kindness of reality and absurd abuse.

an attempt at madness: eccentricity, boredom and anti-reaction. I must work on that film, on that TV show, and see if they are acceptable to WBGU-TV. Who cares, anyway? Benno has his scholarly Ph.D. and a conventional scholar at that.

boarding with nice, homely old ladies, returning to past memories, the joycean stream of consciousness versus the farolan stream of subconsciousness projected by the flow of the unconscious as i perceive with multi-faceted eyes mirrored people in dream reality, in flashbacks of philosophical oneness and multi-dimensional ohmness

the stream is a series of colours in different shades of black and white, grey and dark grey, or colours in red, blue, flashing yellow, pink, full-length insanity projectile readiness lectured ears for 16 speed bikes and cameras clicking dishwashing and smoking unprotruding moments of despair, misgivings, oratory and music.

red white blue watergate affairs; speed reading, speed people, justified repeated sounds of stars and piano players, sounds of visions inspiring-bothering people spiritually

micturition until the bathroom door opens, truthful obnoxiousness to this innocent state of affairs, the teletype continues despite the heat and the wavering defects of mankind, it seems the noise caused from fans and other miscellany has exhumed my system and the women of my life have gone up in smoke, the selection process of humanity,
we are victims,
mixed and fixed marriages,
people all around, friendly suggestions, introspections regarding the personal aspects of life despite the publicity involved, tabloids go to the extent of publicizing private emotions, the drunks and the whores, as i type almost endlessly researching my thoughts as they come flowing within the existence of the bourgeoisie, radio stations and fans blowing wildly in the heat, and after all this, the existence of the flow vertebrates itself until i am no longer relieved by the relief of pissing after trausti has left the bathroom, after his long icelandic bath.

the results are simple, the diary of the noise and the romeo/juliet affairs have been misconstrued by the experts of having to room in mrs. stillwell's rooming house as the marijuana seeds have been related to the existential nature of the forsaken dissertations of the alcohol in my bloodstream, in the quarry, and other love affairs, in the truism that goes: aphorisms are the thing! hope for the best, expect the worse, and the words flow like blessings in this heat, this heat full of clichés, morphisms and anti-truisms in this bohemian explanation of books and other diaries which continue to exemplify the noise from television and mass communication; signitzer is getting a paper done on ANCHORMEN, scholarly, yet absurd, refined, yet ridiculous, for a scholar to stick out his tongue in a fellini movie which i have hesitatingly and reluctantly and repeatedly and redundantly expressed through capitalist commercials.

According to Fromm, i spell his name FROHM as though he were forming foams in his mouth bitten by a police dog with rabies, a half-german shepherd, nourished with purina dog chow, the balanced meal for men and dogs.

i end endlessly

by accepting my subtle state of affairs by accepting hell-like heaven-like the confidence of teletypes that come in big letters, 10 by 75 margins and all the formats that go into a Ph.D. in legal broadcasting citing Signitzer, that the machines have taken over and that boasting in television and boasting in radio that proposals are rejections and of course a bachelor a puritan bachelor must not be horny and make a thousand women happy a sentimental bangladesh politically speaking but california awaits me and the commercials and other sentimental bourgeois crap have been accepted by less radical moments called liberals or if they are projected to people are incorporated in the name of anarchic liberals, half-bourgeois, half-indoctrinated by bureaucratic rules of the game, games people play, like democracy and other examples, JOY, dishwashing liquids and other reflections on how to wash with different detergents.

What follows is an injuncture of words, phyllis diller show, jim bailey and here's lucy shows, interrupted naturally by NBC and ABC.

The reactance theory expressed by psychological dissonance has been corroborated by the theories of the tyler and dick van dyke shows which happen to accept the conventionalities of the pepper and salt shakers, relating of course to the indoctrinated moments of hot summer months, reading books, orderly fashions of guests and other baths (without showers) in a very poetic and anti-poetic show.

Other commercials in other channels: drano and ABC clogs, detroit in channel 7, and other more esoteric shows, TV is in and obviously music has won the hearts of women, madness in a show of delusion, and an accepting knowledge that the effects of personal behaviour have entered grammatically into the use of prepositions, propositions, conjunctions, rejections and other less grammatical dictional words that rhyme and reject themselves in other forms, icelandic or otherwise.

Words, however, have no effect on the melange of winter and the possibility of simplicity, like a beer in howard's and other possibilities. There must be an excitement of things, like make-up and other women who govern men's lives:

are men still the master of yogurt? are men wimps? have they become partial to the repetitious trivialities of Beckett and other misconstrued aspects of witticisms?

i am silent to despair, i only imitate Lucky and his thinking hat, and other cocktail parties and football games in summer. Reject the subtleties of Americans and accept the dire exposition of their souls: simple and almost naive, full of subtleties, universal, like all human beings, advanced technically because they travel and away from the small middle-class mid-western towns, poetic and otherwise.

I conclude: there is simply no answer and conclusion to the trivialities and subtleties of humanity; the fact is that there are other answers, like the answers of despair, the answers of rhythm, the answers of God, and the answers to icelandic chess, profound in their explicit zeroist attitude to humanity, synthesizing obviously the hegelian thesis-anti-thesis of life-illusion-death-and socialist realism.

The pope has been branded a eunuch! Where lies the answer to eunuchs?

In their castration?

Availability, english-style, verses in disguise to aching queries on quarries where girls flirted with men past 21 in an attempt to grab their attention and enter a world of adults security puritan-like kim subtlety of jim baker may he live in peace

it was jesus after half a cigarette and it was an expression of a night of beauty of warmth and existential stupor, of expressions of delight, of the black bureaucracy as the smiles exchanged themselves in commanding english, they appeared absurd, as the blacks exchanged vows of serenity while the rest were 3/4ths drunk. That was as far as she went in my memoirs of american women, an interesting night because i made it so and i made it so because i had the privilege above all others to stipulate the answer of conjectures because i was flattered about the strangeness of my face and reality, and i realize the folly of women, and i smile because we are all jesus-influenced, we are all creatures of madness and mozart divinely inspired by the creation of harmony and words and other more relevant matters.

All those damaged cells and confessions of pasty introspections towards nothingness, I construe forward in the heat of another day in June, that the return to mother earth is not symbolic at all, rather literal, in death, in burial, the source of reincarnations, death/birth of mankind as well as womankind; life and the planets are the result of this oneness; after the earth is united it becomes a microcosm of the galaxy; other planets will intervene to express another oneness, and then more and more planets will join in this oneness, and this is all the circular overpowering sounds of sight and planets and comets and planets and stars burst like amoeba separating themselves into two and four and the multiplication process geometrically takes place, and life goes on, from species to species, from atom to atom because we are all microcosms of macrocosms of reality bursting into new life and returning to the atomic nucleus of existence as in 2001 space odyssey, the last sequence of machines from hg wells to vonnegut and other more contemporary science fiction writers who envision life to come in the vastness of space and time and spacelessness and the timelessness we live in.

And this flow must continue, whether the sperm's in the gutter, and love's in the sink, according to jethro tull, the wastebasket womb, the continuum must express itself like the wind, and the weather, and the expression of day-to-day experience whether it be introspective or extrospective, the importance of aloneness in the face of the world and standing up to it, towards independence of mankind from other species, sex and power, the freudian dichotomy, extinctive-instinctive

extinction of life is impossible from one human immortality will take other human forms and the cycle is a vicious virtuous cycle using Wender's terms because the purpose of Deviation Amplification Feedback is polarized in reactance that has positive and dissonant factors. This happens to be the crux of communications, human or otherwise, because only humans on this side of the planet can perceive, can laugh, can be obscene, interpersonal relationships in the marketplaces of the mind or in the more or less un-obscene places that have shown examples of the deterioration of the body and the mind with time, only the soul is timeless, the madness of men is infinite, and in the light of this madness, a blue or green light that is turned on perpetually giving peace and harmony to the conflict in Stimmel's propositions or mein kampf according to hitler but all in all the theories of social comparison and values of Festinger et al have produce innumerable publications regarding the materials for empirical studies of Addington, Kepke and other Darridian empiricists who are machines and computers counting the number of people who say yes and no and I think I know and other conceptions and/or misconceptions regarding the outburst of emotions and intellectual goings-on.

The point of the matter is that after the black absurdity of last night's beer blast, my memory cells and other brain cells are burned out, I express only what is left of my burned out cells, and they reflect a memory of an elephant as the African lions wee swaying in the blackness of the night, a very bourgeois temperament, not even petite, but out of this world, returning to the past, according to tesh, the passé parliamentary system of the english; and the interesting factor about this was the picture of flashbulbs and people coming and going and laughing and making fun and getting excited all because of these formal trivialities. I played the game. I won.

Returning to more irrelevant matters: the coed was another dire example of a drunken night as she fell with me in the bushes at 620 E Wooster, and as she was frightened by my madness because after my utter shock of her affective perversion, I attempted to simulate a rape scene by which she was frightened because as I laid her on that wooden porch, two other men came to her rescue and in my perverted madness, I screamed and expressed Mozart's 620th concert in formless poetry, music, as the sounds of my gurgling reality affixed themselves in non-conformed rules and games and other junk in the subconscious reality of the minds who were attempting to play psychological games in this simulated madhouse where all humans were computerized and segmented into thoughts and thoughtlessness. Obviously, the poetry was unsuccessful, and the 19 year old coed affair terminated as fast as it began.

In our vocal attempts to play other games, the sound of far-away music expressed a dullness in the early morning as the nerves in my back began to ache, and a summaries of the flow of experience were reiterated not in conclusions regarding the bs on Spanish Underground Theatre, but the stupidity of signatures plotted against "mental thugs", according to Sam B.

I do not seem to remember now the relationship between enzymes and the weather and the sun, and I believe that the weather, especially the sun, is a comforting factor especially after a turbulent experience of rain and snow. The important factor about the sun is that it gives ultraviolet rays which penetrate the skin. Again, the relationship of the sun and the moon and the earth: we are at a so-called age called Aquarius and in this age, there seems to be an understanding (it's about time) of the relationships sun, moon, earth and other planets, because all are interrelated to the human system. In Emil Trausti's treatise entitled THE EARTH, SUN, PLANETS: A DISCUSSION

OF ASTROLOGY, he says that the north polar system was polarized by the ebb tides of the moon, and the fire tides of the sun were expressions of radiation which protruded into the flickering system of the beckettian atmosphere causing depression among human dregs. The conclusions reached by this eminent scholar were simple but profound: the penetration from radiation from the sun to the earth is not only symbolical but parallel to the penetration of a penis to a vagina. Dr. Emil showed the Freudian intra-relationships of these factors by pointing out the scholarly natures of the penis and the vagina, elaborating by giving us an analysis of both the linguistic and social functions of the origins of the two words in the english and icelandic vocabularies. The other reflections reached were the following: the comets who hit the earth occasionally as in "falling stars" are again reflections of certain taboos regarding the human situation. The comets are the sperms, and the uterus, the earth it penetrates into, and therefore, the taboos made by man regarding the "luck" or "bad luck" nature of falling stars reflects the attitude of pregnancy which semen is wont to take when it begins to wander in other miscellaneous areas which are not their own, and thus, the birth of theories such as "why did that sperm enter the 11 year old girl?" and other young children up to the age of five were said to have been stricken by the wandering sperm which was an outgrowth of the thesis propagated later on by Berelson and Steiner on Opinions, Attitudes and Beliefs. The OAB expressed by these writers were proof of the nature of Bowling Green levels of attainment.

It appears that the levels of attainment are low, regarding the mediocrity of the coeds who cohabit with males and other miscellany.

But the mediocrity is expressed by more human, almost bureaucratic affairs, such as the quarry and the slimy fish in the quarry who hate french onion dips and hot dogs and potato chips and like the piranhas of the Amazons, the Bowling Green fish almost gobbled Dick's leg, or toe (to avoid exaggeration). But I love Bowling Green's mediocrity, the middle-class town, in the mid-west, everything is so simple and bourgeois, the crux of happiness!

The aggravating factor about purity and the flow of experience is this hope for a God who forgives, a loving father who forgives after repeated sins of insanity, fornication gluttony, and fantasy-dreaming. We are all pantheistically related to this oneness, as I have reiterated so many times, because alcohol is not the solution to brain damage. Opium deteriorates the body, morphine makes it sleepy, and the final fix, grass and hashish and other like stuff are not as comparable to the LSD treatment (as advocated by the geologist, Peter Gunn, who, by the way, personally amazes me because of his music and incomparable stature to another geomorphologist, Joe Mannix). The acceptance of dementia praecox and intellectual masturbation can be inspired only on Sundays when the relationships and flashbacks of words deviate themselves but are again integrated in the text and/ or context of Georgian reality, and the ultra-violet rays have been tape-recorded by the tapeworms of God and the devil. We are all included in this solution of the brain where the treatise recalled at this particular moment dealt with the fantastical moments of LSD and the mind-solving drugs of computer centres and other cultural centres of hypocritical learning. The calmness and patience expressed by Sunday endeavours are only examples of the copies made by so-called boring friends and poets called Barbara Paymaster et al in their attempts to believe in music and other photojournalistic barbarities.

**At one o'clock, my madness is secure.**

The rejection of the species in an attempt to delve into the enjoyment of excretion, and in the flight of utter despair, the excreted factors of humanity are traversed in maggots that announce the death of winter and the birth of heated summer with its crawling corpuscles of slimy earth.

The aftermath and afterbirth of excretion and that is why they call earth slimy because of its womanish image and the entire metaphorical interpretation of the bible and the figuratively-speaking dedication of the genetic writers and the writers lost in exodus and deuteronomy...

a pilot's prayer:
touch god's face in the skies.

the seeds, the seeds of prayer, the co-pilot's god, 220 pound class, american wrestlers and other quantities involved in gold medals and latent promiscuities, the russian is winning, and the flight is almost over…

my feet are dirty, i'll wash them, i have washed them, i realize i am lost in a certain amount of tobacco and i have to repeat the circular motions of the world by repeating my history: in chapter 1 of my novel written between the years 1965 and 1971, I interpreted in a preface-like discussion and analysis of an interpretation and reinterpretation of my vital state of affairs…DIARY OF A FILIPINO.I gave Sionil Jose the manuscript, he never returned it, where is it now? Then there was the novel ROSEMARY (English for Romero) which I gave to Ning Molina and he lost it…all those early thoughts lost, how can I document my life in those early years, I was 20 or 21 when I wrote those early novels…

in the second chapter of DIARY I described a projected arrival in the Philippines, Christmas of 1987: bare feet on hot asphalt, midnight, lights in a main street, and my shadows disappeared because my other self was projecting into other selves and running wildly on the asphalt/ cement streets at midnight, or after midnight of christmas…

in the third chapter i was historical and nostalgic about Switzerland and my first encounter of snow in the United States more than 20 years ago. In the subsequent chapters, I did not analyze, nor did I express, nor was I poetic. I accepted the stream of consciousness and unconsciousness and wrote them down; the experiential reality of the chapters that followed expressed an entire repertory of mixed emotions and intellectualizations ranging from nostalgia to critical theories of philosophical analyses from Camus, Sartre, Adamov, Arrabal and other similar absurdists.

The novel was accepted for publication by Vantage Press for publication on the condition that I invested $4,000. The fact was that

I did not have that money for obvious reasons, and the novel remains unpublished somewhere in Sionil Jose's files gathering dust and other vermin.

After stipulating the answers of gymnastics and other dance theories, it appears that the steps have been irregular and I interpret simultaneously the jumping steps that rhyme with jumping words and the technical aesthetic functions of gymnastic free exercises on Toledo 11 (an Ohio TV channel for unknown viewers) and the fact is that the dancers have trained and followed the steps of piano-making devices and the style falls/begins/relates/enterprises and analyzes for the Russians and the English in a gymnastic superimposition of art and other more artistic demonstrations of life and other continuities. Paste. Polaroid cameras are examples of epic style justifications and rationalizations, and the facts are repetitive, the realities behind the alka-seltzer ads and other American commercializations, no wonder this country has been considered a myth, only because the PhDs have been graduated too soon, and the women from Connecticut have the same style, very inspiring play, and very inspiring fellow, justified by other sophistries such as the promotions and understandings of the less-token ones. So, a cooperative gest is necessary, respect for the disrespectful, and it seems that the degree has been granted, priesthood is another game in life, and in my personal rejection of God, I find God. In my personal rejection of people, I realize I need people. I ensconce and eschew once again as I spit words that are pregnant with meaning and yet despite my empathy and antipathy I show a certain amount of alienation although many times I am sucked into the orbit of indifference.

But once indifferent I confess I have to be anti-indifferent and then I become sentimental and shed tears of disgust, compassion, tears of melodramas…in this state of affairs the researchers for circumstances in ghettos and mental illnesses are reproduced by distress and other searches for the paralysing loneliness and hostility of concrete poetry. The will and stamina to be alone against the world, to be yourself and not say it but doing it—this makes me cry like a sentimental old fool, and yet in the face of hostility and interrogation i make the most fantastic lies and i confess i act with a certain amount of innocence which almost convinces me that my lies are truths or half truths. After all, lies are truths. Bad faith is good faith. The salvation one confronts before the bureaucratic system has been subdued by lies in order to slide away from paragraphs that begin in the following manner:

"I believe that the important hope behind Midas mufflers is the beauty of digression. After all, we have to shit and piss and then we are ultimately degraded by insanity. Baseball games are animated and the paragraph continues thus:

`I am alone in this mirror that reflects a mirror as the paragraph repeats against thus:

"I have finished my paragraphs within paragraphs, I am bored by this game, my poetry slackens into prose, and my flow is broken prosaically and poetically, I resume thus…

THE MARGINS BEGIN LIKE THIS: WE ARE ALL EXPRESSING WORDS AND HOW ABOUT OTHER LETTERS LIKE 12@#!%&&)&*^&& OR MARKS.LETTERS/MISCELLANY THUS":~}{[]=_))(*&&^L;AFJJFOPEFHOFJ
which bothers and yet proves the non-sensical linguistic reality of this world where no one communicates we are all banished from the tower of babel to speak in gibberish, the non-sensical reality of bushes with coeds and fallen people within the drunken stupor of loneliness and togetherness and other baseball miscellany…

the political consciousness of Allende and Chile's slums of poverty as though there were no slums in the US where americans still refuse to believe that they are lost in poverty, and the poverty is stimulated by the housing projects, tenements, they're called, and the highlights of american life have always been the realities behind the lies, truth/lies, and other such operations, and the cultural centre of the philippines awaits me to make my debut as a professional filipino actor, time is of the essence, how much time is there in timelessness as i ponder my future tediously tallying ticktocks interjected in other countries, poverty, impoverished philippines, time is running out, the end of the world is near and Jehovah will be upon us!

beauty and tourism, the cosmetics of a country in big cities, mythical america, glorious in movies, lost in obscurity, lost in absurdity, 20 years from now celebrating the 500 years discovery of america by columbus, and it makes no sense because the indians were here and america was not discovered by europe, contradictions we cannot construe ourselves...

that feeling of anguish returns, that feeling of angst that makes me sigh a sigh of despair thinking of organizing and getting accustomed to pharmaceutical excerpts of the future, a vital necessity, a maturing in life, words and metaphors taught in school.

**A consciousness is formed, and people are together.**

the poets and the singers waking from this dilemma of the conscious plot to throw away the thickness of the brick into the minds of covert people, the neutrality of phase L is won; the next phase: the mind.

In the mind the ship travels into unconsciousness and after a time of misgiving, there appears a stone's throwback of fruitful faces of memories and other sick and suicidal notes of greenish garbage floating amidst the turbulent tides of poetry and other quantitative matters.

The hot night is affected strongly by the examples given by Rolex and Freedman regarding the scholarly treatise on the Unresponsive

Bystander and the thesis on death and dying by Kubler-Ross in an attempt to pursue the meaning of silence and the motivations of mankind in its thrust towards existence.

After the affair is ended other affairs come in place, affairs are poisonous vermin, archetypal patterns of sweet yogurt, strawberry and nectarine flavours, deduced by heat, misgiven by the aura of extraness and twoness, blondness and summerness, inverness, vertebrate nature of words like fillings on tooth cavities.


today is sunday, 88 degrees, the old woman noticed the icelander coming in at quarter to 4 and my coming in at quarter past four this very early morning after an almost bizarre experience created by my own doing and aided by the creative mind of jim...keller, yes, keller is that beckettian character who has aided me in my travesties both in jerry lewis fashion and in eh joe examples of sordid names and an expression of repetitious family life of names and other miscellany that shows that keith works in the carpet place and mona comes here and mrs. sun was a korean, and there were 11,000 other korean boarders and 12,000 chinese and other asian miscellaneous boarders and germans and tall icelandic characters and 3 million indians and there was george the son of monty and the children who played in the mud and the reality behind the masks and the names continue: jim, jane, chris, flix, crass, bass, mass, lass, dash, florence, nighty, ingale, bergman, emilson, steinson, x-15, y2344, 292, johnny and mary and jeannie and kathy and joanne and other numbers and characters and foreign names like ching, chung, chang, king, kung, fu, fong, ting, tong, shen, shin, chon, fling, flong, fang, prang, brong, and germanic names, herr, benno, heinz, treinz, hegel, Nietzsche, and english names, floy, patterson, scott, van, wayne, and the realities of the fbi spoofs on other seas and other oceans pacific and otherwise, mediterranean and atlantic, indian and pacific, and the pick-ups are expressions of breathing exercises and other exercises of fright and fearfulness and other miscellany more and more like inverness and sojourness and flimflamness and the hat is still on my hear inside my brain and Lucky keeps on whispering the more intense subjectification of reality and other irrealities like production people and other fish caught in oceans and seas as in China the expressionless expression of people and mermaids and other whitewashed and "washed ashore" instances.

It has been repudiated many times and the history of the mind is the history of ideas and this history has been subjugated into other histories and issues of the international contributing to the fishing history of summer and other large listeners.

To continue I must continue: the tarantula eats bananas and bananas are green and the length of a banana is proportional to the trigonometry of algebraic functions.

The conclusion has been reached: the hypotenuse divided by the sides of a square is equal to the world premiere of the fabulous Dr. Fable and the effervescence of diabetes is a doctoral comma, d.h.o., in other movies to come and other ABC programs and obviously the sociological factors involved in the study of diamonds and other words that proceed from the mind's subconscious and eventually the results are programmatic and therefore the supply and demand curves are made of fly swatters and the reality of arms and the man and the different titles of the FBI have been taken in by mobs and other more controversial issues regarding the Economic History of the Philippine Revolution it is approaching it is waiting to remove the discontent of history and mankind owing to the cavernous and tavernous realities of the FBI agents disguised as lunatics in a madhouse and the results become repudiated by the curves that proceed between microeconomics, macroeconomics and the history of philosophy.

According to Quevedo and Valle Inclan, the avant-garde began with such pieces as **The graces and disgraces of a rectum's eye** or **The discursive nature of a Jewish nose** and Valle Inclan's search for the Spanish identity in his **Lights of Bohemia** have precluded the analysis of the Spanish Underground Theatre. Stop. Telegram received. Continue. The results of the damaging factors of the lecherous nature of the old ladies return to express the blond nature of sexual fantasies and other realizations ranging from tragicomic overtures and Japanese NOH theatre in the reality of Japanese Kabuki making the comedy obnoxious and therefore tragically anti-audience.

The results of the musical overture of **Man of La Mancha** synthesizes the fact that we must bring pieces like this into the stage and therefore express the reality of dreams, the unreachable dreams and the unbeatable foes. Stop. Continue. Therefore the stage directions have been preconceived by teletypes and other more morbid expressions of aid and obviously the alliterative functions of madness repeat themselves in such functions as the creative junctures of the sneakerish attempts at oversimplification and the warmth of a summer night and the rains will come summer has begun early in the day with whitewashed chasers all over the more inductive and deductive bulldogs of comedy and anti-comedy.

The flow is typographical in approach, also topographical, quantitative as well as qualitative, anti-scholarly like a film that is not a film but an anti-film. I know now that I can investigate a story according to aristotelian concepts of the well-made play; the anti-play breaks these concepts; the anti-play or anti-film in disconformity to Aristotle's beginning middle and end and the six parts of tragedy— plot, structure, music, etc—have been subjugated by the anti-film concept of plotlessness and other more dire instances of flashbacks and home movie techniques unfocused and de-focused; the Sardou style of well-made plays is a copycat of the aristotelian concept: there must be plot and suspense, a chase, and end and a denouement. Stop. Continue.

The results are vital though inevitably coarse but audiences love this and even movies today and agatha christie novels, etc go for the money because of sardou.

However, anti-films and anti-plays and anti-poems and anti-thesis are hated by audiences because they are purposely anti-audience. The rationale for these anti-matters is a stomach ache caused by excess homemade yogurt.

Having pieced these anti-pieces together, the fruit float and other similar commercials with balloons etc

extend the meaning of well-made films that are epical and topical resulting in re-obscuring the flow of experience manifested by a writer's madness and/or producer and/or director in an attempt to create the creative and ad secluded factors to the P/U results of first-hand notices such as pass or unsatisfactory movies that fall under slipshod or shady deals. Diarrhoea is inevitable. The heat has taken over. Stop. Continue.

The results of madness are discriminatory and apprehensive of context. The acquiescence of other factors such as the acquiring of required courses for the Ph.D. exemplify the suggestions made by Allport and Postman regarding Roger Mudd's report of rumor in the Water Moccasin case of Georgia, U.S.A., a number of years back when blacks were said to have arrived, shoeless, in Georgia and preparing to invade the US government. And now, the divorce rates are high, but statistics quantifies matters without really discussing the more important aspects of the clincher, such as the sand and the sea and the sun in Camusian fashion, and all in all, the psychology of rumor is again nihilistic in approach for the same reason that the entire world is misconstrued by running and chasing forming bulks and bulks of literary trash and vermin, voluptuous garbage and the expression of the unorthodox rumor that the Red Chinese have landed in Mexico ready to attack the US after a UN contingent has laid aside the intervening factors of national defense and top secret watergate issues for the sake of security and the unending experiences of life and other issues which affect the national security of the country, my fellow americans, and therefore, the state rests and impeaches the President of the United States. Stop.


The library of congress has published the effects of the dissertation written by eminent scholars whose dissertations come in ends, from top security to estudiantil rejections internationally published by the Canadian National Library so long as a Canadian flag appears on all the pages of these treatises because the writing effects of summer have overcome the winter effects of reading in Canada so that the realities of the mind and other instances such as the watergate scandal and the bowling green public library and the new site of Howard's and therefore, the answer to propaganda is anti-propaganda and other more examples are: the moccasin and indian militants, the SWP, the communist party of canada and the US which publishes the Daily World, and the comedy hour of ABC TV. The ending of the entire slander and calumny perverted by newspapermen is not freedom; democracy comes in many forms, including the fourth international and Trotskyite movement; in this affair, there is no bureaucracy involved; liberality does not side with anything; it is cynical to communists, Trotskyites and even christians especially the catholic church, tooth in mouth, tongue in cheek, the world is a joke, just for fun, and the entire world must be viewed from a cynical standpoint and aloof instead of committed—the entire section of evangelism comes in death and the experiments must continue, we are not delving into the unknown, we are only victims of time and predestination, we are aware of the realities, we are aware of the editorial we, we know how politicians use we all the time in their speeches so they can blame their constituents, we are aware of the grudging reality behind the victims and the victimless scandals of human nature and we seem to pursue the realities behind the facades and behind other more intricate matters of both concentration and de-concentration; the concentration camps have been disguised by the white house and pentagon officials and the officialdom of intellectuality is almost simple and simply sentimental, we are all part of this cosmos of miscellany conceptualized in a world predestined by a personal god who says thank you to our prayers and are ordered to imitate him and look at life more positively, and continue smiling and being happy and not let go of the saving factor, saving amazing grace and the other sacramental oneness of the entirety of the catholic universe composed of christian planets named after the classical greeks, the universe and galaxies of the mind, the space within us is immediated by the space without, just as we float inside, the entire universe composed of atheistic planets and other important things outside of us float too; we are, i repeat for the nth time, a microcosm of our outer galaxies, and therefore we are not one but part of the whole and it is luciferian pride that drove satan to the end of the world and to tempt humans and subhumans in other planets to rebel against the unmoved mover. STOP.

    DIALOGUES
    this is extremely boring
    what do you thing the us should do?
    I THINK THAT WE MUST RECOGNIZE THE FACT THAT THE ARGUMENTS OF THE REGIME IN ATHENS AND THE COUP D'ETAT AND THE OTHER FORCES...

The armed forces of my country have joined together the single governor and electrical devices for free countries, and part of Athens and the missions have been associated with the importance of survival and other issues and answers.

What is extremely boring about the need for survival?

There must be an answer and an issue.

According to Billy Graham, you have been subdued and used as an example of ridicule. Is this true?

I don't know. Perhaps the abdication indicates something.

Establishment. Do you think that America and the great armed forces show certain allied factors?

The dialogue seems extremely interesting.

Yes I agree and the subject matter is slightly paranoid but the fact is that my country's greatest production the ACROPOLIS made by my forefathers...

Under what conditions?

ANTI-DIALOGUES

The play or anti-play has been interpreted as a stream of consciousness and not as a flow of experience. I summarize the dialogues of the past, each second of the day makes one happy, adjusted to the anti-dialectical system of the aids which grace upon our existence. The problem of recognizing a monarchy is dubious. The coup d'etat is a necessary function of anti-films, and I disagree with your conjectures that Nixon and Marcos have controlled the generals of the world and the rumours that there is not going to be another war, the shaving cream is bad, and the anti-dialectical nature of philosophical thinking is still medieval in nature. The dialogues of humanity are archetypal and thus, boring, because of repetitions.

The play or anti-play seems to have an effect on NBC television evening news in that the oppression of ramifications seems to express certain degrees of alcoholic and apariential realities which deem them correct and anti-discursive. Thank you.

You're welcome.

Stop.

flow of experience 3. continued from flow of experience 2. continued from flow of experience 1. stop. continuing. stop. play? stop, go, comedy, anti-comedy, dialectic tragedy, etcetera, stop, continue, staccato, stop, and go, continue. stop. go.

We will now proceed to poetics: the poetry of life becomes a redundance. Its redundant nature is due to various factors, two of which are poetic and anti-prosaic. From the poetic angle, plato discussed the meaning of light and darkness in the cave in his dialogues and the republics of Greece and other platonic dialogues reflect the historical juxtapositions of Aristotle who came before and/or after Plato in 6 or 5 or 4 or 3 BC and Pope John XXIII who lived before Christ. The juxtaposition of time and space as in the birth of Aristotle in 1876 in the home of Mrs. Hazel Stilwell at 140 Clay street, parents Davender Singh and Davender Paymaster of the Aryan-Indian race. Godfathers: Edmundo Farolan and Trausti Steinsson, North Pole and Asia irrespectively, and the godmother, Benna Signitzer of Europe. The Indians have been besieged after the Grecian coup d'etat in the year 1467, and the historical moment for Mandragola by a famous machiavellian personality, Dr. Emilsson who was Viking on his mother's side and Brazilian on his father's side. The end of the story is the end of the history, the end of mankind, not the bomb, but the threat of ants and other vermin in the house in summer. The results: expertise: H20 and 0xY from chemical reductions and other philosophical conventions.

Continue:

In effect, the moon goes around the sun and the sun goes around the earth according to the revolutionary thinking of Copernicus, or was it the other way around? Facts are gathered in the Encyclopedia Britannica only to inform us that the meaning of reality on Anton Artaud's left shoe, as he was found sitting holding it dead on his bed. William Inge died at the age of 60 after being depressed for a number of years from lack of inspiration and material. The cause: suicide from gas poisoning in his garage.

End.
Begin:

In effect the logic behind the continuum of the socialist nature of the experiential expertise of Mr and Mrs Regino Signitzer happens to be reduced to three sentences obscene in their nature: smelly feet, beards and anti-aristocratic scholarship and conventionality, neckties and other fellowships in BGSU.

Marriage bells ring, but these are rumours because ping-pong is still a a natural Austrian and/or Australian and also Asian and/or Australasian sport. Funny yet we must continue:

The loudness of the fan expresses vinegarred memories of stomach aches and other such aspects similar to scholarly writing of dissertations and other flatteries such as potato chips and piggies.

Canada awaits me.

Only in summer.

Winter there is cold and dreary.

Therefore, the United States awaits me.

Particularly Honolulu and the oily skin of Tahitian women in search of Polynesian freedom poor Gauguin caught syphilis and died happily painting with beautiful colors of tropical hues, and i must wait no longer, fate announces now's the time, jesus will reward me with my sixth knot in the affairs of love and death and the afterlife goes berserk the importance of powder kegs and similar situations of verdure and anticipatory moments of more love affairs movielike in appearance exemplifying the innocuous love affairs shadows of your smiles and other important sojourns.

Suffering passes as in a bothersome cold, pain is not futile but inevitable, the imminent idea of leisure is encompassed by pretentious realities in the light of Dr Brehms dissertation on the distinction of the paradigm theory of attraction and the reinforcement theory regarding Festinger's beliefs in Communications and other practical matters.

One learns film clandestinely and the result is obviously introspective and extrospective unless the communists come and return the powder kegs in order to begin the revolution against democratic fascism.

The linguistic expression of words such as salubrious as in the Spanish sabroso expresses a certain amount of English sophistication, simplicity and a down-to-earthiness which can only be subsumed in the first moments of love and enjoyment. Womanhood is the answer to the meaning of manhood and its historical development.

Is it callous not to feel sorry about women who are abused and raped? Is it disgusting to be a chauvinist and say "They deserve it?" Is it the privilege of man to force himself like a cave man unto a woman in order to continue the propagation of the race? If a woman refuses to propagate, is that her problem and not man's? Is it the inherent fascist right of man, being the stronger mammal, to force himself into the female of the species?

This human state of affairs was discussed earlier in this introduction and the reasons are summed up thus:

comets come wandering down mother earth etcetera etcetera and therefore if Mexican bandidos force themselves on gringas they say they are guiltless because they want revenge for American cowboys who rape Mexican women; Spanish culture also dictates that it is in the due process of English parliamentary procedures and puritan ethics that rape becomes a crime punishable by 0 to six months imprisonment. According to Garcia and Garcia, a chauvinist cerdo from the Bronx, plain women become gay libbers, but women in general, particularly the less plain women, remember their instincts (as was the example of the 19 year old coed last night) and it is a free and wilful decision imposed by predestined instincts. It is primitive because God created woman not necessarily in the image of Brigitte Bardot, but he did create a law that must be imposed on his creatures, and his creatures,must be punished by God for rape, but God put the devil to tempt man to rape in order to propagate more rapists which gives us the answer to the dilemma: who came first? the chicken or the egg? The answer: the vicious circle of an egg is neither visionary nor vicious and we should now revert to terms such as rape and seduction by giving them fresh meaning in the light of modern times, a more positive meaning, so to speak, and there are positive instances to reality that must be taken into consideration such as psychological damage, physiological reaction, attitudes and beliefs,, silence, and the obscenity of continuum.

And now, a critique:

There was a slight flaw in the plot of the TV movie **Powder Keg** starring Rod Taylor. There was a lack of continuity in the train scene when the lady who was raped by the Mexican escapes him and an absurd sequence takes place: the abductor (obviously because he is the villain of the plot) is shot only in the arm. The reason for this is to allow the villain to suffer a more voluptuous death under the American WASP hero, Rod Taylor, as he prepares the powder keg for the climax of the story, coming up in a few minutes. The entire sequence was an absurdity, and the 73 people in the train must have been killed by now by the wounded Mexican villain.

Writers have a way of putting fantasy into reality. That's why I'm a writer. Writers lie. They lie a lot. Lying is necessary for fantasy which brings us to a discussion, a poetic discussion, I must add, of the relationship between poetic lying and moral lying. Distinctions, in reality, are irrelevant because lying is lying, whether it's poetic or moral, but for the sake of argument, granted that metaphysical lies are not moral lies nor poetic lies, what is a lie? A lie, generally defines, is white or black in color. Poetic lies are fanatasy lies, and thus, coloured white. Moral lies are black because the colour of guilt is black. The colour of conscience remorse is also black. Metaphysical lies transcend both moral and illusory lies in that they perceive the world from a cosmological angle, and therefore, they are abstract and colourless. Metaphysical lies are exceptions to colourful lies because they cannot be deciphered for the simple reason that this type of lie is and is not, a somewhat paradoxical situation, so to speak.

Now, an anti-critique:

I am disappointed by novels because they try to idealize the West without taking into consideration its defects. Take for example Montana. I was in Montana, but the problem with writers in that they make Montana appear like a romantic resort when in reality, it is a backward state and I feel the reason for romanticizing it is to attract people to live in these backwoods, and I see no reason why people have to live in these backwoods. We will be intruding into the lives of another form of living species: the backwoods animals. We already have violated the rules of humanity by intruding Indian Territories of the West through trickery and greed.

What's to be done, then? Alienation. Alienate yourself. Human nature is corrupt. We thrive in corruption. It is God-created but devil-influenced and our father is a romantic version of the Western vision of idealization, and we run away from concrete reality, and to a concrete mind, the loving God is unacceptable because it is too romantic, and Jesus movements are for idiots like me, the romantics, the nostalgic, the sentimental, the idealists who look for personal saviors and friends, the idiotic fundamentalist, the positivist, faith hope and charity and the greatest is charity for life and the afterlife, let me dream of positivism, no more negatives, dream on, dream on, the simplistic approach to forgiveness, without the catholic rituals and sacraments and indulgences pray directly to the loving forgiving father and not through the catholic priest who listens to your gossip in confession and the loving saviour christ who has saved us that we should go and save the world after receiving him in our hearts despite the fact that we reject him constantly in our daily greedy actions, and so there should be no need for depression because of the thesis don't worry be happy our father watches over us, oh how peaceful, oh how positive…(FOOTNOTE 1: the fact is that my personal interdictions are expressions of the tragicomic situation of the universe and my microcosm when I mix styles in the same paragraph/sentence/word to bring about the dichotomy of both my life and others which is FOOTNOTE 2: life is emphatic and alienated either at the same time, i.e., spontaneously, or logically, i.e., one after the other in logical sequence).

The point about the footnotes is well-brought because this expresses my alienating/emphatic character regarding this flow of experience which delves from religion to philosophy and more materialistic matters like machines that type letters, computers, business and economics, in that logical order. Chemistry and biology are scientifically are scientific endeavours which include the left hemisphere, but the left hemisphere of the mind and the world are in a somewhat descriptive and graphical nature so that the result is an entangling or better still entwining of both spheres (which, by the way, proves the circular mode of the universe including this planet earth and other such planets as pluto and mars) and also the continuous flow of the stars and other forms of the galaxy which are divided into light years. But it is good to stop the flow which is characterized by music and the Eastern or Right sphere versus the mathematical or Western sphere, e.g., Europe and the United States. I am, pardon the personal interdiction, a scheme of both hemispheres encompassing the entirety and wholeness of the world, being thus Edmundo (meaning the world and therefore symbolic of both hemispheres) and Farolan (meaning the light bearer, the World View, so to speak, of this world, and my character of Eurasian nature covers my interntional sphere being east and west under the mestizaje brand of being Eurasian which, by the way, is the most beautiful and wholesome race, and I'm not being conceited.

After almost half a gallon of drinking water to recompensate the slight diarrhea which I suffered a few moments ago, I drank myself into gluttony only to feel more secure with the warmth of the flowing water in my vertebral system and the flowing motion of the fan which is circular and therefore reputed to be extremely philosophical as it includes and excludes the world and the squareness respectively and therefore paragraphs in the name of legalities.

Being an agent myself, I find that the entirety of words must be cut from the more Latin Influence of Spanish to the more staccato nature of the Nordic approach to PhDs and life in general.

A medium must be stipulated: a medium called mass,
where hardware must be in proportion to software.
The east has too much software,
the west has too much hardware,
so we must compensate: hardware must be shared with software. The problem is that the right hemisphere of the mind cannot be recompensated by the hardware of its left hemisphere by the simple reason that the mind develops a million even trillion and infinitely trillion times faster than the mathematical computations of techno-evolutions and other mathematical endeavours. I am not saying that I am partisan to the right hemisphere of my mind, but I cannot help it, limited human being that i am, to be an agent of the right side of my brain which at any rate encompasses the left side of my brain since the left side is partial to the wholeness of the right side according to the theories in humanistic studies which have developed in neurology in recent years. The limitations of Einstein and other geniuses therefore must be rejected because their limitations mathematical-wise were genial which brings us again to the universal human dilemma: which comes first, the chicken or the egg?

And the universal dilemma is reflected by the clicheic aphorism: vicious circle. But the circular reiteration of this thesis only proves the circular nature of the mind the planet earth the other planets and the minutest atom; the molecules of our body are also circular which proves and confirms the superiority of the roundness of the right hemisphere versus the squareness of the left hemisphere.

Talking of reflexes, the mind is too subtle to perceive unconscious reflexes. Dreams for example take the shape of reflexes. Reflexes may come in three categories: Freudian, Jungian and Farolanian. The Farolanian theory synthesizes the theories of Freud who said that there are two basic drives of man: sex and the desire to be great; Jung who stipulated that reflexes are expressions of archetypal instincts of the human drive, developing the theory of the unconscious stream which Joyce later develops but adds to the more objective aspect of humanity by abstracting Freud's theory; Pavlov whose studies were empirical and was known as "woof", or the reflex theory applied to dogs, (and dammit, I hate dogs!) and other slobbering creatures like laughing hyenas; Nietzsche whose Superman theory transcends the instinctive reflexes as I reiterate the Hegelian thesis-antithesis-synthesis syndrome which has been the format used in academia and other intelligentsia ever since its formal format advocated by Hegel. The Superman theory gave rise to the Comics character Superman in American Pop culture, a being born in Krypton and American instituted in his disguise as Clark Kent of the Globe newspaper, a bespectacled, timid, bungling newspaperman who at the sound of an alarm would change to his Superman personality and costume and save the human race from the "bad guys" and mad scientists like Luther, Stimmel, Einstein, Emilsson, Signitzer and Steinson. The Krypton effects on Superman weakens him since he was originally transported from the planet Krypton as a baby, landed on earth with foster parents Kent who are the only ones who know his superhuman secret. As I said, I strongly believe that this science fiction character was inspired by Nietzsche's Superman combined with Jesus Christ Superstar, cognitive, prophetic of the end of the world when Christ the Superman will return in his full glory and power. Fact or Fiction? I say fact.

I will now process to answer the dichotomy of Remington shavers. I will demonstrate in Shakesperean fashion the idealized nature of reality and the blonde approaches to the kinetic nature of the weakening aspects of life and reality.

Let me digress: I need to jump to another approach, more objective, more epic and alienating, an approach taken in brechtian fashion, used for theses and dissertations. This whole treatise of the "flow of experience" is an example of what a dissertation or a treatise should be with disregarded footnotes. The theory behind originality in dissertations must be conceived from a different point of view, whether the name of the game is honesty or dishonesty, but there must be more honesty and "originality" in dissertations instead of the uncreative garbage produced in formats of green and bureaucratic universities etc and perhaps such dissertations are needed in order to be able to understand deeper its futility and the need for an anti-dissertations so to speak as in this case of flow of experience.

Digressing now from the digression, we return to the point being games people play. We are empty of games and we must proceed to understand the use of Indian spices and other miscellany for good Eastern cooking. The use of dregs and anti-dregs, drugs and anti-drugs are necessary for the existential nature of the human race.

Regarding people branded as "insane". Someone was caught stealing and when he was asked what motivated him he answered " I am a messenger of God!" Many interpretations may be given to this man's answer I will only delve on a few, in fact, only one: being a messenger of God may mean from a christian standpoint that the devil (this is particularly the case of fundamentalist christians) made me do it, using the black comedian Flip Wilson's and that the devil put the words " I am the messenger of God!" in the victim's mouth as an excuse for his crime. But the point of the matter is well-taken by the christians. True, it is the work of the devil but the fact that the devil is a creature of God makes the devil the messenger or harbinger of the victim and therefore indirectly by saying he is a messenger of God he truly is and only he is a messenger through the devil. Academically speaking, this is a very Jesuitical approach being from a Jesuit-educated background and liberal the way Quevedo and Hitchcock, both Jesuit products, were liberal and cynical about their Voltaire (another Jesuit product) approach to God and the Devil.

The unsuspecting fact is that this is God's writing through me. But again, is the devil intervening? That remains to be seen. I am intellectually convinced that only the Creator is directly involved with me and I say I am convinced from the Virtues of Faith Hope and Charity, the three, but the greatest is Charity (Matthew or Corinthians?) I suspect it is a Corinthian verse.

Manipulation is quite devilish and perhaps the business manipulators of mankind are devilishly inspired. Machiavelli looked like the devil, if we consider a beard and a goatee and a moustache as a stereotype of the devil, but we need not fear if God is on our side the devil's on our feet and the only thing God can do in his perpetual game of hide and seek is give us hope and grace as the devil tickles our toes and he can do worse things of course WITH GOD'S PERMISSION but god won't permit anything supernaturally if we are not supernatural enough to face or confront the Job-tortures of the devil. So, I conclude by saying PRAISE THE LORD and AD MAJOREM DEI GLORIAM, those beautiful prayers of Ignatius and Xavier stick to my mind in formulas and abbreviations ptl, amdg, that i repeat over and over like a chant until i am brainwashed and my life is lived fuller from this religious experience.

Manipulation ends this treatise temporarily.

The attack is there quickly manipulated and let to die as the last moments of blondish promiscuity crawls from the evil of her face and her natural womanish outlook to make people die can be so cold people can be just watch and see but still the general concept is that the world is good and this is the Western white concept the white god concept, an intermediary that perpetual question of evil as a creation of god, true or false, but the concept of god as a supreme being is accepted and if people do not accept this they live in apprehension and other fears but the conviction of God's existence rules fear out especially if this is a powerful loving and friendly god personal in your side.

Returning to the intermediary force the devil the black magicians and other primitive rites of india and africa and haiti and asia rely on this type of devilish machinations and the directness of God-man relationships in the case of western culture only proves the superiority of the Aryan race because of its discriminatory nature believing in more facts than one that god's existence is punitive and that the relation is direct.

Granted therefore the existence of a super-being the dilemma is short-lived the absurdity of it all becomes a game and a personal jest the experiment has been played and the results are nil but the consequences are anti-nihilistic, there is no alternative but growth in the belief of the super-being right after you have put your foot down in initial belief.

**On the circulatory nature of jobs and job-hunting:**

**It seems that all of us have a niche in life and therefore, we must not pursue that niche which is already predestined. We are all equal because we end up in that niche; some might have nicer niches, and others, just a simple hole in the ground. So also in life: everyone has been predestined. As McLennan said: we'll all get there sometime or other; some take longer, and according to Master Reddy, the longer we wait, the more valuable the happening or state of affairs, or whatever label you may put into it. So it is not rationalizing; it is another instance of the flow of life**

and humanity and other affairs whereby we are not destined to teach or to be worked upon shows that there are greater fortunes in the future.

**Guru has spoken.**

**On the philosophy of soap operas:**

The dialogue is almost bestial., "goodnight, I'll call you" then there is organ music playing and then silence, and then a technical sentimental line: "if the board strikes at this point, the victim is unattended", no way without risk, and doctors and nurses and other affairs stimulated by shock and other dialogues of subservient nature; the plan of mysteries but some become too romanticised as the organ music is played cameras zoom in fade out and another almost disgusting commercial, Tide, and the edge of night continues with its intrigues and other miscellany. Then another soap opera follows. Its philosophy is inestimable. It pursues and attempts to pursue, so it zooms: "We heard you", "Oh well…" "How is he", "Oh, he's fine", "but it's going to be some time before (mumbles, mumbles) and the week before I visited him (knock, knock) "That's probably the paperboy giving stories why he's late.oh hi! it's you" "I'm late because (mumbles, mumbles)" "John, what is it?" embarrassing silence fade in ANOTHER WORLD fade out commercial BACK TO THE SOAP OPERA AND PATIENCE AND OVERPATIENCE IS NEEDED.

"The divorce…"

"only if the judge needs you"

"John did you request that my maiden name be returned?"

"Yes it's absolutely…"

"It's very humiliating."

"John, you know that I am young and I'm going back with him oh excuse me (Lawyer comes in who is in love with the blonde wife who now lives with parents)

"Honey, what's the matter?"

"Once my divorce is over…"

(Organ music)

shitty sentimentality: "We'll return to our story in just a minute"
(Announcer's big voice)

*commercial (every five minutes)

As you may note the philosophy of soap operas appeals to the most intellectually-inclined housewife who loves organs of all sorts, music and otherwise, the pace is extremely slow, it is extremely boring which is a challenge to the middleclass housewife who begins to perceive the fact that she has to wash dishes while one ear is glued to the sound of soap operas in televisions and other miscellany, and obviously the brands become promulgated there are no bourgeois attempts at kindness the fact is that they get lonely and stuck with soap operas in television and other miscellany like jeopardy and the price is right and they start to talk like soap operas and discuss the unintelligible circumstances of the wedding gossips and who did this and who did that and the newspaper boy this and the woman next door and i am embarrassed to even delve on all of these as my stream of unconsciousness produces soap operas because i watch too much TV and i see myself metamorphosis as a housewife as I glue my ears to soap operas and at the same time concentrate on household duties such as listening to my thoughts simultaneously with the soap operas. John is always mentioned in this soap opera, john has been mentioned 2,148 times, all i hear is john, john, john, i don't even know who john is and i was intently listening to this soap opera, and now the woman looks at this other woman who is going to marry john and the look looks devilish she is trying to be as un-boring as possible by changing her tones, words, words, words, "do you want a church wedding?" "That's too small", "we're not inviting people", "I like to have a feeling of space", "Let's get married in your house", "I'd rather not", "Is it because of Alice?" "Well forget it", "I know what's happened" (Silence) "Do you really want to know?" and on and on and on and the man gets mad and there is this hot silence and he apologizes.the terrace.outside…I mean, I mean…(he stutters) something may happen so we must…what could happen?.well…my brain, my brain.Ha, ha what a ridiculous situation people get caught up in this state of affairs…the soap opera continues with the nagging mother saying don't let whatever happened between you and stephen turn you against love" and she answers "mother believed in love he lied to me about everything he was with rachel the day i lost my baby, i will never trust another man as long as i live, well aunt alice did i say something wrong she wants a divorce but she never can believe she can love anyone else (music, fade out)…

I'm sick of this topic i'm turning off the tv and take a bike ride. (one hour later)

I open the tv with a glass of lemonade in my hand, the commercials continue, and it appears that the only women taken for tv are beautiful women and the ugly women watching tv are attracted by the beauty of the women and are said to be so dumb that they believe that just because the products they advertise express the beauty of women they are convinced they can be as beautiful as them but once born ugly you're ugly for life and these commercials just are big lies and since ugly women comprise 85% of our population of the female species they end up buying these products and that's how commercials work. End of commercial lecture. Mass Media 784, BGSU. Open to graduate students in Speech and Journalism.

A movie begins.

Another depressing movie.

letters: there are funny letters and sentimental letters. The best letters I wrote were sentimental letters. only absurdities and jokes and other things related to humor. This is a lie, of course, because I write only depressing letters.

immortality.

IMMORTALITY has been a problem delving/besieging mankind; so I will only delve on it for a moment. In passing, memory is immortality, and in a given poem, the search for immortality was expressed (footnote 3: "memory is immortality; he lives only in the minds of people and he slowly dies as he is remembered less, pleading when no one cares any longer". The Rhythm of Despair and other poems, Edmundo Farolan page ?).

The fact is that immortality exists/does not exist, depending on one's outlook. For some, it is immortality in the form of children and the continuation of the species; for others, it is reincarnation (buddhism, hinduism) and for others, it is the afterlife (christianity) in the form of life with the Father and His Son, Jesus Christ. I might term my views as synthesizing, eclectic and slightly stubborn and scattered. There are no answers because the situation after death is unknown, thus another view—mysticism. Mysticism may take two forms: hope and optimism, or beckettian despair, where the spiralling effects of life end in death, and life dwindles into nothingness. And yet, despite the pessimism of beckett, he states in **Endgame** the fact about grain upon grain, piling one after the other, in conformity to Zeno's philosophy of the man who collects sand that is washed away into the sea, and like the myth of sisyphus, the process continues: like the rock, like an ant, man strives and continues his struggle in meaningfulness/ meaninglessness. The meaningful aspect radicated by christianity whereby progress ensues, not material but spiritual thus in conformity with other religions where individual, spiritual progress is attained from constant meditation and surrender to the godhead (footnote 4: **Sri Isopanisad**, a look at Krishna philosophy/religion). The struggle must continue, and man must continue patiently to survive; the existentialist point of view might be an approach—there might be a hope in a pessimistic point of view as long as one's approach is optimistic. Thus, christian existentialism with Marcel and Teilhard de Chardin conform to the fanning process of humanity in relating this particular aspect to Jung's archetypes of humanity. Where is the answer? No one still knows. But a patient peaceful struggle must go on.

insanity.

INSANITY may come in various forms: the quiet insanity of paranoids or the anguished despair of schizos. The result is this: when one reaches a bureaucratic status, there is no escape but a quiet acceptance of self; but there is so much too soon, and so much to lose in a bureaucratic state; there must be an answer. Sanity and insanity are terms. The existence of both aspects are possible in the same human being; we cannot categorize insanity. Insanity is Sanity if taken from a dialectic point of view. Even doctors still debate the moments of normality/abnormality in their patients. There are more moments of insanity in a paranoid patient, and that seems to be the only difference: the degree of moments of anger, impatience, etc. but from a standpoint of sanity, it is almost impossible, except for very rare instances, that a man has perfect control of his senses. Even the americanized term "horniness" is an example of "going out of your norms of sanity", since horniness is a rare situation, and the fact that you release certain emotions due to weather and other influences only proves that there is no such thing as a perfectly sane human being or other beings. Everything is insane, only some are more insane than others, depending on freudian moods, weather temperatures and other such external factors of environmental stimuli.

history.

HISTORY is a subject matter which cannot be discussed because history is not argumentative but rather deductive and/or inductive. It is an enumeration of past facts and events. But history may be taken as a presential form if current events are taken into consideration. The fact is that literature on history is incomplete because it only takes into consideration such factors as the "sparks of the past", meaning, the more glamorous aspects of history such as independence of nations, wars, and other extremely outrageous happenings of mankind. History must in fact enumerate all of reality second by second boring and not boring outrageous and not outrageous, but since this is impossible because observation is limited only to certain facts, history therefore becomes prejudicial, subjective to the whims of the historian who writes what he wants to write. Thus no matter how comprehensive history or the literature of history may be, the fact is that history is never comprehensive nor objective to all of mankind's databank.

criticism.

CRITICISM is argumentative and discursive. The debatable aspects of history or certain points of view such as the debate regarding the size of a thimble in the 17thcentury as compared to its present size, or the theological debate of the fathers of the church who debated years and years on how many angels can fit at the edge of a pin, or other debatable aspects as who came first the chicken or the egg—these are matters for criticism. We comment on them, and many so-called "critical works" are not faithful to the true meaning of criticism because there is no subjective synthesis within the discursive sections of the discussion, which makes criticism criticised in some other label. Modern criticism is no longer logical—you write what you like to write. Modern criticism also is a copy cat, quoting quotes and therefore it becomes a documentary criticism, no longer the free for all personal criticism. Critics also have always had problems with creative writers because creative writers say that critics have no imagination and cannot create, so they end up being sourpusses and therefore, critics.

poetry.

the existential views of poetry are labelled, we cannot be poetic if we label, we must not label poetry as either romantic or existential, absurd or religious, we must search different labels, create new labels such as zuk to mean existence and frk to mean non-existence and thus a poem like this must be considered true poetry:

zuk fruk exunked bruked blouk ksdlo fu ldkf dxcid dh83 ads77f adod9did idufusuf

now, the above is true unadulterated poetry but that is how poetry should be patterns of perusal and statements like the quality of inequality is an expression of mercy and gramercy and...

now this type of poetry that rhymes in verses inner and outer are examples of extinct poetry according to modernists but actually the world is round and we go back to the old ways because originality stems into disoriginality in poetry and i say disoriginality because the word originality and creativity no longer has meaning, no valid standpoint, originality has been proven and disproven by Jung because man repeats and repeats himself throughout the whole course of mankind so one must not repeat himself in other words he must be dis-original.computerized poetry, concrete poetry, machine poetry all types of poetry have been experimented on and this new form i call 39did djjskkdkdj in other words, a subtitle
wwdi394728374483.

This attempt is eclectic but i refuse to be poetical eclectic or anti-eclectic since such forms have been expressed: examples of dis-original poetry are:

spwiiwieiroqi jfdjkf jfojf jfur8fho 9862^^^^^^^^^^^^^^^^^^^^^^
^^^^^^^^^^^^^^^^^^^^^^^^^^^^^^^^^^^^^^^^^^^^^^^^^^^^^^^^^^^^^^^^^^
^^^^^^^^^^^^^^^^^^^^^^^^^^^^^^^^^^^^^^^^^^^^^^^^^^^^^^^^^^^^^^^^^^
^^^^^^^^^^^^^^^^^^^^^^^^^^^^^^^^^^^^^^^^^^^^^^^^^^^^^^^^^^^^^^^^^^
^^^^^^^^^^^^^^^^^^^^^^^^^^^^^^^^^^^^^^^^^^^^^^^^^^^^^^^^^^^^^^^^^^
^^^^^^^^^^^^^^^^^^^^^^^^^^^^^^^^^^^^^^^^^^^^^^^^^^^^^^^^^^^^^^^^^^
^^^^^^^^^^^^^^^^^^^^^^^^^^^^^^^^^^^^^^^^^^^^^^^^^^^^^^^^^^^^^^^^^^
^^^^^^^^^^^^^^^^^^^^^^^^^^^^^^^^^^^^^^^^^^^^^^^^^^^^^^^^^^^^^^^^^^

^^^^^^^^^^^^^^^^^^^^^^^^^^^^^^^^^^^^^^^^^^^^^^^^^^^^^^^^^^^^^^
^^^^^^^^^^^^^^^^^^^^^^^^&%&$^^

In this beautiful verse you will note certain patterns of Martian influence, could be other extraterrestrial influences from other planets, as I noted down in **Rhythm of Despair,** still unpublished at this point in time, where I definitely confirm the existence of UFOs and other aliens from other planets, and just as our moon influences the sea and we have the term "lunatics" who have been moon-influenced.

This kind of poetry continues and transcends all forms of poetry because it is dis-original. The word creative has also been abused and we must stop using such words unless we use them to quantify meaning, e.g., reality of Pluto and other astrological notations since words cannot transcend only expressions can and if expressions are written they can only be transcribed in the following fashion:

89907(*^&#%$44^%&869&87&(*()8 ojdmfal ca_*8967810928 04091274746283464149^#@!$%&^*()+_)OIOHOHkjhsojdosjf 11!!177&9

Thus, speaketh poetry…

saltpeppers.

saltpeppers are chemicals which are neurological in meaning and christian in context. People eat saltpeppers because they are grey and therefore gloomy. The salt pepper tradition has been Polynesian in origin although some sources have expressed the origin to the aspects of nature which originated in India and china sources however say that indochina was the source of origins of both india and china or vice versa thus the word indochina.

incense.

the queen of scotland ate incense, the queen of england ate incense. the children of asia have been besieged by incense. once upon a time the smelly incense reached the scottish metaphors of madness and the english accents were substituted by incense accents and these accents were made interesting by the effects which the weather in Bowling Green caused upon the issues and answers of comfortable situations and the restrictions have finally showed certain parallels to bohemia and other countries such as malta. the malt liquor of Malta was an influence from incense. Incense cannot be thought, it can only be smelled; it may express certain reminiscences of other smells in life, but the incense of India superseded smell, and therefore, the queens of the world became fairies and vanished after smelling the incense of india.

hot dogs.

hot dogs originated from germany and pepsi cola is taken with barbecued hot dogs, and the nutrition and other diets of the US become very becoming of the health and bodily movements of Americans. That is why health becomes good in the beginning, but old age removes the health of Americans, and America is for the young.

old age.

old age is related to paste. when you paste paintings into old age, a result is a repetition of new affairs such as the birth of staplers when their death is construed by the rebirth of potato chips and nail clippers. the carpenters who paint and who make wood from trees are exceptional sub-humans and therefore there are courses for the mentally retarded and paper becomes other kinds of materials such as burned ash and burning people become aged and like piggies they become toasted by summer and summer becomes an expression of a flow from one reality to another and then one gets used to old age because old age connects and disconnects. The. Man. Becomes. Staccato. And then the old aged people become and then they vanish and then they return to a certain nirvana from televisions and beds and other bohemian tricks and then bells ring and then they vanish and then they return to a certain nirvana and then thoughts flow but then the reality of it all is in the mind and old people are young at heart while young people are old at heart, and emotions, and realities such as brain drains become forced into sentimentality and other emotional criticisms and old age is a philosophical concept.who is old? who is young?.because it is a becoming, a DEVENIR or other such instances as passing from infancy to old age and in this life we only see birth and death and old age and youth and after old age there is a watermelon and other fruits to eat such as corn and nectarines and peaches and the names of old people are mentioned and enumerated by other instances such as the expression of vice presidents and other presidential affairs which are befitting to the man and the woman who are young first and then middle-aged and then old and then a breakdown of the realization of other people and we are concerned only with ourselves and other friends and when we feel the ache within us we thank someone the same way Father Back thanked someone and that someone seemed to be my student trying to settle his anguish shen each one has his own personal anguish about old age the continuity of the species and i can no longer think of my species or the propagation of my species i can only conceive of the madness of the diary of the friends who write and who become part pf the repertory of the conventional history and the researchers both critical and historical in their attempts to synthesize the facts about old age and reincarnation and the hope is still there we must keep on smiling idiotically and take time as a passing juncture of indian poetry and music and everyone must participate in this theater of madness and in this old age which awaits us in the future and i have ten years to live to write and to say what i felt at the moment and i feel that i am old and i feel that i am full of knowledge and i keep on expressing this flow and this flow is no longer a flow but a quantity of words reflecting despair and hope and other similar junctions of reality i cannot stop and i cannot go and i cannot publish and i just live on day by day thinking of my material needs, the immediate influences upon me day by day, today, as i eat and cook and eat and drink and cook and continue the lifelong search but the immediacy is what counts and ants and vermin are reflected by drums and humdrums and other manifestations of old age as an old woman slowly lives out her days and i am ready to leave from this place in search of new places in order to wait for a few more months and the duties have been done and i have to continue my training without remembering that old age awaits me and we are concerned day by day until one day we realize we are wrinkled and old and we are alone and yet sometimes aloneness is happiness, in the midst of our days and other reputations and youth passes by and the purity of goodness and the jesters of old people as they laugh slow and walk slow and shake their hands, as old houses are filled with ants and maggots and the smell of sickness and the people as they pursue evil and women become men and men become women and we all become spirits in this flow of experience, flow of life, flow stream of mankind as we attempt each moment to breath and to realize that in our breathing there are other external factors because breathing is life and we are mediate in our affairs and we only think of what happens to us and not others and we slide by in the encompassing moments of history without realizing that each second relieves us of despair and we do not want these seconds to pass i ask that these seconds pass and they do not, i ask that they do not and they pass on and on into history they move into minutes hours days years and before you know it you're old and grey and we can only pretend to stop time in our minds the brutality of time and the consequence is old age the inevitability of old age like time and space they must go on and there is no timelessness in our reality and we can see ourselves in the mirror reflecting ourselves and yet we do not attempt to be aware we are afraid to face the inevitable, fear, but there should not be fear but fear itself, the fear of the inevitability of death and we await heaven and other surveys whether we are ready to die or not, whether we are ready to go to heaven or not, and we make deals with friends to come back after death and tell us what's out there and we are afraid because they don't come back to tell us what's there, and we are afraid because of rumours of what is there.a light? nothingness?.and faust said **let this hour be but a year a natural**

**day that faustus may but live and save his soul** but it was too late he was committed to the inevitabilities of death and the imminence was there and there was no other choice but to accept its inevitability and the fear can be lessened by accepting the fact that we should not care for anything material or pretend to care because we are facing the inevitable what we have is not ours and we must continue even without books but only our thoughts and the continuity of experience and a certain hope and smile in our faces despite long hair or baldness or grey hair which comes in old age.

the day passes.

another day, another night, another heat wave, and there is no consolation

but a fan and a TV and a bathroom and then it rains then there is a thunderstorm my retreat from the world is coming into me, and the transcendence of all is beginning to come, there must be some way of opening up in other fashions, in saltpeppers and old age and history and criticism without adding the word ANTI before them, without having to synthesize anything in Hegelian terms, there must be a capacity for happiness that is even beyond transcendence because i cannot express neither indifference nor happiness nor metaphysical lies nor sadness nor anything in this heat wave, just a mere exemplifying of words and feelings and experience, as i contemplate on the heaviness of the fan and the exemplifying reasons behind meditation and the closing of eyes and the transcendental meditation and other types of meditation that brings one to a heavenly sphere giving restful sleep to the awareness of the mind and of the soul. I must begin to meditate and then to write of the awareness of meditation, as though the reflection of a reflection comes and goes and stays and grows and grows until a supreme height is reached, a majestic height that cannot be deciphered into words, a mere opening up completely, but these are dreams, we must learn to put these dreams into reality, we must make the mind completely part of this reality and fly because we must fly and dive and swim and fly especially fly into the heights of life's madness and envision the entirety of existence in one finger and in one tow and observe every second of the day as the night passes by as the day passes by without being aware of time nor space just this feeling of being forgiven by Ohm and by the supreme being and then entering his realm of timeless weightlessness and other aspects that go into anti-gravitational thinking and other incumbencies of thought and expression and we are lost in this state of having to try to search weightlessness when in the mind there exists no weight nor gravity and no one can take out the dreams and the fantasies of the mind because it stays there and only when it is affected does it vegetate and even vegetables live and think as the thinking plants and the suicidal Venus flytrap and other more injunctive forces of self-predictions and prophecies of the mind...

one needs discipline in this state of affairs and not rambling babbling senility and in senility there is reflection of old age and i must be alone without anyone because i must discipline myself to be strong and self-sufficient and not only alone because i must be alone, self-sufficient, the ubermann attitudes of Nietzsche and who knows where there are others who consider nirvana as something too personal while others consider christian salvation the reality and who knows when there are others who consider salvation reachable by only one way who knows and there are others who consider that the only way of reaching the thoughts of mankind is by computers and others who say they are unreachable and who knows when only hypnosis can go so far and that the individual mind cannot be reached after a certain point only the individual himself, who knows, and that others constrict and i like it but who knows that i like it and i never express my individuality as much as others and i express my dis-individuality and then i realize that i am part of a whole and that no man is an island and then i rebel because then i am isolated and who knows this is mysticism because i am trying to be monastic, solitary like monks and people don't know me i only show parts of a book and i rationalize and say i am afraid of certain things and i'm not afraid of others but who knows writers lie and i am writing and lying and asking who knows when i know the answers or do i and do i really do not and i pretend to know other answers and i really do not and the thunderstorms come and they are caused by the waves and the waves are caused by other things like heat waves and the heat waves form into clouds and the clouds cause thunderstorms and lightning and then it rains.

# CHAPTER 2

# FLOW OF EXPERIENCE 2

IN MY ISOLATION i do not make an effort to reach people, to socialize and other similar functions, and so i attempt to justify my isolation by attempting to realize the other aspects of reality and i stay alone watching television and typing seeds of thoughts that may develop or die like flowers and the birds who are reborn in spring and they die like flowers or bears who do not really die but hibernate, merely dormant in winter and winter is like death and we are only dormant and how is it that saints are not rotted and why is it that they stay alive without their rotting bodies what makes a saint and there are no illusions to sainthood there are strong intentions towards faith and other more religious aspects of life enter into non-being, the non-being of reality and then there are other ghosts of reality that exclaim movies and movielike versions of reality and the vertical aspects are horizontally expected to be verticalized because i still do not comprehend the difference between vertical and horizontal, i still cannot make out the meaning of double negation and triple negations where a triple makes a negative and yet in other cultures such as the Hispanic as negations quantitatively increase, the more forceful the negation is.

One must not premeditate the thought processes because this is nihilistic and in order to find one's personal salvation he must understand why ant killers eat ants and why the Johnson commercials are exceptional factors regarding ant killers and other such aspects as personal salvation in order to beget children and immortality the flow continues in varied forms such as the existence of stipulations and court issues which cannot be engendered and must be stipulated against court appeals which are warped by lawyers who need dramatic experience.

On cooking barbecue and icelandic fish i immediately forget the experience that occurred in my mind as words were flowing in loudly as I ate the mushrooms and other cooked vegetables, and the onions were delicious and the garlic was freshly cooked as my bourgeois stomach ate and gobbled the exotic oriental dishes with barbecued meat sliced in pieces and almost professionally did a gourmet dish come out of it which brings us to the point of fish. What was the relationship of having silent fish barbecued? Why was fish discussed early this afternoon in the kitchen of 140 clay street? It seems that in my silence words were being reproduced since it was early afternoon and I was preparing another gourmet dish. It seems that there are so many sides to interests. Some people like good food and others like good women. I like both but the problem is I can't always get both, which brings us to the dilemma who came first, women or food? I try to console myself with the fact of chance meetings since chance rules man-woman relationships, chance rules our lives since the unmoved mover is said to know all and decide all. But isn't knowing deciding? How did the Aristotelian unmoved mover know? It is because he transcends all limitation we are told in basic theology-philosophy books, but the reality behind the supreme being is he wants us happy so long as we conform to his mode of happiness which brings us to the general contention that the world is generally happy and good, good is the word, linguistic derivation from God and God-good seem to prognosticate the weather which is almost 90 degrees fahrenheit and the thunderstorms come and go and the people in the house have gone except for me typing my flow of experience, limited experience as discusses two thousand pages ago in a footnote regarding the fact that the flow is not continuous because one has to defecate twice a day, eat twice a day. drink lemonade and orange juice four or five times a day, watch old movies on television with the fan subconsciously controlling the mind of a dreamer as he is sleeping in the attic/garret of a bohemian house which is close to the roof and the heat is extinct from the heat of the Brazilian amazons and African deserts and the only good part of this heated roof is the privacy involved with the radio playing WJR at 5 or 6 in the morning with the sound of the fan whirling away, drowning it, and i am privately amused by my thoughts of **sautéed** and other Brazilian flashbacks, and I am disappointed by the flow of thoughts of women who have loved me because love is different from sex, and sex comes normally as love becomes a forgetful experience, as one looks at the moon on television and contemplate the existence of moon men or lunanites or such scientific terms which HG Wells used in his novel/story/science fiction—THE FIRST MEN ON THE MOON, being english of course, due to his english heritage, if not nationality. But the late late movie was followed by a late late late movie and this was followed by the the crow of the cock who crowed twice at dawn after Peter denied Christ twice. And after biblical instances, I try to reproduce the facts of the flow of three hours ago without hesitating because it seems that I can only hesitate when the flow is discontinued by other dreams, like the exceptional thoughts of me and you and the dreams of slow-motion and other films which justify the rationale or irrationality of fellini and his numbers. The fact is not only to transcend but to de-transcend the esflumen of facts and other realities because the doctorate is not enough one must plot the death the death of oneself in order to be admirable. The suicidal factors of existence can only be measured quantitatively. The use of the word measure for the qualitative aspects of the mind is a contradiction. Therefore, the cats begin to scowl in the afternoon, or early evening, as the breezes have descended but I refuse to stay in the midst of the breezes because I am egotistically involved in this hot, almost insane room which expresses the bohemian atmosphere of my existence and other miscellany such as a goatskin bag filled with tar, empty of wine because of its leaking effects. The efforts have been tried; the entirety of my creativity is numb because

I refuse the egotistic and almost eccentric view of people who are aware of the eccentricity, who view the facts of life in the state of depression and it seems that the wildlife counterparts of humanity is an exceptional power-stricken poverty of life and existential joy and the fuller meaning of existence and essence, without going into Being and Nothingness and my studies of epistemology, cosmology and other Jesuitical studies from ferriols and other philosophers who have begged me to wander in their minds such as Fr. Non, very symbolic of nihilism, a good jesuit friend, and a friend of the family. I have portrayed my life in a few minute-seconds, expressing the now or the immediate past or the immediate future which is inevitable and I can consume my madness and anguish as I relate weather with my existence since I am very consummate about weather and I only attempt to conspire in my state of madness, as I click the camera of life where god is exceptionally the essence and the goal of my contradictions, and i cannot explain my life, my decisions have been predestined from a positive angle, and my positivism is a subjectivism which is expressionism surrealism dadaism creationism ultraism and other isms such as symbolism and experimentalism and objectivism and other such isms which only quantify words in limited fashion. When there is a smile from my face, a certain amount of mysticism is expected, and we are victims because of this aloneness, we are victims in a hick town, and I must consume myself after having observed and observe the differences of mid-america and the concepts of puritanism, beer-drinking and other such orgies which reflect the standard state of mankind, and we are thrilled by the fact that in summer, one must seduce, and in the midst of concepts and cultural innocence, one is drummed in with indifference, despite the observations in gigolo and 4 d's and other such examples as the noisy hog-kissers such as jim keller as he was making out with that fat slob and i was a mystic, tender and insane as usual, as i made out with the nineteen year old who had breasts as small as a child's. But away from that, and we now proceed to the more sublime aspects of American culture such as the predominance of chauvinism, and the utter absurdity of socialist movements and the definitions of liberalism and bourgeois examples of babies who are blonde and exceptionally interesting in the midst of technical photography. Hardware/software one must learn to be precise, and in New York, there are many software characters, the fact that New York has become the center of photography and pornography, the cultural center, the center of the world's cultural character, and I was in New York, and a certain amount of sadness because of the heat and the aloneness and the prostitutes who waited to be picked up in Broadway and 52nd, and I passed by only awaiting the chance effects of food and other such dishes as cultural activities and programs of bystanders and i could not focus on other instances since there was a milieu of things going on, as i fantasize new york, a few days before i proceeded to middle america and acted in a very good company of people. Huron and more huronic people i rebelled against because of the naiveté, because i was not participatory in my professional or semi-professional ways, i needed to be dragged by the hand as these people had problems, educational and otherwise, and of course I am reaching too far when i must concentrate only on the effects of my existence at this very moment facing inevitable time ticking away, and i ask what's to become of me, and Campus Crusade now looks at me with a smile and I feel that i have received a more powerful answer to my despair, an answer which once used to be "janitor in a drum" or other answers such as " I don't know", and I always was in despair from a nihilistic angle if only i had thought of Beckett I would have been more positive but now even Beckett cannot answer the hope of the fat lady or the ugly fat lady or the bearded gentleman because there is an answer to Matthew and other biblical sources regarding a futuristic hope for mankind, especially the rapture which fills me with tears and bliss as i remembered the tears and bliss of humanity as all looked forward and never backward looking at the future stars hoping for the rapture of mankind when all will blend blood and soul body and bones with the everlasting eternity of the creator and the angelical music will resound and tears will be dried and there will no longer be the traces of maggots and sins and parasites because the body will become life and there will no longer be need for sex as there is a strong need for it because of our maggot bodies wanting to penetrate greasy keyholes, as in dick's comments on kamal and other arabic factors which have to deal with women, since women have always been subservient to man, therefore there is a strong need for a woman's body near man and we must free ourselves from this reality since man cannot be freed by the anguish he now encounters unless he leaves all anguish aside and look at the praises of the lord without being fanatical because only through madness can one reach everlasting bliss, only through the stars can one encounter the madness which Perez Galdos foresaw in FORTUNATA AND JACINTA and in the bliss of these contradictions, one experiences the pangs of delight and torture of happiness, and in these states can we be inspired to express the inexpressible and only express the delight without feeling delight, only then can there be a certain amount of happiness even in dreams even in coming and going and even as words are formed from mouths or from our minds, the hair disappears, and yet the brain remains to console the feeling of distress and the ending of flights from heaven and hell, and the continuous tirade of meaningless and meaningful delights shall encumber our ecstasy.

In order to secure our madness, we must now clandestinely conclude the flow of experience which is this: I conclude that I cannot conclude because I cannot stop the flow of thoughts which continue endless, even if they end, the spiral ends/begins to discontinue and then continues again, whether in poems or afterthoughts or aftermaths, they are all thoughts, they are all emotions which are uncontrollable even if they are controlled through censorship and literary effects, they cannot be controlled by the mindless efforts of the mind and the emotions and we prefer to predominate over all these, we do not discuss, we are silent because in silence our thoughts continue to show certain amounts of un-conservative and de-consecrated grass, hashish and other mental drugs such as sneezing and coughing after a rainstorm comes and goes. In the end, when he reaches the middle, there is moralizing: the point of no return is the moral of morals, it is the message of messages, it is the war of all wars, because it is at this point that the flow of experience becomes tedious, redundant, it is at this point that the stream of consciousness is neither subconscious nor conscious, it is at this point that poetry blends with prose, it is at this point that life is comic and tragic. It is at this point that I have reached the conclusions of the point of no return, but the answers have always been those of despair, although now, one must no longer return. Now, I do not despair of this point of no return because I know I must move forward like the quixotic strife which drove him to continue the fight and to continue without turning back because there is only one way, forward, and that is the only way because one cannot and should not look backward; if he does, his sentimental past full of regrets will encroach upon him. Thus, the lecture on life and death and immortality continues in certain amounts of synthesis, lemon juice and orange juice, because the lessons are always moralizing whether there are messages or not, man always has to rationalize his justification to survive and exist in this cruel/uncruel world, whatever counterpart, he has no other exit but forward, and the forward exit is not of doom but of hope, of a future hope of morals, prayers, maggots and parasites who are drowning in ant killer juice and other miscellany. And so I stop and I continue, I stop and continue the flow of mankind on this earth from evolutionary amphibious animals to land animals to erect animals, I continue the evolution of the consciousness of humanity, and there is something more human and humane than humanity, and that is, the animal, for we are all animals like Sancho Panza but we must strive with lessons, lessons of good and evil, lessons of morality, lessons of the facts of life like the birds and the bees, and we must continue smiling with or without whiskers, with short hair or long hair, we must be idiotic and laugh in different ways, in hysterical ways, in guttural ways, in noisy ways, and there must be a difference in sexes from homosexuality to heterosexuality to gay liberation and women's liberation, and we must be liberated from maggots and vermin and other disgusting factors of humanity that crawl on the face of the earth such as acne, pimples and other cream factors that are made, remade, cycled and recycled like trash and newspapers and other things in bottled or plastic forms in order to continue the reincarnation of man and christianity and the humanistic efforts of ants and grasshoppers and man and names of men, women and children, and typical examples form boring books and PhD dissertations and anti-dissertations and anti-poetry and anti-television and anti-guerrilla television and anti-anti-pollution and dirt and contradiction and silent expressions and sensitivity and other emotions and unoriginal poems and poetry in numbers, in computerized forms and old age and summaries and anti-summaries and anti-anti-anti-conclusions and transcendence and over-transcendence and transcendental transcendentalism and there should be more conclusions to the human and animal and plant and mineral states of affairs like gold and copper and tin and zinc and silver and brooks and streams and names like boredom and Turkey and Russia and Siberia and the Philippines and Timbuktu, Congo, Janie Josh Jesus, Johnny, Matthew, Greg, Montez, Hazel, Emilson, Steinson, Signitzer, Farolan, triumvirate, Freud, Jung, Berelson, Steiner, Angola, Biafra, Bangladesh, Vietnam, and we must proceed to name biological functions of the body in used and unused and overused terms, in terms which may be categorized categorically, allegorically, muscularly, bonely, anguishedly, mentally, overly, existentially, and anatomically such as excretion, tumition, micronesian, polynesian, enumeration of facts such as the events of General Electric fans and the Olympic games and football games and other repetitions of Beckett's Lucky and letters that may be categorized in different fashions, with red or green ink and other eccentricities like billiards, pinball machines and the tilt, free style or otherwise, and a promise to be silent, or to practice silence, and to keep insanity only from a distance in order to deceive people, in order to observe people, as the phone rings and expresses a certain amount of melancholy at the way one expresses even in a conscious state the parts of the body that cannot be deciphered but goes on inevitably faster than typing a dissertation and other such factors as attempting to categorize the effects of atomic bombs and the next program of channel 7,534 and UHF channels such as WTOL TV channels of understanding such as public broadcasting system and other educational channels which cannot be expressed except among exceptionally retarded children and the fact is that they are the ones who express death and destroy the intelligence and awareness of the

Master's degree in psychology or a doctorate in speech and the ways one can communicate oral interpretation and get lessons of diction and English and speech and teach interpretation and teach language materials to so many people who apply for jobs and the possibility of getting contacts and part-time teaching possibilities in Seattle and the jobless situation in the United States and the opportunities and possibilities for creating jobs in the Humanities and there are journals such as the PA or the MID or the XGH or the IOL or the POLKO or the PMLA or the YTR or the ETJ and these are scholarly journals as can be seen with their scholarly abbreviations.

And so I continue my summary and conclusions and synthesis. I accept. Calmly. Patiently. Staccatowise.
It stops.
Begins.
Stops again.
Like a drip of water.
Like the grains of sand.
Like poetry.
Or prose.
or opportune moments.
or prose poetry.
or poetic prose.
or essays.
I begin.

I stop.
I continue.
In tree-like fashions.
In commas.
In words.
In positions like kamasutra.
in prepositions,
and handouts,
and green sheets,

and other states of affairs,
like kant,
and handke,
and peter nero,
and eddie dumas,
and people's realitites,
superman,
alter ego,
ego,
man and woman,
the stories of reality,
the consummate reality, of nirvana,
and other fungi,
virgae,
libra,
virgo,
capricorn,
goat,
me,
foat,
froat,
cloat,
float,
moat,
sought, nought,
brought,
laugh,
loop,
cloop,
moop,
nope,
lope,
loooooooooooooook
booooooooooooooooooook

beyond the beyond awareness and magic-magic and anti-magic and occultists god and the angels and in heaven and the afterlife and the creation of goodness and the imagination in madness and suicidal attempts and other such attempts to drown oneself in either sorrow or drink or both or madness or awareness to sink deeper in thoughts to repeat summarize conclude synthesize the meaning of messages and experience and the poetic gestures as paraphrases and paragraphs are read from one end to the other in chemical flows and in lemonade manners without expecting the solution to be solved but rather to continue the venom of existence such as the speech in experimental languages such as to be or not to be in icelandic, Swahili and ten other divisions of tongues such as the pentecostalists and the aids given to jesuits and other religious orders and the vocation and the practical justification of aids and money-made and man-made spaceships to the moon and mars and venus and other jars made of honey and saltpeppers and medieval spaceships because i hate to end and yet there is no end to madness like the stars like light years and they continue to appear and disappear and we look upon humanity and shake our heads in a benign fashion as we save ourselves from embarrassment and only look upon the glorious aspects of history the history of mankind without realizing that there are other sad inglorious untold stories of heroes good and bad introspections other comments from TDR and other relative misinterpretations and friendships with editors who publish because of friendship and there are always excuses for publications and contacts to get a PhD to overpower or be overpowered that is the question no respite to reality to life a certain amount of disgust prayer and un-prayerwise because we ask and it shall come the sixth and most heavenly queen of the universe of our soul our reality as we continue and apprehend the endlessness of our despair comprehending apprehending and returning to the routine of teaching boring grammar and then only to reject the offers made by Carolina universities and then to bring the entire family here to decide and not to decide because i feel that there are answers to non-answers just as there are other dimensions of the mind of our bodies in different realities that may either transcend or non-transcend the conclusions of anguish are the introductions to happiness and the ritual is a circular hierarchy the circle of fear and joy and the antonyms and synonyms of fear and hyphens and interjections and the wide vocabulary murdered by the mind and burning brain cells because we look at life only from this limited fashion and are disgusted by the philosophy of others who have made life a patterned hell without realizing that the force is not a block but a living force that lives on day by day consciously or unconsciously and in the silence of prayer or meditation a constant commitment because it is only through commitment that we psychologically ensconce our life and then there are scholarly words pretentious words like C students and levels of awareness such as karma and veda and other kinds of knowledge both theater and otherwise in speech and radio tv and film and human communication continues should there be communication or not? should there be only a certain amount of disappointments or not? should we pray constantly or wallow in unconscious prayer, in dreams and in the realities of the brain as we remember past dreams childhood dreams and ambitions and other disappointments that come along the way without having to stop about dreaming and sleeping and eating but rather living life fully without routine going out and evangelize and know people and quarries and cement and ants and grasshoppers and yellow beds and yellow rooms and plays on canizo and kierkegaard and john bosco and caged dreams and the plays continue both in flows of antioch club members and reality dreams in the form of resignation and humanity and trials bringing our ego out curing ourselves of egotism and other drugs and poisonous and blasphemous healthy visions and visionaries and poetry and fans and the fact that i have been bewildered by the fact that the days are longer than the nights and that i have precluded my reality from other realities from other ambitions and the facts that the devils have conquered the realities of people's minds and that we must try to remove ourselves from messages and morals and amorals and anti-messages but live and stop rationalizing even if i do even if others give unconscious messages and the important thing is to care and to go on and to struggle and to exist and to justify and the facts are thin or fat and the limitations are small big little and there are cars that pass and phones that ring and there are no longer interruptions to the films that must be edited and stopped from being used and unused and seen and a desire comes and goes and there are no more interesting factors to life that is planned/unplanned related/unrelated such as the materialistic factors behind the use and abuse of christian warehouses and landlords committing atrocities in the name of christianity like smoking pipes and getting stopped by the typewriter as a sign that i must change the subject digress from my digression and delve more into the sublime and think about words and meet other minds the seat of originality the seat of exceptionalism the fire always glows when he is around and there are others remembered and remembered again and the process continues without end in staccato fashion in straight fashion in curved fashions waiting for the realities to diminish and give life against from one flow to the other from one state or existence of a former life which still delves in my unconscious which must be brought out so i can live again and enjoy the qualities of my reality and the prayers must continue in the minds and backroads of minds my mind the sub and un conscious levels of mankind's mentality and essentiality and there are no justifications there must be silence

and the quiet of the night
and nature taking its course
and there are no more decisions to make
because decisions are superficial
there is a higher decision
which cannot be challenged
and we are again moralized
cut down
experimented upon
befriend the flow
befriend the flow of experience
the continuum is never at a loss
it begins
ends
and remains
at a point

of no return.

I stop.

# CHAPTER 3

# CATEGORIES

There are categories. Different categories. Categories of enlightenment, categories of distinction, s.u.r.y categories, mathematical categories, enumerative categories, hegelian categories, emphatic and empathic categories, underlining categories, kantian categories, rational and irrational categories.

Enlightenment is one form of category. Enlightenment assumes a state of mind, a human state of affairs, and a repetitious and tedious state of affairs. The Watergate hearings are categorical. They express enlightening categories. The Reddy-Steinsson-Farolan hearings were categorical imperatives. The imperatives were reduced to questions. And the questions were reduced to answers. The answers were subtle. We are dragged into favours. Patronage. Favorable and unfavorable. At five o'clock the meeting is to be adjourned. At four thirty the meeting was adjourned. A certain amount of categorical knowledge ensued during the meeting.

There are categories of distinction. Distinction is either biological or metaphysical. If it is biological, it assumes posterity. If it is metaphysical, it also assumes posterity. Therefore, distinction is nihilistic. The nihilistic distinction of good and evil. The distinction of awards. Fame and distinction are categorized either as historical or ahistorical. If it is historical, then dialogues are presumed. If it is ahistorical, then non-entities are assumed. Therefore, distinction is again nihilistic.

S>U>R>Y> categories are East Indian in nature. If an Indian is red, he is American. If he is brown, he is Eastern. Therefore, South American Indians are either Aztecs or Mayans. If an Aztec is not a Mayan, therefore a Sioux cannot be a Cherokee and it logically follows that enlightenment is a form of Apache Indian. It is also logical that Apache Indians may be categorized under distinction, biology, history and sury.

Mathematical categories are enumerative and numerative. The numerative function of enumeration is numerical inform. If two equals two, therefore one equals one. If a radio is not a television, therefore it can either be a stereo or a vacuum cleaner. Since it is not a vacuum cleaner, therefore it must be a stereo. A stereo is either considered a Gerrard or a non-Gerrard. If a Gerrard is of superior quality, therefore a cross-examination may not be necessary for a non-Gerrard. Thus spoke Zarathustra.

Enumerative categories are basically mathematical in nature. Superficially, they may become distinctive or anti-historical. If they are distinctive, therefore they are Cartesian. If they are not Cartesian, therefore they are Hegelian. Subsequently, they become Kantian. And consequently, they result in categories of stereos and other household appliances. Such appliances are: radio, television, air conditioner, fan, oven, stove, refrigerator and vacuum cleaners.

Categories underlined by emphatic and empathic are distinctive in the first sense of the word. Thus, empathic categories are categories worthy of emphasis. For example, if yellow is red, therefore black cannot be white. Empathic categories are categories that are not alienated. If empathic categories are put to an acid test, then Nixon is guilty. If emphatic categories are put to an honor test, then Dean is guilty. Empathy is theatrical.

Underlining categories mean two things. They either subjugate or surrogate. If they subjugate, they are imperative and therefore must be underlined with Indian ink. If they surrogate, then they cannot be underlined unless pencils are used. If absurdity is a synthesis, therefore it is transcendental.

Kantian categories are imperative. The categories of the mind are a result of Christian upbringing. Such upbringing may either be resuscitated or elucidated. If it is resuscitated, therefore it can only be rational, but not irrational. If it is elucidated, therefore it must always be educational. Logic is a category of the irrational mind.

Hegelian categories are either amplifying or transcending. If they amplify, they cannot transcend. They are stated. If they are not stated, they transcend. Therefore, Hegelian categories are anti-Kantian and pro-cartesian.

There are rational categories. Rational categories may either be irrational or logical. If they are logical, therefore they are exhaustive. If they are not exhaustive, they are logical. Thus the biological approach to reality.

The biological approach to reality is construed in a number of ways. These ways may be referred to as "theses". "Theses" are small versions of dissertations, and dissertations are methodological in style. If a style is not methodical, therefore methodology is an absurdity. If absurdity is anti-theatrical, therefore it is mathematical.

Mathematics is a growing process of biology. Anatomy is a construction of brain cells, therefore, an anatomical analysis is void. If the muscle cells are cohabitants of the bone cells, therefore calcium becomes a by-product. If by-products are reproductions of excrement, therefore sexual intercourse must take place through more erudite means. Thus, ear fornication, nose fornication and tooth fornication.

Veins are products of blood. The hip bone is connected to the jugular vein and thus the bone muscle becomes of the brain muscle. The sex muscle becomes an erection and erection becomes ejaculatory. If ejaculation is prayerful, therefore it becomes an interjection. Interjections become prayerful if conjunctions are subjected to prepositions. Prepositions are grammatical transformations of biology and other related sciences.

Botany is biological in approach. This approach may be irrational as the explication of the body is a mental process. If the mental process is subjugated to the categories of the teeth, then the gums rebel, and a conclusion may be reached: gums or teeth are categorical, therefore, biological in essence.

If urination is biological, therefore micturation is botanical. If drinking is chemical, therefore saturation is a form of induction. Thus, subtraction results in deduction, and consequently, the process of induction begins. The synthetical/categorical behaviour of the process is abstraction.

If categories are biological, reality becomes a hair. A hair may either be public or otherwise. It is pubic if it is adolescent, and otherwise it is adult. Thus, the birds singing at dawn.

If entertainment is enlightening, therefore life becomes irrational. If two radios make one television, therefore biology makes two philosophers. Thus, excretion equals urination and therefore, the biological function of today becomes a process of tomorrow.

Creativity is a categorical and biological synthesis of anti-synthesis. If thesis equals anti-thesis, therefore dissertations are light bulbs. If botany is biological, therefore plants are animals. Thus, if a mouth and the sounds of the throat are antiseptic, therefore marijuana becomes a state of mind. The results are obviously logical and rational.

If irrationality is creativity, the categorical function of biology is null and void. Pauses become pusses and poses are results of pussies. Cats are either dogs in disguise or biological manifestations of the evolution of reality. Beliefs transcend attacks on Watergate hearings. Thus, Benno shaves at three a.m. because of the heat.

If Shakespeare wrote Macbeth, therefore biology was a form of alchemy. Alchemists were nurses in disguise. Alchemists were medieval chemists. As a result, English was spoken only in India while England and Spain discovered America. Medicine is an outgrowth of biology. Therefore, the dialogues of the mind are categorical, and the crossfire is a thorough cross-examination of witnesses testifying to their testimonies of five and a half days. Thus, Shakespeare was false.

If Shakespeare died in 1928, who died in 1616? If 1616 was Lope de Vega's death, what was Calderon's reasoning for **Life is a dream**?

If universality is a common affair, what isn't?

If poetry is anguish, what is existential?

If categories exist, what are words?

Biology equals literature. Literature minus Shakespeare is no literature. But literature plus Calderon minus Lope de Vega is Doctor Faustus. Marlowe minus Goethe is Handke in Pinteresque disguise.

Normality is rationality. Therefore, Abnormality is Irrationality. But logic is misconstrued because the construction of destruction equals two minus one and the Newman Center is a Ping Pong table in the guise of pinball machines and weightlifters. If bike one equals bike two, therefore twenty hours without sleep equals ten hours of sleep.

If dreams are categorical, therefore spontaneity is a simultaneous deliberation of critical analysis. Literary analysis is a manifestation of Marxist products. If techno evolution is Semantics, therefore Mass Communication is Guerrilla Television.

Shakespeare equals categories equals Calderon equals Biology and Anatomy, resulting all in logic and common sense.

If death is the be-all and end-all of things, then life is a walking shadow. If life is a dream, therefore Shakespeare was Calderon in disguise and Macbeth Hamlet in disguise. If bike one was stolen, therefore bike two was bought. If Jews were converted gentiles, therefore writing is futile. If two levels of awareness are intelligible, therefore transcendental meditation is unintelligible. If my handwriting is legible, therefore Mr. Reddy's is unintelligible. If literacy is the opposite of illiteracy, therefore the categories of words may be expressed either biologically or mathematically. Thus, the subject was roses and the man of La Mancha came from Cervantes' novel.

A novel is a play if it is written as a flow of consciousness. If it is not, therefore an invitation becomes boring. If swimming is the conclusion, therefore escapism is a challenge. And if one escapes, he abounds. If he abounds, he rebounds, compounds, rounds, counts, flaunts, bounces and rolls.

Thus spoke Shakespeare.

"Do you speak English?"
"In a strange fashion I do".
"It's the same old thing".
"I am disillusioned with the hearings of last night".
"Master Reddy underwent a thorough cross-examination."
"Dr. Steinsson, the moderator in the proceedings, agreed with Dr. Farolan that digression was a state of mind".

"Dr. Farolan agreed with Dr. Steinsson that a thorough and minute cross-examination of Master Reddy's untitled short story was an imminent necessity in order to get facts off the case."

"The truth is what matters!"

"But how can I bring the surface of the truth if I do not delve into the details?"

"I refuse to comment on the details leading to the sexual act."

"Master Reddy, you are out of order."

"Master Reddy, you are not to refute the court's decision. The committee feels that you must answer Dr. Farolan's questions."

"But I must say one thing..."

"You are not to say anything. You are only to answer the questions thrown at you by the critic."

"I vehemently refuse!"

"Mr. Moderator, what is your judgment at this moment?"

"I feel that since we are not getting anywhere, we must proceed to other questions."

"Master Reddy, what is your favourite colour?"

"I have no favourite colour."

"Do you like red?"

"Yes."

"Do you like black?"

"It depends."

"On what?"

"On the situation."

"What situation?"

"Well, black is good in certain fabrics."

"Do you like blue?"

"Yes."

"And white?"

"It depends on the situation."

And now, presenting Trausti Steinsson (anti-dialogs):

once upon a time there was once upon a time

life is a suspension of pain
suspension of an acute toothache
tralalalalala
life is a ping pong
life is a gameabalabalalaba
sael vertu systir
hvad er ad fretta
hvad er titt
hvad er nytt
segdu mer allt af letta
Himinn
hve oradjupt bu syndir
ut i eigin blama
allra atta
og vidattunum hverfir
inn i eigin hvelfing
um mina smaed - utar skynjun
inmar - a endalausan veg
television is a good way to waste time 1118e77adiayuidy duyud
shdjhdhak3y8yjkhbxj
Jon...


And now, back to me:

The precepts of incommunication.
The negation of truth.
The rebellion against eternal awareness.
The position of positive reality and negative meaning.
The tedious expectation of a typed dissertation.
The stubborn limitation of eastern thought.
The results of convictions.
The sticking out of one state of mind.
The reflection of reflections.
A state of reconstruction.

A negation of positions.
The reality of dreams.
A state of blissful ecstasy.
An enumeration of facts.
A stern carrying out of one conviction that life is a worm.
A categorical state of anti-dialogs.
A catalogue of tags.
Tagging tags.
A result of reductions.
Withdrawal.
A flow of experience.
A categorical state of mind.
Exploration of old age.
L & M, new experiences, KOOL and other miscellaneous Bowling Green, Bonded Station cigarettes at 40 cents a pack.
A feeling of feeling lazy to move out.
Exorbitant rent rates.
Exorbitant grass rates.
Gas rates.
Telephone bills.
New sheets.
A dramatic reading of Joe Flex.
A night at Kaufman's.
Comfortable but disgusting Howard's.
Charlie's blonde wife.
A conviction of conventions.
A reduction of subtraction.
An honest attempt at communication.
Crossfire.
Cross-examination.
Filipino doctors.
Filipino friends.
Trite trivialities.
Trivial trifles.
Incestuous incense.

Prisoner of Zenda.
Two views. Cowardly and Brave.
Two views. Black and White.
Two views. Awareness and eternal void.
Awareness and unawareness.
Growth in old age. Bourgeois pursuits.
A meaningful waste. Wasted day. Fuller lives.
A leap towards bad faith.
Is Sartre senile?
Is Beckett senile?
Who wants to be old?
Who wants to be committed?
End of chapter 3.

# CHAPTER 4

# BOWLING GREEN, WINTER 1972

BS!
Canuck suffers from having a horny male dog on the other side of the door.
J.D. has missed a ball with a beautiful 18-year old; so he tries with Canuck.
I'll tell him now.
No, don't tell him.
Discriminatory differences: Canuck is suffering from being comparted with Jim Dickson.
This is a sexy night; I am left with Canuck "twilone".

25 February 1972

(K=Kissinger; W=Walters, Barbara)

1. Moderator: Benno
a) 1. Question: Can you imagine K being an aid to Brezschnev?

T: Yes, definitely; because he is of the diplomatic temperament, adjusting to circumstances; the amor fati type.

E: No, because the circumstances of the Kremlin will not allow diplomatic attitudes prevalent in Mr. K's personality.

B: Full agreement with T.

2. Question: What is the major element of K's ideology, if any?

E: Political Machiavellism.

T: K. doesn't stick strictly to any ideology but if he does, it is on an international scale.

B: I do not agree (for methodological reasons) with either. K's ideology ("ideology" defined in a very extensive sense) lies in his basic assumption of the existence of a "system of order".

T: What I meant by "ideology" was some ultimate political end like communism of national socialism as an absolute (metaphysical) end. If K has any ideology then it is an ideology of compromise between extremes (which would not fit the traditional definition of ideology).

E: In disagreement to T and B, Machiavellism does not ideologize K's systematical "order", the sense of his being a chameleon.

3. Question: What **verbal** statement of K in the TV interview with W did support the most your above-mentioned opinion of K's ideology?
T: K's double-talk at the end of October '72 (**Peace at Hand**) which manifested his diplomatic compromise with, on the one hand, those he was negotiating with, and on the other hand, the American public.

E: In accordance to August Comte's sociological statements, a writer must be "free" and "deaf" and "blind" to ideas of others. Therefore, paraphrasing K's last statement in the interview: "My political life does not interfere with my social life".

B: K's attempt to fully understand both the ideology and the political tactics of the so-called enemy (in the TV interview he showed this understanding by respecting China's rejection to participate in the Salt Negotiations).

**Second Moderator: Trausti**

Fourth Question: What do you think of Dr. K's approach to the differentiation between **foreign** and **domestic** affairs in the aforementioned interview?

B: K's statements showed that his notion of "system of order" ("Balance of Power") can only be conceived on an international level with capitalist nations as its constitutive element. He gave a priority to international affairs. K's morality ("ideology") is the following: everything that enhances this balance of power is good; everything that does not is not good.

E: In supplementing the atypicality of K's **Weltanschauung**, as expressed by Dr. Signitzer, I think that the "yellow pages" of President Nixon are adamant and therefore, Dr. K's evasion to the foreign and domestic policies attempt to reflect diplomatically and escapist ambiguity to an American TV audience in order to prescind from the top secret "yellow pages" of the fascist dictatorial dicta of Mr. Nixon.

T: Dr. K. referred to this differentiation while discussing the topic: "U.S. Aid to North Vietnam Now That the War Is Over" (which is reminiscent of the Marshall Aid after WWII plus aid to so-called "developing countries" and political / "ideological" allies). Without committing myself to any "ideological" conviction concerning "imperialism", foreign aid tends to degenerate developing countries while not contributing to their progress. Without committing myself here and now to any such conviction, I declare that it is very desirable and even essential to have people with Dr. K's attitude around. This attitude is broad-minded/wide-sighted (i.e., **not** narrow-minded, **not** near-sighted). He has an international overview and knowledge/ education at his disposal to back it up. And I like Dr. K's notion that "we never become perfect at home". Being confronted with severe problems abroad might challenge American politicians and the American public at home.


3) **Moderator: Edmundo**

Question 5: Please summarize in less than 50 words your opinion regarding the above-mentioned interview.

B: Summarizing this discussion, I should like to leave the mere whirlpool impressions I have gotten in this interview. And I would like to attract your attention to K's laughter to W's question regarding who his real enemies were. This laughter told me more than anything else.

T: My impression to this interview was that it was a platonic asexual intercourse between W and K.

E: In relation to the above-mentioned comments, I opine that K's asexuality and his indifferent exposure of his personality only reflects the Machiavellian, Jewish - German attitude relevant in a diplomatic, democratic and Nixonite situation. Therefore, I conclude that the essence of K's relevance and personality preclude the synthesis of the above-mentioned interview.


-2648-

**On the Relationship Between Talking in the Student Union and Listening to Distraction.**
**Or Incoming and/or Outgoing People**

~~The anatomy of a bad habit may be analyzed in two systematical ways: first, being distracted by people we don't know; and second, listening asystematically to Mardi Gras in Bowling Green. To proceed from this premise ... er... we.... eh... George Meany~~ .oh. but even . eh . from . laymen

.eh. . (non-philos...)

"Okay, but aren't we all leather balls in the long run?"

Tryggvi passes.

"I cannot commit porque somos lahat sapagkat uki na da amin"

"TV cameras are patient, Canuck is patient, Dave Clark is patient, absurdity is patient, Jim Dickson is not—f...ing is a matter of patience, right, Edmundo?"

"I think Cornelius Cash could.Kornelia.but by the way, f....ing isn't all that, is it?"

"Exactly, intellectual masturbation is the ideal situation."

"Vi a Trigvi con una mujer el martes pasado.entonces que paso? Tinira mo o hindi?

"Der mond ist aufggangen die goldnen Sternlein prangen am Himmel hell und ver der Waldsteilibschwarz und Schweiges und oues den Wiesen steigel del WeitsNebel Winderbor Claudius. German nostalgia is penetrating the softness of this summer night which symbolizes and categorizes the end of the end. Trausti is going to write more than I—skip the following—therefore, it won't be worth reading."

"What is this language we call language? Communication? Maybe. We communicate only by what we do not say. What language shall we speak tonight? The language of obscenity? Schizophrenia? Perhaps we will create a new language."

"No words."

"Where is the innovation? Where is the creativity?"

"You consider 60 cents innovative?"

"No, a necessity!"

"Necessity conflicts with life!"

"Absurd!"

"Who was Alexander Graham Bellsky?"

"The first telephone pole."

Beer transfusion

Eight ball cologne.
Silvia smokes her KENT.

We all smoke cigarettes.
Statistics thrown around by Barb & she wired it!
The sun feels yellow and the grass smells green
And the breeze plants the Kiss of Spring from the

Shores of Consciousness.

Terry Tan, John Body, E. Farolan

This is a heavy and dirty joke: The elephant fell in the mud puddle.

PUN POEM and/or either of which is alliterative allegory

Perilously upon Pisanello's Polecats
The Pisanello pilfers polecats from pizza pagliai.
Perhaps putrid putrefaction personifies piss.
Oedipustic ramble angles avidly atavistically afterwards.
Two transient turtles toddled toward Toledo.
And before being brutally broken basically they borrowed beautiful beasts of burden.

Sadism on Silvia

8-ball is unlucky because her eyes thanked me sarcastically for my bitterness.

# CHAPTER 5

# LIES

Lies may be amplified in artistic forms. Artists are liars because they need to fantasies, and fantasies are a form of lies. Metatheater is antitheatrer in disguise while film is anti-film in reverse. If we outline antitheater, the scheme would go as follows:

**ANTI-THEATER**

LiesMetatheater

FilmAnti-film

-reduction
-subtraction

1. fraction
2. white lies
3. black lies

a. dogmatic
b. unorthodox

In other words, anti-theater is a projection of two facets— lies and metatheater. Both lies and metatheater are subdivided mutually into Film and Anti-film which are categorized in two deductions: reduction and subtraction. Subtraction takes the form of 1) Fraction 2) White Lies and 3) Black lies. The latter may either be dogmatic or unorthodox.

At this point, it may appear that subtraction is directly related to lies. This is true, although the diagram does not show it. Subtractional/ fractional lies are projections of grey lies; in other words, lies that are neither black nor white, but rather a vague combination of both.

The question now is: how can we give concrete examples of anti-theater as a projection of lies, metatheater and film/anti-film. The motion is circular: it begins with anti-theater, proceeds both clockwise and counterclockwise to lie and metatheater, and locks in the bottom part of the circle through a clockwise (metatheater to anti-film) and counterclockwise (lies to film) deduction/induction. Thus, if a film is a lie, then it is anti-theater. If the SOUND OF MUSIC is a fantasy (lie) therefore it is anti-theater (anti-reality) whereas FELLINI 13 AND 3/4 is a play of illusion and reality (metatheater) then it is anti-theater (anti-reality). Thus, the circular motion.

Film therefore must be anti-film. And these project two actions: reduction and subtraction. If anti-film is a reduction, therefore film is a subtraction. For example, if SOUND OF MUSIC is a fantasy ( it subtracts from reality in that it does not contribute to reality, since people are not likely to sing in everyday life) and if Fellini 13 3/4 is a summary (in that it reduces fantasy/reality in a nutshell by projecting subconscious and unconscious reality as expressions of flashbacks and farts), then both are lies, but in two different levels. The film SOUND OF MUSIC is a lie in an un-esoteric sense, while FELLINI 13 3/4 is a lie in a more esoteric, erudite sense, because it is anti-film which is therefore anti-fantasy while at the same time deducing reality in a nutshell making it both fantasy and reality, and therefore, circular in its metatheatrical, antitheatrical, lie-film-anti-film motion.

Proceeding now to the relationship of the Theater of the Absurd and Lebenschaung. Instead of outlining, we shall only refer to it. Such a task is called **referieren**, where only references are referred to, such as names, movements, eruditions, life styles, erections, and lies. Lies are referred to the theater of the absurd in the same way lies are circulated through film/anti-film. Thus, the theater of the absurd may be referred to as unorthodox or dogmatic. It is unorthodox because it is unconventional; it is dogmatic because it refers to certain Lebenschauung which we might refer to as personal and subjective, i.e., from the author's standpoint.

Continuing with our task of REFERIEREN, let us mention a few authors of the Theater of the Absurd: Samuel Beckett, known as Sam B., 5'7", Irish by birth, approximately sixty, author of ENDGAME, EH JOE, and others such as WATT, MOLLOY, MALONE DIES, poems and other trilogies. Cartesian in approach; anti-Cartesian in action. Eugene Ionesco known as the French Rumanian. Bald-headed, logical in approach, illogical in Weltanschauung, both logical/illogical in Lebenschauung. Others are Genet, Adamov, Tardieu, Arrabal, Grass, etc, etc, etc.

Esslin overlooked three upcoming and important absurdists: Steinsson, Farolan and Signitzer. These three may be referred to as the "winter common mind" because they wrote their best works in the winter of 1973, together, in an attempt to put logic in an illogical fashion, by writing poems, essays and other miscellany in alphabetical, neurophysiological and babbalabical order. Their movement referred to as Twoism/Threeism was short-lived because of mitigating circumstances, such as the birth of Spring and the death of summer.

Now let us proceed to our discussion of the film of the absurd. This discussion will attempt to clarify film and the absurd in relation to lies. We shall not endeavour to make an outline, and therefore, the entries will be spontaneous.

Spontaneity is an essential factor in the film of the absurd. The spontaneity must not at all be planned. Thus, in the editing room, one must be free to pick up the garbage lying around and include it in the film. This garbage which is extraneous materials from past film of others, thrown there because they are not useful to them, may enhance the quality of the absurd. It will make the film more of a lie because the dishonesty involved (that of plagiarism in that one steals from a garbage can materials from films which are not his) gives the filmmaker added incentive regarding the cross-examination of Dean and Mitchell in the Watergate case. Thus, if the Watergate scandal is a digression, it must be included in order to make the film Absurd. Absurdity is the relationship between digression and non-digression, and if a film can proceed to begin a story and not end it because of perpetual digression, its absurdity is enhanced.

After having plagiarized different films and put them in disorder, since disorder is the best motivation for films of the absurd, then editing them is an essential. There are two ways of editing films of the absurd. The first is by editing them. The second is by anti-editing them. Editing them means putting glue in them. Anti-editing them means cementing them. If you are a professional filmmaker, you will use the word "cement" and therefore, your film will be absurd. But if you use glue, then your film will not be absurd, and thus, amateurish. Your film is either absurd and professional or conventional and amateurish. Therefore, glue is in direct proportion to amateur filmmakers while cement is in indirect relation to professional filmmakers of the absurd.

Editing films may be a lie. The film-editing room is a room of lies. You may either lie verbally or physically. If you lie verbally you are dishonest, and therefore, absurd. If you lie physically, you are honest because you are tired. So you lie either on a table, on a floor and most commonly, on a hammock in tropical countries, or on a bed in other countries, especially European and American. If you lie physically, you are instinctive, and therefore, honest. But honesty connotes non-lies, and therefore, conventionality. Conventionality, in turn, is a film of the amateurs, while unconventionality (moral lie) is a film of the absurd, and therefore, an honest dishonesty because of its spontaneous deliberateness.

Experimentalism is a lie. A blatant lie. A one-way ticket. I have to pay my debts. The debts of the past. I cannot grow unless I fill in the gap. The past's gap. But I'm stuck, stagnating here in summer, awaiting a long trip. And I'm tired of travelling. I just want to go because I have to, not because I want to. It's all the same, anyway. If I experiment, it will be a lie. If I travel, it will be the same; if not, it doesn't matter.

I don't need words. I need silence. Silent words. Communication Theories are disguised in technicalities to avoid communication.

In my Eurasian disguise, I lie. My Eurasian state is a state of meditation, a searching of oneself, some moments to think, to experiment truthfully for art. For life. Lebenshauung. Intuition in life. Yoga. Rest. One month for that. Making every moment a reality without having to wait for it to pass on tediously.

"What is humanity?" Intelligence asks.
"What is intelligence?" Humanity asks.
"Is there something more than synthesis?"
"Perhaps chance. Drift."
"Indian relations. East Indian…"

And the relations continue. They come and go. Faith, life after death, the Virgin of Fatima was the same Virgin at Lourdes. She talked to me. In my heart, in my vision, in my soul, in the white snow, in my eyes, in a friend, in Paradise, and scepticism lives, courage…

"Coraje, hijo."
"Sí, mamá. Necesito tiempo para comprender y creer."

And then there is silence. The silence of years. The silence of nostalgia and subtle love. And expressed love. And bikes in the dying summer. And other things to sell, when I only have manuscripts scattered all over, from the north to the midwest to the east, and friends, scattered friends like scattered thoughts. And late movies, and Australian adventures. And waiting more: rituals, confirmation of Faith, and other outrageous feelings. Feeling sleepy, creating milestones, quantitative milestones, labelled milestones. Hit the core...

"Labels, labels."
"Working inside of you/ impressionism and expressionism. What you see and what you feel."

Trams and cars and the weather and heartaches. "I have to go, to travel, to cease from writing, to know people, to grow old, to prescind from commitment, to drag my typewriter, to write a few more words, new variations of the same old theme."

"I reckon."
And the ping pong games go on.
And new characters in my novel.
And more poems.
And more television movies.
And more thoughts.

"And then, what?"

# CHAPTER 6

# AGE

And she died when she was 95, or around there. And I lived with people who aged with her. My grandmother died, and I wrote a poem. And I stopped writing. For just a while. And then I wrote again.

I aged.

And others died. Heart attacks, old age, alcoholism. And I continue living.

I live: in a certain age, and then, in another age. Smoked age, smoking now, having a beer now and then, making a business from bikes.

And fans blow; old fans. Aging wind, hot wind, decaying wind of summer.

"Are you discussing age?"

"No, I am discussing obnoxiousness. Deliberate obnoxiousness."

"Why be obnoxious?"

"It's a natural trait. A zest for life. A disgust for it."

"Life…"

"Is life obnoxious?"

"Yes."

"I don't know."

"Yes, no."

Only age can tell. Age and experience. Beauty is external. Age isn't. Age is internal. Especially old age. Middle-age is semi-external/ semi-internal. And I ask why I write.

"And I say it's an impulse."
Or an urge.
Or just a profession.

But I don't force it. I watch TV and I have to write. I sleep, and when I wake up, the urge returns."

It returned a few years ago. And tonight it returns. In bits and pieces. Like bacon. And I don't resent it. I write for faith. Faith in visions. Faith in pizza. Faith in summer, and the sea, and a fresh cigarette. In decisions. indecisions. In riding bikes and carrying on philosophical/ semantical discussions.

And then a brief silence.

And the games continue.

And then I am overcome by people and swimming pools and digressions, digressions into life, away from death, to walk, to meditate quietly on mushroom pizzas with other items like olives, deluxe pizzas and spicy spaghetti.

And then I leave quietly.
Or noisefully.

Noiselessly I travel. I squander thoughts. And make decisions, and meet new people, and reminisce on old people, old friends, aged friends, potential friends, no friends. Everyone is an island.

"No man is an island."
"False."
"Moderation then?"
"False."
"What is true?"
"Boredom, reality, repetition, imitation."

I bow to the inevitable.
Tears flow.
Life goes on.
Novel goes down the drain.
And it goes on.
And on.

"Why must it go on?"
"Chance."
"Determination?"
"Life is chance."
Or half-chance.
And I decide to put in the six-ball. At 35.
Green ball. Green for life. The eight-ball is black. Black means death. And you put black in at the wrong moment without wanting to. And you lose the game. Chance has taken over.

"No discussions".

"let me think."

And summer goes on. Slowly first, and then it goes faster, and faster, and a new season comes, like last year, only in a new variation. Everything is the same, I've thought of it, you have to put a stop to it, greet sweet/bitter death with open arms, say goodbye to sweet/bitter life.

And more incense is burned.

And life is perfumed temporarily. Time passes. Age grows. The back aches. The bones ache. Arthritis settles in. Barbecue and beer. Girl meets boy. Boy falls in love with girl. Girl dies. Boy is alone. Boy dies of a broken heart. Another boy is born. Another girl is born. And it continues until old age races, rat races, donkey races, and words are repeated, the same phrases said, "I love you", certain gaps, certain moments for thinking, sharing, slowly thinking, slowly digesting, and the body becomes the mind, and the mind flies. The body remains behind.

The smell of pizza is there. And then it goes away.
Pain is there. And then it goes away.
Age makes smell go away.
Age makes people forget.
Age makes pain go away.
Age makes time. Time makes age. Time is age.

Formalities are issued.
Semantics age.
Aged formalities.
Informalities age.

Youth dies into age.
Age dies into death.

# CHAPTER 7

# ANOTHER WOUND

**Cut from the past. From the memories. From daffodils and the weather. He reopened my past, and I was passive because I challenged him. I asked the questions, and he answered me with pain, a pain that cut through.**

All my fault. A fault from the past. From my upbringing. And I wanted to confront it again because I wanted to. I wanted to because I was mediocre. Indecisive. But deciding on indecision.

Three incense sticks pointing at me. And I must continue to withdraw in order to understand myself. In order to decipher more calmly the roots of my being, of my innocence, of my limitations, of my failed attempts at machiavellism. I knew I had to act on bad faith and I felt good. My ambiguous state of mind whether I was fearful of guilt and other enterprises was an intrigue in itself.

But the wounds hit strong. He talked about the past. And the past was almost forgotten. I decided to cut myself off. But the roots grow again. And again. He knew, at least unconsciously. And I admired him. I knew, I was aware, that this caged life was another monologue, a solitude of passing trivialities, laughter, justification, lies, soap operas and other trifles. I wanted to stick to my principle, my one principle in life: a joke. A big, passing joke that will end abruptly.

Locked in like junkmen while the history of power and regret remains unfocused.

It's more than just having to remain focused or drunk. It's even a complement to be in utter despair, to be called an alcoholic. An alcoholic because of utter despair, despair because there is no exit, passing the bucket, the reflection of doubt and pretension.

Whether I must be dead or stereotyped alive. Whether I must contemplate on a way of life, a poet who repeats himself in meaningless ways, reiterating the history of friends and mankind.
And mankind dies away in his mind.
Like false tears in death's passing away.
Or false gaps in the fear of having to live tediously from moment to moment.

What is boredom?

Another inspired poem,
inspired by depression and cut wounds,
from the past,
and in the moments to come, I choose this ambiguous state of indecision, of repeating myself ambiguously because I decide it,
of asking myself why,
of shaking freedom in droplets of fear and cowardice.

I simply nod and go on.
And then ask why.

# CHAPTER 8

## ON THE INTROSPOECTIVE ANALYSIS OF A DUNN 10-CENT CIGAR AND/OR THE ARROGANT WRINKLES OF A PROFESSOR OF POLITICAL SCIENCE

Escapist arrogance manifested in his wrinkles: he was scared! The ten-cent cigar was lighted from the rectal Weltanschauung. The professor was scared in the company of proletariat representatives sitting tie-less at his table. In their economic inferiority, they were his superiors. So, he kept on showing off his forehead wrinkles, signs of respectful age and assumed knowledge and wisdom. In despair, he kept on gossiping about Lenin's "blood thirsty" taste for music. We, the proletariat representatives just looked at him with scorn in our eyes, through the smoke of our cigars which we blew into his face. His whole performance was ridiculous. The graduate students, anachronistic and Trotskyite, were sympathetic to proletarianism and broke the crumbling walls of the professor's bureaucracy. Meanwhile, the ten-cent cigars continued ruminating around his wrinkled, defensive face.

If he only admitted he could not discuss and say he did not have the specialty, instead of the ridiculous ambiguity of his argument... the cigars were honest but he refused to admit to this honesty.

Theory without practice is useless but practice without theory is valueless because it is nihilistic. For example, the Russian Revolution:

Serge and Trotsky wrote after the Revolution. What is the alternative if professors from Bowling Green wrote in the IVY TOWER situation?

It is therefore necessary for critics to unite—critics from outside to challenge the situation. It is democratic. Trotsky allows this; Stalin wouldn't. Stalin didn't tolerate this "treason".

Meanwhile, the first ten-cent cigar is about to extinguish itself in Howard's. Opportunism: alienation of people—join it, why alienate? These are petty bourgeois opportunists attempting to capitalize their personal attitudes. They alienate themselves because of capitalist domination. They deserve scorn.

From a psychological and sociological point of view, anthropologists seem to also capitalize un societies, and therefore are decadent because they alienate themselves from the essence of mass struggle. Discrediting all opposition is reactionary. The argument is political. The tongue is burned, and another cigar is not an inducement. The point is: you do not give fluid currency. Capitalism parallels professionalism, a system that uses money in competitive societies. Labor is more productive in Russia: bonuses, etc. for more incentive in economic patterns.

Like a cigar smoke, the circle circulates, like the extrospective vicious cycle of systems and philosophical/personal/critical/analytical human hypothesis.

# CHAPTER 9

# ESSAY ON MAN

Death is an expression of hope on this side of the railroad tracks.[1] Strolling up and down the street to show his pretentious idleness, throwing his pitiful spite on the faces of the walkers—by, he, with his Napoleon hat on his head, toddled home to his den to write on the angst of Christianity.[2] In reference to footnote, F...Jaspers for having stolen the idea from this collective mind![3]

Nietzsche's wisdom is in his nostrils because German culture is indigestible: they never finish anything. **Referieren**[4] ECCE HOMO[5]

We are sure Jaspers, Kierkegaard and Sartre could not have liked hot dogs.[6]

By the way, how could we expect this table and/or pepper shaker to transcend its mind?[7]

Therefore, concluding unscientific remarks (Kierkegaard), we summarize and conclude the following: **Ding an sich**[8] negates **Ding fur sich**.[9]

# CHAPTER 10

# ALIENATION[10]

The paradoxical note of separatism: identification is or is not. Therefore, indifference.[11] Analytical expressionism.[12] Therefore, our identification to fellow human beings is indifferent[13] because P 1: we are thrown into this world[14] and secondly P 2: no meaning is imposed to our lives from outside.[15]

# CHAPTER 11

# HAIKUS

## A POEM ON A NEW HAIRCUT

Timing is essential—
Haircuts must coincide with warm weather.

Cold weather prohibits haircuts.
Secret conspiracy between barbers and weathermen.
Everything depends on everything.
Everything is interchangeable.
Everything is a structure.

Nothing is isolated.
Nothing is innocent,
Nothing is pure.

Haircuts and weather,
barber and weatherman;
Edmundo and accent cuts,
accent man and language.

Benno Signitzer
**ATTEMPTS AT HAIKU**

Laiku

Sometimes I sit very patiently trying to find out what price I have to pay to get out of going through all these things twice.—Larry D.

A Match

The sixties rock striking sentiments of life-death reincarnation.—E.F.

Jethro Tull

Flutes; sponta-nei-ty; improvisation and Pink Floyd: "realistic alternatives".—E.F.

Seventeen

A mystical tune is played in the sky. I see a blue spoon: the moon.—T.S.

# CHAPTER 12

# SPONTANEOUS ILLUSIONS

Love manifests snow-white illusions of wind, bicycles without strings and alleys.

My sky-above the snow-country-how deep you swim into unconceivable eternity. The universe is an illusory balloon. I am a gatherer; I gather human hearts with indifference IDs.

I am in awe!
Awe with the red softness of Kaufman's!
Awe with the wind blowing in faceless Bowling Green!

Avoid fatal introspection.
Generate good feelings.
Eliminate hostility.
See how arbitrarily Bowling Green has been thrown like a little stone unto the surface of this earth.
Illusions vanish with the pain of humanity when we perceive the tragic nostalgia of **saudade**.

I know where a woman can take your soul, but she can't take you any place you already don't know where to go to.

And I know an organist who lives in the house behind other houses; his soul is a purse—a little pearl embracing the universe; nobody has ever seen this house.

In the deep recesses of the soul's mind, eternity lurks like a happy anguish while we wait indifferently for trivial death which is just a mere final incident in a long train of incidents.

(The poem has reached its climax and the codetta faded away...)

Larry, Trausti, Edmundo
2-26-73

# CHAPTER 13

# IMPRESSIONS
# AND DISILLUSIONMENTS

ß ¥

Kaufman's, Monday 2-26-73

E. and the dirty plates are BS a…s in relation to the Camusian dilemma suffered by T. who owns half of the apartment.

T. A trifle expanded into explosion of latent and long-hidden emotions.

E. Alienation from 618 E. Wooster is the temporary solution to release the above-mentioned emotions.

T. Different characters confront each other without any mutual comprehension.

E. a philosophical artist vs. a quantitative left-hemisphere chemist.

L. I do not feel very profound. I feel very restful.

T. Shallow.

E. The pretzels await a second round of red matches in abundance; cashed for ten dollars at a Savings and Loan Association.

T (moving from the initial issue.)

E. Triviality must be learned to be taken indifferently.

L: You've got to live behind your eyes. So, make it a nice place to live.

T: I don't know if this trifle should be commented on any further. It would be a favor, to much of a favor to... in order to be able to appreciate what's in front of your eyes. And you also have to sublimate your basic drives. But sometimes, wisdom is manifested in the nutshells of trivial things.

-End-

# CHAPTER 14

# SIGNITZER

On Kaufman
Signitzer

Kaufman is not explaining Nietzsche, but using him. Nietzsche is not arrogant; Kaufman is. Kaufman is the first to fully understand Nietzsche. Nietzsche is the second one—after having read Kaufman. The relationship between N. and K. is the relationship between an ass and an asshole.

**Signitzer 1**

I hate it here,
no fog pollution, just cleanliness
and the good smell of life.

Decadency died yesterday—
how can I continue to live,
how can I possibly.

A sad lively life
Decadency where have you gone?
Decadency makes life meaningful,
decadency—only.
What a decadent world,
what a ridiculous life—
sweet decadency,
sweet mortality.
**Signitzer 2**

On commitment

A POC[16] considers himself free in both Sartrean and Nixonite sense. He commits himself to commitment. The concept of commitment he takes from both the Sartrean an Nixonite Universe. In so far as he shares the freedom of a POW. Kissinger's accent can liberate POWs, not POCs, POCs can only be liberated by an Austrian accent.

POCs transcended their poison, they regress to ideas, to illusions, to god[17], to the devil, to mankind and/or humanity. They do not mind making logical leaps and tricks; so, be tricky; that's one of the essential traits of a POC; that is his justification and/or excuse for existence, for his taking away the good air of the community. The only justifiable commitment is the commitment to death. But this commitment need not be called a commitment, because death itself is already a commitment to life. Every commitment beyond this basic commitment, I mean the commitment to death and/or life, is ridiculous. In the light of the above explorations…and I do not explain anything, I only explore…I, again, in the light of those explorations, strongly commit myself to on-commitment[18].
**SUB-FOOT LONG NOTES and/or sub-long endnotes**

## ON HANDNOTES (Signitzer 4)

We have surpassed the stage of footnotes; nevertheless, we do not regret our having used footnotes. Footnotes are very important for our development. But after a certain time we have to change our approach to the universe. Footnotes no longer seem to be the appropriate means to cope with our intellectual outcomings. Therefore, hand notes are in order. There is a tremendous advantage of hand notes—hand notes can be handled more easily—especially with respect to the usage of hands which is dominant in our African civilization.

Ed's note: Therefore, hand and foot notes are neither European nor Asiatiedensteinian and/or Andorran.

## ON THE RELATIONSHIP BETWEEN THE LAST POEM AND THE LAST POEM (Signitzer 5)

The relation between relation and ship is the same as that between a prisoner and a prison. A prisoner who wants to escape in a ship will have a hard time to overcome the jealousy of the relation. The same is true with poems, especially the last ones.

Ed's note: It's before eleven and I have just received a letter. The mail has made my decision not to leave for Chicago.
CONCLUSION

## ON THE RELATIONSHIP BETWEEN THE LAST POEM AND THE LAST ESSAY

The interrelation between intrarelation and goats/sheep/Noah's ark is different from the Liberation of Men/Women/Freedom of the indifference of Camus and the Quixotic idealism of office metaphors. Therefore, absurdity is tragic and inexplicable from the viewpoint of Ph.D. students in Blue Mexican Grass.

(The following is the poem "referiert" to in the past two essays:)

The walls in Howard's have ears. They listen attentively to everything the proletariat intellectuals sitting in the cell in-between them say: the law of gravity eventually applies to these loudspeakers; they will fall apart, disintegrate, disappear and the ears of these walls will get new young boastful tongues to listen to. The smoke sucks red prose-poetry from the walls that breathe/perspire/sing and puke with blood
and discontented methodology.
Smoke.
Lights are dim with neurophysiological decisions.
The fog announces tragedy and Samba in passing Brazilian women with skin painted brownly with sun-saudade.

—Steinsson/Farolan

STEINSSON X: This fog embracing Blue Green in March reminds me of London where I used to hunt rabbits and pheasants during the war. This fog is so romantic.so melancholic. so beautifully decadent that it turns my mind to Acapulco which swims into the {pacific where everybody lives on everybody like vampires. So it goes everywhere. Thus this fog inspires my mind.

STEINSSON Y (NOTE 3 ON COMMITMENT): As a matter of fact Gogol used to write in his **Diary of a Madman** especially posthumously that chess should never be played in the early afternoon; that might lead to too much commitment.

**THESIS (Signitzer)ANTITHESIS (Farolan)**

I was thinking and thinkingYou were not meditating nor
and/or thinkingliving nor dying neither/nor
or thinking,exisitng.

Now I know
That
ThinkingWe are dying/flying/and/or
and thinkingexisting
and/or thinking
or thinkingAdds pictured poems
Leadsand poetic spaces


onlynever
toto
thinkingin juxtaposed
andmeditation/premeditation/
thinkingtragic skits of Japanese and/orMarcel Marceau and conflicts
thinkingbetween East/West
or thinking.hemispheres of the mind.

Now I know.Now/never will you expurgate.

### SYNTHESIS (Steinsson)

En-soi + pour-soi ± ding an sich X ding fur sich = Zero
Zero multiplied with zero equals synthesis which furthermore equals Austrian sub-dialectical continent which is the Absolute Spirit transcended into Being and Nothingness which equals the ultimate synthesis of **Existenz**.

# PART III

Many events and narrations in this 3$^{rd}$ part of my memoirs are based on facts but I have used some true-to-reality names, events, etc. perhaps to remind myself that truth and fiction are two figments of the mind divided only by a very thin, threadlike line.

This part of my memoirs is written in the 3rd person. Frankie is the main character. He narrates a story of how his maternal grandfather first came to the Philippines from Spain during the turn of the 19th century. This is the first segment I entitle "Palali".

The second segment aptly entitled "Frankie" is a more subjective almost diary-type of narration. Frankie in his memoirs and in his diary recalls his life, his thoughts, his parents, brothers and his sister, relatives and friends, expressing through them his thoughts and ideas, nostalgic, philosophical. Sometimes, narrations and dialogues are in Spanish, Tagalog and Ilocano in order to capture the mood, a slice of life, as it were of the memoirs.

# PALALI

**palali** \'pa-la-li n : *a tropical wild flower known by its scientific name delleniaceae; commonly called katmon*

## I.

*Ronda, 1884*

The sound of horse-drawn coaches on cobblestones. The sound of horse hoofs on the streets mingled with voices and a guitar playing the flamenco. A gypsy dancing accompanied with the clapping and "oles" of her partner.

Young señoritas with their white veils and colourful dresses—red, violet, pink while old women in mournful black were all leaving the old church at Calle Santa Maria on their way for their "paseos" at the Parque Central. A couple stops at the bridge and leans to look down towards the Tajo 500 meters below to watch blackbirds hovering over the Guadalquivir. They kiss passionately.

The young ex-Cavalry lieutenant Francisco de Paula walks sullenly towards the bridge. He has just been discharged dishonourably for insubordination. The punishment: exile to the Far East— to the farthest Spanish colony."las islas filipinas."

Rumours abounded. Some said that his superior had commanded "Gallop!" but he went "trotting" with his horse. The captain insulted him with "Son of a b.!" That, he couldn't take. He drew his sabre and slashed his commanding officer on his right shoulder. He was a short-tempered, impulsive young man. The impulsiveness of youth. Youth and its restlessness.

Francisco was the eldest in a family of eight. His youngest sister Adela noticed his distraught face as he approached their casa solariega on Rios Rosas No. 8. She was looking out the window watching the gaiety in the streets when she noticed him coming. She turned around as he came through the door.

"Hi, Paco," she greeted him quietly.

"Hi, little sister". He kissed his sister on the cheek, and sat down beside her near the window. They were in the living room. The room had the quiet sensation of medieval discomfort—high ceilings, thick concrete walls and when one spoke or whispered, the sounds would echo down the hallway.

Adela spoke in her soft, feminine voice. She was sad for her brother who was leaving.

"Filipinas, what are you going to do there?"

"I don´t know. Self-exile, I guess. It was quite serious. Mama knows about it. She was very upset but she can't do anything about it. At first she sympathized with me, but then, because of the consequences, she decided to let me go. She wrote Tio Miguel, and then, gave me her blessings. I'll Most probably work with Tio Miguel in Morong. Only God knows."

# II.

*Malaga, 1894*

He was surrounded by his mother, *La Condesa de Ronda*, his brothers Abelardo and Diego and his sisters Maria, Antonia, Concha, Pepa and the youngest, Adela. He was getting ready to board the train express to Barcelona. From there, he set sail on the Galeon Manila for the Philippine Islands. His favorite sister Adela was in tears.

"I'm going to miss you terribly".

"I'll be back in two years. I'll bring you back one of those nice velos manilenos, the famous 'Mantillas de Manila'. He hugged and kissed her.

His brothers embraced him and wished him well. "Good luck, Paco." His other sisters kissed and hugged him. "We'll see each other soon. Very soon." He assured them.

His mother, a sad smile in her face, kissed her son. He felt the warmth of her lips. He embraced her. Neither knew this was the last time they would see each other.

*"Ten cuidao y vayate con Dios!"* She whispered in her Andalusian accent.

*"Gracias mamá. Nos veremos en dos años."*

The trip to Barcelona was nostalgic. He looked out from his window seat at the orange orchards blossoming under the hot Andalusian sun. He remembered his boyhood days in the *hacienda*.riding his horse and sometimes that funny, stubborn donkey that wouldn't budge no matter how much you tried …the sweet smell of orange honey from the blossoms of the citrus trees and in the fall, picking up the oranges and lemons as his mother used the peels to make marmalade with toast and coffee with goat cream for breakfast.

It was now summer of 1884. The colonies were restless; many Spanish American colonies had gained independence after fighting bloody revolutions. Only a handful was left—and the Philippine Islands was one of them. But these islands were also on their way to independence. The Spanish friars were giving a bad name to Spain, abusing their ecclesiastical powers, taking advantage of their friar lands to gain political and economic control of the Filipinos under the name of Christianity. The Filipino intellectuals, the "the enlightened ones", were beginning their propaganda against the friars and eventually, against Spain. This was the start of the Philippine revolution against Spain that was to break out in 1896.

Francisco was going to a country in turmoil; a country where anti-Hispanism was the in-thing among the masses. While Spain was slowly losing her colonies, a new economic power was on the rise: the United States of America. This new empire was going to take over and dominate the world, thought the young Francisco de Paula.

*Destiny*, he thought. Many times he would sit in Church and instead of listening to the friar's sermon he would pray directly to the Crucifix and say *Your will not mine*. He found it difficult to believe that one needed to go through a priest in a confessional to talk to about your sins, your hopes, your psychological problems… He found it difficult to believe in the sacrament of confession. It wreaked of gossip and political machiavellism.

In this regard, he was a rebel, a "protestant" who didn't believe in asking forgiveness through an intermediary, the priest in the confessional. Instead, it was more pure, more natural to directly communicate with the Almighty.

*Destiny*, he thought again. He was on his way to one of the colonies. A feeling of hope surged within him.

# III.

*Morong, 1891*

The young Francisco de Paula put his residence certificate in his pouch and was on his way to his uncle Miguel. His uncle was the governor of the province of Morong and had previously received a letter from his sister in Malaga of Francisco's arrival and if there was any way he could be of service there. The governor had written his sister back and said that with his son's background, he would certainly need him in Morong. Francisco's engineering background from his military training at the Military Academy in Zaragoza was definitely a great advantage at this time. There were roads that had to be built from Manila to Morong and the outlying towns around Laguna de Bay.

He spent seven years acting as an engineering consultant to his uncle and these were seven fruitful years in his career. One afternoon, his uncle called him to his office.

"Good morning, uncle. "

"Hello, Paco. How are you? How's the family? " They embraced as they exchanged greetings.

"Everyone's fine, including myself, thank God. Mama, as usual, always nostalgic, and in her last letter she complains about Adela, with so many courting her and yet she hasn't decided who to marry. My brother, Abelardo, is now assigned in Madrid. Mama says that they might assign him as Commandant at the Military Academy in Zaragoza."

*"That's* great! I'm glad things are going well with the family."

He continued: "I asked you to come because I'm leaving the Islands. I've been here for more than ten years, and the governor of Malaga recommended me to take over his position. He is being transferred to Madrid to be one of the King's chief advisers."

"Congratulations, uncle. That's great news."

"Thank you. Now back to you. Do you want to come back with me? You can stay on if you want. You're doing a great job here in Morong."

"I'd like to stay longer in the Islands, *tio* Miguel. I like it here. The people are kind and gentle. I do miss mama and my family a lot, but maybe two more years. Then we'll take it from there."

"Did you want to stay on in Morong?"

"I don't think so, *tio*. I'd like a transfer. For a change. I'd like to work up north. I visited that part of the country last year and I loved it there. The mountains, the sea. The road from San Fernando to Baguio reminded me so much of the zigzag roads from Malaga to Ronda. Have you been up there?"

"Yes, I have. A few years ago, I visited too. I know what you mean. It's
beautiful out there."

"Can you get me a post in that area?""

"I can talk to the Director of the **Tabacalera** in Manila when I go and see the Governor General next week. He'll surely need someone like you in the Ilocos region." "

Thank you, uncle. I appreciate that. Well, I'll see you later then. Okay? Goodbye. "

" Yes, of course. I'll see you around. Goodbye, Francisco. "

A month later, Francisco de Paula was on the train for San Fernando, La Union. He was assigned to manage the Tabacalera branch in La Union. As he boarded the train, he was struck once again by that feeling of destiny. Something awaiting him there, something that would change the course of his life.

Little did he know at that particular moment when he boarded the La Union train that this would be his final destination. He was going to live there the rest of his life. Roots. Roots he never before imagined he would implant permanently in this fair land. Roots. Roots of his seed. Little did he know that up here, he would marry, have eleven children, and die in this mountain province he dearly loved as much as he loved his family. Palali. Baguio. So reminiscent of the hills and the *tajos* of Ronda.

The train ride was again reminiscent of the trip from Malaga to Barcelona seven years ago. The towns the coastline—how much of Spain this part of the islands was—how much of Andalusia—the sea, the mountains, the hills. He particularly remembered the hills of Palali when he took the bus ride from San Fernando to Baguio the year before. He loved those hills in Palali so similar to the red hills of Ronda, and the zigzag road to the pine city of Baguio, winding like the winding road to his birthplace. Yes, he told himself, this was going to be his new home.

# IV.

*Luna, La Union (1894-1901)*

These were the best years of Francisco de Paula's life. His career as Manager of the **Tabacalera** flourished. He had three children: Antonia, the eldest born in 1894 a year after they were married. They adored her. She was a beautiful baby, white as sunlight, her hair chestnut brown. The second child was Abelardo, a handsome boy, born in 1896, the year Jose Rizal, the national hero was shot by the Spaniards, the year the Philippine Revolution broke out. The third child was Maria who became the mother of 15 beautiful mestizo children. She was an ideal mother who brought up her children with kindness and gentleness. She was born at the outbreak of the Filipino-American War where Roosevelt and his "raiders" took over Cuba, and Puerto Rico was annexed and the Philippines, a victim of the Treaty of Paris.

All these turbulent events were going on around the world, but in Luna, life went on as usual. Don Paco was enjoying prosperity. He had just acquired in this period the area now called Camp Allen; it was bought by the Philippine Government from him a few years later when the Philippine Military Academy or Constabulary at that time was set up by the Americans. This was the beginning of the American brainwashing of the Filipinos, in accordance to President McKinley's dream that the Philippines would be annexed to the United States just like Puerto Rico.

And so, as the Katipunan was waging war against the Spaniards, and Emilio Aguinaldo, Adela's first cousin, was fighting the Spaniards in Cavite and Manila, Don Paco was prospering from the profits of the **Tabacalera** in the Ilocandia region.

*"The sea that touches the wind,"* mused Don Paco in his farm in Palali.

"What's that, Paco?" asked Adela.

"Nothing at all…I was just thinking of Ronda, Malaga, my family there.*"*

"Why don't you go and visit?*"*

"I'll see if the Company will give me time off.*"*

# V.

Paco received letters from his mother and sister Adela almost every month. He had the habit of answering their letters immediately. He had a brick-coloured wax which he melted to seal the letter, and with his ring bearing the family's coat-of-arms, he would stamp the wax.

This month his sister wrote a letter which was a big blow to Paco. She wrote to tell him that his mother was very sick; her health had deteriorated in the past three months. Since she had her first heart attack 10 years ago, her health had started to deteriorate. This time, wrote Adela, she had a bad attack that almost killed her. *"Come immediately! Mamá is very sick"*, she said in her letter.

"Adela, I have to go to Spain. Mama is very sick. Do you want to come with me?"

"Yes, but what about the children? Who will take care of them?"

"Could you ask your mother?"

"All right. I'll talk to her."

That same month, Paco and Adela were bound for Spain. They arrived in Ronda on a hot day in March. To his grief and disappointment, his mother had just passed away a few days before his arrival. They had arrived just a day before the burial.

Paco, being the eldest, gave the eulogy. His voice was sad, low-keyed, cracked. He thanked on behalf of his brothers and sisters the friends and relatives who had come to attend the requiem mass and the burial. He then expressed his deep sadness for not arriving on time to see her alive. He stopped. He could not speak for a few seconds. Tears started streaming down his cheeks. There were audible sounds of weeping from his brothers and sisters. He forced himself to continue:

"I deeply regret and I find the death of my mother truly painful. I don't know whether to feel remorse for not having come earlier, knowing that she had been sick these past few years. It was my work, my family, but…no, no more excuses…"

He paused for a moment.

"I feel guilty, very guilty."

He looked at the serene face of his dead mother, and started to weep.

"Mother, forgive me", he wept.

His tears were now streaming down. He no longer could talk. His wife helped him to his seat. The priest, amidst the weeping and tears, went on with the requiem mass.

It was a hot day in March as the funeral procession brought them to the Ronda cemetery. The hot, dry weather of Ronda in March. Family and friends attended the burial. Paco and the two Adelas stood by the priest as he read "The Lord is my shepherd I shall not want…".

Paco and Adela stayed another week before returning to the Philippines. He met his in-laws for the first time—the Izquierdos and the Corrales who were married with his sisters Luz and Concha. Abelardo was with his wife Teresa. Abelardo was still in the military and was now a Colonel. Adela despite all her suitors remained single.

"Well, little sister. How time flies! And you never married?"

"Someone had to stay home to take care of mama."

"You did well, Adela. Mama, in heaven, will help you the rest of your life."

Indeed, that was what precisely happened. Before dying, her mother had left half of her possessions including the house in Ronda to Adela. She left Paco a small inheritance which he later used to build his house in Baguio and buy his farmland in Palali.

Before leaving Ronda, Paco showed his wife the farm where he spent many happy moments when he was a child.

"My happy childhood", he told Adela. "I remember picking lemons and oranges during harvest season. Mama would make my favorite desert: lemon and orange marmalade from the peels."

He pointed to the olive trees at the side of the hill. "Look at the olive trees. I remember those huge green and black olives which the farmers would pick and then later on prepare olive oil, or marinate the olives with vinegar to give it that special bitter-sour flavour. And that pure olive oil tasted so good with the *bacalao* my mama and my aunts prepared during Holy Week."

His thoughts brought him to his mother again —Death. The inevitability of death. You are born, you live, you die. All part of the human cycle. All part of the divine plan.

The day after, Paco and Adela returned to the Philippines.

# VI.

Paco returned to the Philippines a broken man. His grief and feelings of guilt devoured him, and he took to drinking heavily to drown his sorrows. His moods were also unpredictable; sometimes he would remain in a melancholic state for days without talking to anyone; then he would just whimper by himself in the middle of the night, or cry like a child being punished, screaming and shouting Why? He was no longer the happy, jovial Andalusian Adela met ten years ago.

In his drinking bouts, he would shout at the servants "Puñetera la madamdama"; his temper was short; he acted impatiently and rashly; acted irascible at little things and bark frequently at the servants blaming them for not doing things right. Adela would talk to the servants afterwards and explain to them that the *señor* was going through a bad period because of his mother's death, and to be patient with him. They understood, nodding, saying, *wen, señora.*

His mother's death had a terrible impact on Paco. He would spend days just tearful, remembering his boyhood days with his mother in Ronda, the *paseos* with her to the beaches in Malaga, the *Semana Santa* processions where they would walk together and sing the *Salvat.*

Paco, after a month, decided to go back to work. He worked even harder to distract himself. He felt he was ruining himself and his family with his moods and irrational behaviour, and work was the only way out to distract himself. He worked 12 hours a day at the **Tabacalera,** sometimes more just to forget the serene face of his dead mother in the wake before her burial. Flashbacks of her face came back to him, but work and his cognac made him forget his grief and pain.

On weekends, when memories came back, he drowned himself with a bottle of Carlos Primero to numb his mind of thoughts and memories of her. Adela was his only salvation. She was kind and understanding and stayed by him through these months of torment and grief.

His grief slowly diminished when his fourth child was born in 1905. He named her Luz, after her jovial sister by the same name. He still remembered the curls in his sister's hair, exactly like the curly hair of his newborn daughter. He smile and called her "gitana".

At times, he would cradle her to sleep and sing *I dreamt …I dreamt dancing for you in a night of love because you had the voice of an angel I saw…,* and the infant Luz would quietly go to sleep.

It was as if the birth of his daughter Luz gave new life to him. She was his salvation from the grief he had bore inside him for three years. From the death of his mother, he saw her resurrection in her daughter Luz who grew up to be a caring person to all her brothers and sisters, nephews and nieces.

# VII.

*Baguio, 1910*

Don Francisco de Paula was reaching his middle age. He was well known and respected in the small community of Baguio towards the beginning of the century.

There was a quiet elegance to his commands, to his posture, —the way he crossed his legs and held his brandy glass.

One day, he was in an especially bad mood because his son Paquito had a fight in school with one of his classmates. He came home crying, his nose bleeding, and the old man was upset and angry and told him to go back and settle the problem himself. Paquito did just that. After receiving the almost divine go signal from his father, the father-like-son Paquito retaliated with a vengeance that made his classmate yelp like a dog with his tail between his legs.

After hearing about this, Don Francisco felt family honour recompensated. His anger subsided now. He sipped his brandy and recalled the train ride to Barcelona when he first left home almost 30 years ago—the summer fields of Andalusia, the sea along Valencia, Costa del Sol, the arid almost desert-like terrain of Castilla with its olive groves like those in Morocco, the kind family riding with him in the same train compartment. They offered him some home-made wine while they were having their *bocadillos* for lunch. He smiled

351

and declined their offer and said he had his own home-made *tinto*. He showed them his goatskin and joined them with a *Salud, pesetas y amor...y tiempo para gastarlos* as they laughed and drank their wine, and as he pressed the goatskin up in the air as the wine flowed through his lips. They were a happy Andalusian family, as all typical Andalusian families are—happy, joyful, energetic, that Southern Spanish zest for life. He remembered his childhood days as he saw the girl and the boy playing with their toys.

"Papa", Paquito was all smiles now, "I hit him back and he didn't even do a thing with me. He just cried and ran away."

The old man smiled. "Now you know what courage means."

"Yes, papa."

"What's going on, Paco?" asked his wife Adela.

"Everything's fine and resolved", answered Don Francisco. She took Paquito by the hand and attended to him.

Was it almost twenty or more years ago? he thought. His shy wife Adela. He remembered writing his sister Adela to tell her that he met a Filipina he fell in love with, and coincidentally, her name was also Adela! He wrote saying that he fell in love with her voice. He was in church one Sunday and he heard a beautiful voice in the church choir singing the Ave Maria which was so beautiful that he had to meet the senorita who had sung it. He was told that she was the daughter of the *gobernadorcillo*. From that date on, he would wait in his balcony for her to pass by — the beautiful Adela, with her Maria Clara dress and her payong riding the calesa from church to home, from home to church. Then, the courage to go and ask the gobernadorcillo for her hand in marriage. Yes, he thought, she will become Dona Adela Aguinaldo de Paula.

But the young Adela who was only 15 did not want to marry the Spaniard from the Tabacalera. She pleaded to her father saying that she was too young to get married, but to no avail. Her father's word, her father's wish was her command. She had to be the dutiful daughter who would not and could not go against her father's wishes. For Don Graciano Aguinaldo, this was a privilege that a distinguished Spaniard had asked for his daughter's hand in marriage.

Adela's mother consoled her. She told her she would be happy once she had children. "Your children will be your happiness", she said. Adela remembered this the rest of her life.

Don Francisco mused as he sipped his brandy, smiling as he remembered how his young bride refused to give her finger when he was about to put the ring in. It was only when she looked at her mother and her mother giving her an encouraging nod did she finally surrender her hand to her groom.

"Remember to teach each of your daughters this: if she marries a rich man, she should know how to manage the household. But if she marries a poor man, she should likewise be able to do the household chores—cook and care for her husband, take care of the children, and everything a good wife should know and do".

Dona Adela remembered her mother's counsel because she lived it at home in the fifteen years she was educated by this wise and good mother and wife. And she made sure her daughters would likewise grow up in this tradition.

# VIII.

The years following the birth of Luz were prolific years for Paco and Adela. She bore him 7 more children, and as each was born, he saw his mother resurrected again in their lives, and slowly, his grief dissipated. Conchita, named after his sister Concha who married into the Izquierdo family, was born in 1906; Paquito whom he named after himself, his "junior", 1908; Miguel, named after his uncle, the politician, the governor of Malaga, 1910; Lolita, 1912, named after his aunt who loved to sing and dance the flamenco; Aida, 1915, named after his youngest sister and also the "junior" of his wife; Josefina, 1917, named after his aunt Josefa, an athlete and indefatigable community worker of Ronda; and the youngest, Diego, named likewise from his youngest brother.

These were again happy years for Paco; he no longer needed to distract himself with his Carlos Primeros; he had his children to play with after he came back from work. He was overflowed by their love and respect. Although he was a strict disciplinarian, he was more so a compassionate, loving father. And his children loved and respected him. His word was his command, and for any minor infraction, he would take off his thick leather belt and whip his children, especially the boys, when they would run all over the house in their hyperactivity and break things, or when they would lie and be disobedient.

A year after Diego's birth, Paco prepared for his retirement from the **Tabacalera**. He was nearing sixty, and at the advice of his doctor,

354

his liver condition was deteriorating; he was also diagnosed for diabetes. He was advised to avoid alcohol. He heeded his doctor's advice for a few months.

He decided to build his retirement home in Baguio. He had bought around five hectares of land there in 1901, and thought of building his home close to the Municipal Hall. In 1921, the home was completed, Paco retired and he took his whole family in exodus from Luna in honour of the Luna brothers, Antonio, the General who had fought with Aguinaldo in the Filipino-American War of 1899, Juan, the famous painter, and Joaquin who later became the Governor of La Union.

The house he built in Baguio was a magnificent three storey stone mansion with nine bedrooms, six bathrooms. Adela and Paco occupied the top floor with their young children, Diego, Aida and Pepita accompanied by their *yayas*. The older children occupied the second floor: Luz and Conchita in one room, Miguel and Paquito in the other.

The other room was reserved for Abelardo when he came and visited from his travels in the US Navy. Maria and Antonia had already married. Maria had married Manolo Montecillo, a young, handsome, dashing lawyer who was the Fiscal of Trinidad. They were in love, and Paco had no qualms about their marriage. He was happy for them and gave them his blessings. They were blessed with 15 children. Antonia married a railway employee, had three children—Francisco, Cesar and Alberto and lived the rest of her life in Manila.

In 1945, before the Liberation of the Philippines by the GIs under General McArthur with his proverbial "I shall return", American planes bombed cities where they thought the Japanese were still hiding. Baguio and Manila were the cities with the most bombardments. The magnificent de Paula mansion was reduced to rubbles. It was again rebuilt in 1951 this time in pinewood and still stands today.

Abelardo had joined the US Navy when he was only 17,much to his father's disappointment. He married a kind and gentle caviteña, Teresa, on one of his trips back home. They had no children. He was barely forty when he died of diabetes. His brother Miguel married the widowed Teresa, and she bore him twins—Miguelito and Luisito. She died with her son Luisito of malnutrition in July 1942 while they were running and hiding from the Japanese.

Miguel was a guerrilla officer in Baguio, and he and his family were constantly on the run. The tragedy finally caught up with them. Miguelito was brought up by his grandmother, Adela, and his aunts Luz and Aida. In 1971, his cousin, Angeling, daughter of Conchita, helped him immigrate to the United States. He became a successful entrepreneur in Al Capone's Chicago.

Don Francisco sent his two daughters, Conchita and Luz to board in an exclusive girls' school in Manila, Santa Isabel. Luz learned how to play the piano there. She would later on recall how strict the Spanish nuns were, and every time she hit the wrong key, her music teacher would spank her hand with a wooden ruler.

With his pension from the **Tabacalera**, Paco managed to support his family and still support a cook, a chauffeur and 2 servants. In 1925, the American Government was looking for a site for the Military Academy, and had asked him if he would sell the property, which later on was named Camp Allen. He sold this property and with part of this money, bought 200 hectares of farmland in Palali, a barrio in Sablan.

Palali. Paco loved Palali. He put up a small farmhouse and during weekends, he would go there because the air was ideal. It didn't have the cold humidity of Baguio, nor the hot, steamy climate of the lowlands of La Union.

The brick-red color of the hills reminded him of his hometown Ronda. He would go here regularly for the rest of his retirement years, to breathe the fresh air of Palali, to bathe in its warm sun, to enjoy the cool, quiet nights, sip his cognac and be at peace with himself, to remember, to be nostalgic about Ronda, to look back at his life, and whenever he walked up to his favourite place in Palali, overlooking Lingayen Gulf, the hat-shaped hill called *Kimalugong*, he would look up towards the bright blue sky of Palali and talk to God, thanking him for his blessings, his children, and his well-spent life.

At the age of 70, Francisco de Paula died peacefully surrounded by his wife and children.

# FRANKIE
## I.

*North Delta. December 20, 1992*

Postcard. Outside. Looking. Through his bedroom window—-Douglas fir trees, their fingertips reaching out towards the white snowy sky. Snow falling some more. Snow-covered trees like Christmas cards.

Thank God for these eyes that see the beauty of His creation! This wondrous snow, this clean happiness, pure, child-like. Children now with their sleds playing outside. Fresh, clean snow. Started last night. The weatherman was right this time. He predicted snow, thick snow overnight. Snow all over; now, spits of snow falling from the white opaque sky.

Memories of his mother brought tears to his eyes. He accompanied her to that last pilgrimage to Lourdes, Fatima and Compostela. October 1988. Month of the Blessed Virgin Mary. He didn't want to remember. Too much grief. So much grief when she died just four months after the pilgrimage. The mother he loved so much. He regretted painfully not being able to show her how much he truly loved her. But she knew. And she forgave him.

The spits of snow were falling, thicker now. Snow flakes now. He remembered that stopover in Weed, California. December 1987. Just before Christmas. He stopped the car—his father, his son, his mother and his tia Luz. How they all went out to receive the huge snowflakes. How he faced the sky with a huge smile and opened his mouth for joy, pure white joy to receive this white, soft cool manna from heaven. His communion with God, his search for innocence, purity, as he stretched his arms, crucifixion-like, surrendering himself to the whiteness, up in that mountain in Weed, the overwhelming whiteness of the falling snow. And then the laughter afterwards. Teasing Carlitos. The merry old aunt Tia Luz putting an aluminum wrapper on her teeth trying to play with Carlitos. Carlitos was only five then. We had just visited Disneyland.

He looked out again at his "postcard window", watching the snow flakes drift sideways, now downwards in slow motion. Christmas. The radio playing nostalgic Christmas songs—Nat King Cole…"they know that Santa's on his way…I'm offering this simple song to kids from one till 92…Merry Christmas to you"…

He was "fathering" now, not babysitting. Christmas in 5 days. Sad Christmas. Christmas was no longer for him. Christmas is for children, as they all say. His children. The children of his world. Hijos del mundo.

The postcard picture window no longer portrayed Christmas. It rained all day today, melting yesterday's Christmas fantasy. Frankie picked his pad and pen:

"It's 12:56 a.m. I'm glad I have my own space, my own room. I can wake up when I need to write, turn on the lights, watch TV, smoke a cigar, sip my brandy, without anyone telling me to turn off the lights, or stop smoking that stinky cigar. I need this space and freedom. The only way I can think. And write.

I went to confession today. After so long. I don't know why I did it. Return to the state of grace? Back to the faith. Vicious cycle. The Church has changed from the way it was in the fifties—the Latin mass, the priest celebrating it with his back to the people, the mystique. Now, everything's so open; priests are too informal. Everything obvious. Sometimes too obvious. Their dark secrets revealed—the media and their sensationalist, explosive stories about homosexual priests, paedophiles, their perversions...

Indeed, the world is coming to an end. Or is it my end? Is it the cycle of youth and its rebellion mellowing into old age and tradition? Is that why things are going too fast too soon? But it never was like this before. Nothing makes sense anymore. People in the nineties talking about the nostalgia of the eighties? That was just a decade ago! Just two years ago, it was the nostalgia for the sixties; and five years ago, the nostalgia of the fifties.

Things are happening so fast. I can't keep up. I'm just living it now minute by minute. Just telling myself "That's life". Sadly.

Too many earthquakes now. Too many storms. One day, I imagine the sun exploding. This will truly be the end of our world. The end of our solar system.

Generational sins. We inherit the sins of our forefathers. My grandfather—a full life. Died of natural causes. Respected by his family. Respected by his community. From the dark moustache of the young man from Andalusia to the bearded old man sitting in his veranda in Palali, white beard resembling Hemingway. His life was his family. Those bygone days when honour and family took top priority over anything else. Values apparently meaningless today. Today's youth, computerized, devoid of sentimentality, character. Values considered today as "corny" and "old fashioned". A full cycle. Generational gap. Never thought this way 20 years ago when I was myself the one saying how "corny" tradition was. Now I say 'you've got to have values, something to lean on; without them, you're wishy-washy. Values strengthen the soul, the character of the person.'

Principles? Dead! Spoiled, spoiled brats, this new generation of mankind. Getting worse and flakier with time. Degeneration. Time degenerates generations. Generational sins get worse as time goes by. Time. And after this life, what? Timelessness. Perhaps the timelessness of eternity.

*North Delta. December 25, 1992*

He watched his children with quiet amusement as they excitedly opened their Christmas gifts from Santa Claus.

"I love Santa", said the little one, six year old Alexandra.

"Why?" he asked.

"He gave me all these nice gifts—the treasure troll watch, this nice drawing book and a paint brush and all the watercolour paint, but I love this treasure troll watch the best."

She showed him the pinkish hair of the troll stuck to her quartz watch.

"I can tell you what time it is. It's 8:36."

"That's good."

His son was already in his room playing with the rocket Lego pieces he picked up earlier from his Christmas stocking. He pressed the top of the rocket, and blue and red lights started to blink alternately with a taped voice coming from the control tower, "Blast off", and then the sound of a rocket ship taking off.

"Are you happy with Santa's gift?"

The ten year old boy smiled. "Yeah. Wicked and awesome."

"Did you like the pearl necklace and pearl earrings and pear bracelet you got from Santa?"

"I didn't get the pearl necklace and the pearl earrings and the pearl bracelets from Santa", said Alexandra.

"What do you mean?" asked her dad.

"You gave them to me, not Santa."

"Oh, yes, I forgot. They were under the Christmas tree and not in the Christmas stocking, right?"

"Right", she smiled.

"This is rad", said the boy.

"What's rad?"

"This police car chasing the scary racing car." He was playing with a toy that his crazy aunt Millie gave him under the Christmas tree. She was crazy, but not in Christmas, said the six year old.

He remembered his wife. She died after giving birth to Alexandra. Was that only six years ago? He felt a single tear from his right eye trickling down slowly towards the corner of his mouth. Memoria selectiva. Selective memory, he thought. The happy moments together. Tagaytay. Baguio in New Year. Tennis in the summer. Her epicene body in the hospital. Lifeless. The funeral a week after. Spring. Spring in Montreal. Cold and dreary. It was utter shock for him. Shock that didn't rub off until a month after. Then grief started settling in.

His parents came shortly afterwards to help him in his grief. Help him with the children, especially the infant Alex. And just when the grief was dissipating, another tragedy. February, 1989. Just three years after. The death of his mother.

More than another three years had passed. Alex was now 6 and Carlos 10. His father had gone back home. He wanted to follow suit—go back to him and share his grief. But there were so many things to do, to think about—the children's schooling, what would he do back home, he had a comfortable job here that paid the bills, but it was destroying him, his creativity, his way of life. He felt stagnant in this cold country that wasn't his. He felt almost useless, a stranger in his own land. The children can adjust easily. But he no longer could despite his twenty years in this cold, strange land he now called his own.

He was caught in-between—the readjustment possibilities of his own homeland, or live his routine life style here. Maybe this was the lesser of two evils. Or perhaps, the utopia—live the best of the two worlds.

Or just take life a minute a time and see what happens with Destiny …the alliterative fickled finger of fate.

"Estas loco para ese nino", he remembered his mother telling him that, and he remembered replying: "Es que le tengo lastima. Es flojo. Igual que su madre."

That was why he stayed on with her. He was more concerned about his son. He was the reason he was still with her. He recalled telling that to her. It broke her heart. There was a fight. And he felt guilty. He never cheated on his wife. He didn't know if he really loved her. He remembered his mother saying: "La mujer con quien se casa contigo es un martir."

A year after, his wife died in childbirth. He remembered the guilt he felt. He broke her heart. And that killed her. "No, it's not your fault", his friends and relatives would say. But deep inside, the guilt gnawed on him.

He left his children with Ruben and Lydia in Montreal right after the funeral of his wife and left for Chicago to try to forget. Chicago was his safehouse. Whenever he felt gloomy or depressed, he would take time off and visit his cousins there. In 1971, he visited his cousin Angie in the summer to get away from his work in Bowling Green. Like all graduate students, he had just worked in a tomato factory that summer and he wanted to get away before classes started again in the Fall. He had nightmares in Angie's apartment in Magnolia—the smell of cooking tomatoes, the heavy boxes he had to carry and was never used to, but the smell of tomatoes being cooked night and day haunted him that entire summer. His cousin Angie was a kind person and didn't mind hr cousin spending two weeks in Chicago. She was the only family he had.

"How are your studies?"

"They're okay. Two more years and I'm done."

"Will you be able to find a job when you finish?"

"I think so."

"I'm asking because you can come here if you want to and work at the hospital. They have an X-ray Technician program paid for by the hospital. You live in the hospital, meals are free, you get a monthly allowance. After a year, you're hired by the hospital."

"It's quite tempting, Angie, but honestly, it's not my line of work. I've never liked hospitals. They're too depressing; they smell of sickness and death."

"I understand".

The next summer, he visited again because his cousin Migueling with whom he grew up with came to Chicago aided by Angie to take the technician's course. That was a fun summer. Together they travelled to Bowling Green where they biked all over the campus, met Frankie's friends. Then there was Teddy who just came down from Canada visiting a girl friend in Cleveland. They borrowed her car and drove all the way to Chicago and Eddie, Angie's brother, had also just arrived. They met more friends—the Barmaceas who were distant relatives and that was a happy summer. During Christmas break, he again hopped on the Greyhound for the five hour ride from Bowling Green to Chicago to spend Christmas with his family that was growing bigger in Chicago thanks to the help of Angie who brought all of them from the Philippines. Later, her mother, Tita Conchita followed, then her sister Elsie, then Alice, then Mary Rose—the entire Baguio clan was in Al Capone's "untouchable" city. The song "The night Chicago died" played on all the radio stations that summer.

Chicago, Chicago of many memories. And now summer of 1986 he was here forgetting the guilt of his wife's death. Chicago, his safehouse again, to forget the pain and the guilt, to be with his cousins Eddie and Migueling for consolation.

Chicago of his consolation. The summer picnics, but his heart was not in them. The visit to Noli's property in an exclusive subdivision of Chicago, parties here and there, the friends were quiet about his wife's demise, they were kind and never brought the matter up. He was passing through a painful transition in life.

In September, he returned to Montreal to pick up his children and left for Vancouver. There, he waited for his parents and tita Luz to come.

***

Frankie drove his parents in the Fall of 1987 to Mexico, visiting friends and relatives along the way—Uncle Johnny from Stockton who recalled memories of the hot-tempered Spaniard, Don Francisco of the Tabacalera. Uncle Johnny was 90, and one of the early immigrants to the United States in the 1930s when passage from the Philippines to the United States didn't require visas, since Filipinos, like the Puerto Ricans, were under the U.S. Commonwealth. Then there was his cousin Joji in Vallejo who had just been inaugurated President of the Surigueno Club in the Bay area. Then Marcial, a retired customs officer, a close friend of the family in Los Angeles; he had retired and was living with his children there. The Barmacheas had also moved there from Chicago, Benny, Minda, with whom he had happy times together with Urong and Migueling and Eddie. He remembered visiting the hospital where Benny's father was dying. Frankie remembered his mother talking to the dying man on his death bed in the hospital in Los Angeles.

He then recalled the raven that perched on the fence of his Langley townhouse.

"They say someone in the family is going to die. Those blackbirds are bad luck."

He only had memories now—summer of 1987 when his parents came with his tita Luz; they arrived in June; a few weeks after, they travelled, Chicago again, on time for Migueling's birthday, recalling that call from the Philippines—tita Lolita had just died and Frankie's mother cried bitterly, feeling the guilt and the conflict with her because of the Allen property; and Frankie's brother, Robert was there with his whole family, a rendezvous in Chicago. Frankie from Vancouver, Robert from Toronto, meeting at the central point—Chicago.

For the first time in months, he was happy again. They travelled all that summer—Calgary, Saskatchewan, Manitoba. In Winnipeg, they visited Arthur and Pining—the reception was excellent and they were still grateful because Frankie's sister who worked for the Canadian Embassy in Manila helped them immigrate to Canada.

From Winnipeg, they went on to Chicago. Angie was no longer there; she had returned with her mother tita Conchita and Elsie who were not happy in Chicago. They returned to Baguio. Tita Conchita died shortly afterwards in 1985.

From Chicago, they travelled together with Robert and his family to Toronto, then Montreal then Toronto again where tita Luz stayed with Maria in Waterloo where she was finishing her Engineering course; then it was just Frankie and his parents travelling, los tres mosqueteros, back to Vancouver, with his father helping him drive. The drive was happy and sad—Idaho, Montana, Washington then up to Vancouver. The children were like little gypsies—Alexandra was barely two, and Carlos was six, two little gypsies like their grandaunt Luz travelling with the three musketeers, sleeping when they felt like it, hardly a peep from Alex, except when there were diapers to change. It was another happy summer in his life.

Happy, sad, happy, sad. Two conflicting emotions necessary for living. Indeed, how can we know happiness if sadness is inexistent?

His children, children of Canada, how lucky, how fortunate compared to the dying, starving children of Somalia, he thought. Somalia and the US GIs, the saviours, the kind, compassionate Americans of Bush. After Bush, what? A wishy-washy democrat? Clinton. Wait and see.

Snowflakes bigger than ever, just like those in Weed, rushing faster downwards and sideways. The farmer's almanac was right again. No El Niño this year. He was here last winter and the weather was fantastic. Fantastic. Van der Zalm gone. Fantastic, his expression. Van der Zalm and his Fantasy Gardens. Gone. He was a good man. Good men never last long in politics.

\*\*\*

The snow, now weighing heavily on the fir tree branches, breaks away in clumps, falling, powdery in their slow motion descent as snow keeps falling turning the gigantic live green Douglas fir trees whiter and whiter.

\*\*\*

The children now at play in the snow, throwing snowballs, screaming "eenie meenie minie mos". They are tired watching videos and playing computer games and are now running, shouting, laughing. Children. Happy children playing. He remembered his mother once telling him "Let them play and laugh". She enjoyed her grandchildren's "noises" despite the annoyance felt by her son.

Now he looks back, understanding why in these mellowing years his mother enjoyed the children's "noises". It was the last passage to innocence, her last bridge to youth, energy, life in its fullest. In its more biblical sense, the words of the Saviour: "You have to be like children to enter my Kingdom."

All of a sudden the annoyance he felt from children at play transformed to joy as he remembered his mother's smile as she observed her grandchildren play, as she gave them the "forbidden" chocolates and other gifts which later on Carlitos, visiting his grandmother's grave, 90 or 100 degree heat he wasn't accustomed to, wept, tears in his eyes, later confessing to his father: "Grandma was kind to me. She always gave me presents."

He again looked back and remembered how much his mother pampered his son Carlitos. Carlitos was her joy. She loved the child from the first moment she saw him as an infant in their home in United Paranaque to the time she threw coins to his friends on his sixth birthday in the townhouse in Langley, four months before she passed away. Carlitos of her life, the grandson she loved best of all.

His tears were now streaming down his cheeks as he remembered the last days with his mother—the champagne on New Year's Eve, as she danced with him, full of energy; the warmth of her kiss at the Vancouver Airport, the last time he saw her alive; the long distance call, her happy voice, just a week before she died; and that mysterious flash of light, her spiritual appearance, her last farewell, perhaps, letting him know she had released herself from her body, when all the lights in her bedroom upstairs in the townhouse just went out for no reason at all, that sudden unexplainable flash of light downstairs—her spirit visiting her son for the last time before flying away to eternity, to another galaxy, perhaps, a more superior, superhuman kingdom, the realm of the Almighty— an enigma he would one day unravel.

Then there was that painful trip back home to attend her funeral. He was accompanied by his youngest brother from Toronto, his brother who had, in his grief, drank continuously in the plane and had become drunk and obnoxious. He sympathized as he felt the same gnawing grief and begged him to remain calm. He quieted down and said "Ok".

There were no tears . He controlled himself all through the funeral. His father broke down quietly when he looked at his wife of 46 years for the last time before the casket was closed and buried. Everyone threw flowers as the casket descended. Everyone except his eldest son. He just stood there, frozen, beside his father, his tears contained, staring at the casket as it descended slowly to its perpetual grave. It was a hot, steamy day. The beginning of summer.

# II.

Frankie wrote in his memoirs:

"I was swimming and I remembered my childhood days in Nichols, swimming in that old pool, in the old Officers' Club. Undo and Rafael and Rolly. The tennis courts are still there, at the back. I would bike there, swim, eat a hot dog, and play billiard with the gang. I was 10 or 11 and 12. There was the movie house there too; it's no longer a movie house; they converted it to a gym.

I had athletes foots, bad case, and I didn't go to school because I couldn't walk; I guess that was later on when I was 13 or 14. My feet were infected. Friends visited me. I had a certain charisma when I was young. I felt like I was a "golden boy" in those days, I was handsome, conceited. They were happy days.

There was an altar in my parents' room. We prayed the rosary, I don't remember if it was every Saturday or everyday. When Fr. Peyton came with his rally "A family that prays together stays together", we started praying.

My room was downstairs. It used to be part of the garage but it was renovated to put an extra bedroom and a bathroom there. That became the room I stayed in until I left the Philippines in 1965.

I remember Dad telling me war stories—how he was in the death march from Bataan to Capas in the second World War. He survived the concentration camp there, but suffered malaria; how he was flying one December day reconnoitring and when he was about to land, noticed all the potholes in the airstrip. The Japanese had just bombed all the air bases in the Philippines hours before. It was December 8, 1941. He told me about how he landed a C-47 in Baguio at night. He was the only pilot who dared do that. Cars were lined up in the airstrip with their headlights on because the Baguio airport in Loakan didn't have lights; it was meant to have planes land in the evening because of the dangerous mountain ranges around; how Claro Mayo Recto was grateful for this and sent him a special letter. Recto had asked Dad to fly him because his son, Clarito, had a motorcycle accident in Baguio and was dying in the hospital. He died, but Recto was there when his son passed away.

I remember Dad taking me to basketball games at the Rizal Coliseum when I was 10. He would pay for a full seat for me; the other fathers didn't do that. They would just let their kids sit on their laps to save on tickets. I remember the teams—YCO, and some players— Loyzaga, Mootoomul, Arroyo—so far away, so long ago, memories carry me back almost 40 years now. He loved me because I was his eldest, and the smartest of his children. Smart like him. I was always compared to him—my dad, the brains of the family. And I admired him a lot. When she was a little girl my sister called him "genius".

He was away doing an MBA in the States when I graduated from High School. But he sent me a lot of things—a pair of nice suede shoes, jackets, and so on. He brought more things for us when he got back after a year in Bloomington.

He would fly to Jolo and come back with a lot of fruits—lanzones, mangosteen,durian. We left the durian in the garage because of the strong odour.

Memories, all memories now. I am just witness to these, for my children, and my children's children who may want to know who I am, and who my father was."

Frankie wrote:

"Delta. January 26, 1993.

Dad's devotion to mom was extraordinary. Never have I known a man as dedicated and devoted to his wife as dad!

I remember how concerned dad was during our pilgrimage to Lourdes and Fatima in 1988. His mom had taken a shower in one of the hotels close to Luarca in northern Spain, and caught a cold which made her cough and sick throughout the rest of the trip. In Malaga, mom got really sick and dad was always with her, every minute of the day.

I did the groceries; I wanted to leave the hotel room because I felt sad hearing mom cough and once, she coughed too much that she vomited. She couldn't eat anything. I knew she was very sick but not matter how much I prepared myself, I refused to believe she was dying. To me, mom was immortal. Even today, I know she lives; her spirit hovers somewhere, guiding me, perhaps smiling, freed of the burden of bodily sickness, and telling me how wonderful being a spirit is.

Dad was upset with me because the trip had made mom sicker; but mom defended me and said she enjoyed the pilgrimage.

There was so much guilt in me when she died; my sister consoled me and said God forgives and if he forgives, I should be able to forgive myself. I went through the Life in the Spirit seminar in 1990 to unburden my spirit of guilt. I was unburdened, I am now unburdened, except for moments when I look back and remember the trip we made, and how really stressful it was on mom. And my guilt returns because I wasn't really helpful. My driving all over made me hot-headed and this affected my driving, making mom even more nervous and sicker during the trip.

I remember Dad telling me in confidence how mom was really sick; I was just quiet; what else could I do? The incident in Valencia when they broke the window of the rented car made her even more nervous. We were on our way to Andorra and the trip up the mountains was nerve-wracking; there was even a long tunnel, and this time, it was mom consoling dad and I asked why, and mom said, "Your dad is afraid of tunnels", and I presumed it was because of the war.

In Andorra, I had the car window fixed and left mom to go shopping; when I picked them up, mom was so pale. She just wanted to go home.

But Dad's devotion was incredibly beautiful when, on our last stop before taking our flight home in Amsterdam, Dad bought mom a diamond ring. Mom had given her diamond ring to my sister for her wedding, and it was a beautiful gesture, a few months before mom died, for Dad, here in Amsterdam, the very same place where they were together 25 or more years ago on some kind of a United Nations assignment of dad, where dad again bought her the diamond ring. What beautiful dedication words cannot express! What unfathomable love! As though there was some kind of a feeling that their golden wedding anniversary was not going to happen, and here in Amsterdam, I saw that beautiful glow in mom's face when she showed me that perfect diamond, wedding ring!

Oh what sadness, what happiness!

The day after mom's funeral, Dad and I drove to GSIS in Quezon City. Dad was telling me how hot it was, and how just a week before mom died, how mom had difficulty breathing because of the heat;

he felt guilty that he had taken mom along. He told me that perhaps if he hadn't taken her along, she would probably not have died. I didn't know what to say. We were both in deep grief. At that time, I was still in a state of shock, so unbelieving that mom had passed away without saying goodbye to me, except for that brief moment in the Langley townhouse, the day she died, she visited me to bid me farewell. A sign—a sudden light which the old man my father-in-law saw; and the unexplainable lights that just went off for no reason at all in the bedroom where she spent her last days in Langley. The next day, Robert called to say mom had died.

# III.

Frankie looked at the 45-year old photo his Tita Aida just sent him. He looked at the black and white photo and memories started streaming in his mind. He was probably five then. His Uncle Diego was holding him in his arms. He was wondering whether this was the Officers' Club in Lipa, because that was where he was living then at that time. His father was, he recalled, a training pilot in Fernando air Base then. He remembered his Tito Diego squeezing water from the pool with his hands and producing a makeshift water fountain. He learned that trick from him.

In his later years, tito Diego was entering fits of depression and would lock himself in Baguio. In the summers in Baguio, he remembered his uncle ordering Migueling harshly to get more "pyang-pyang" from the corner liquor store. Migueling resented this. Migueling resented being shouted at. He resented Tita Aida also because of this, but he liked Tita Luz because of kind and gentle ways.

Tito Diego's best friend was Johnny Montalban, from the Forbes Park "group of 400", the select class of Manila Society. When Don Francisco was still alive, he belonged to this select class, and Baguio's "high society" counted on the de Paula children as the cream of the crop. That was how tito Diego met Johnny. Together, they became the playboys of high society and were the darlings of the 400 group.

When the family fortune started to decline after Don Francisco's death, the contrary occurred with the Montalban family. The Montalban Cement Factory prospered, and Johnny who was a born businessman, raked in millions. He later expanded into real estate, construction and residential subdivisions.

Meanwhile, his uncle Diego had squandered his inheritance money, and took to the bottle. At times, Johnny would take him off his depression and offer him management positions in the different parts of the country where his business flourished. In the late fifties, he accepted Johnny's offer to manage the cement factory in the Davao branch. But his uncle didn't run the business well; his sojourn there was complicated by an affair he had with a Davaoena who was love struck with him and wanted to settle down. But this wasn't his time yet, and so he left her and returned to Baguio.

After some time, Johnny offered him another job at the Rizal factory, but Diego found the job boring and lonely. Frankie remembered visiting his uncle there. It was sometime in the late fifties. He remembered the smell of rum in his breath.

He returned to Baguio to be with his aging mother. He knew he was the black sheep of the family, being the youngest, his mother's favourite.

He returned for the last time to Baguio in the early sixties and in one of his drunken moments, fell down the staircase and was brought to the hospital. He met a kind nurse from Pangasinan who took special care of him in the hospital. When he came out, he courted her with the natural charm he had always had with women. They married a few months later. He was 43; she was 21.

Frankie wasn't at the wedding in Dagupan in the summer of 1963, but he was shown pictures by his aunts in Baguio.

—Kitaem ti rupa na. Nakaesteng pay. Kasla itsura ni Bagatsing.

Frankie laughed. He had always liked his uncle; he was kind to him and always gave him toys when he was a child in Lipa and Nichols. Always showed him tricks.

A year later, Maria was born. She was the darling of her father. When his wife went to work, he would care for her so affectionately. He would change her diapers, boil milk for her, lull her to sleep. As Maria grew, he became more fond of her. But in the evenings, he couldn't control his depression, and took to drinking again. He tried to stop; and when he tried, the desire to drink became stronger until it enveloped him completely. He became more and more violent, but he would not direct this violence to his family. His fits of anger caused by drinking were directed to cookware and tables and glasses he would smash, and when the violence subsided, he would just go to sleep. The next morning, he would not remember anything, and spend the rest of the day being affectionate and extremely kind to his wife and daughter. Dr. Jekyll and Mr. Hyde.

In 1968, his liver finally gave in. Frankie was in Toronto studying at the university there; his parents were in Montreal where his father was a diplomat for ICAO. He saw the picture of his uncle in the coffin, and recalled his mother commenting, "Why would they take his picture inside a coffin? They shouldn't have done that, or even worse, sent it to us." His deceased uncle was wearing a suit. This was the first and last time Frankie saw his uncle wearing a suit.

Four years later, Dona Adela Vives Aguinaldo de Paula died.

Frankie looked at the black and white photo again. He remembered his tito Diego driving the whole family to Baguio . He was a careful and excellent driver when he wasn't drinking. He was quiet, cool and reserved in his manners. He recalled those drives from Baguio to Poro Point, then to Luna. Those were his happiest summers during those childhood years—the crystalline waters, warm Pacific waves of the China sea at Poro, and the strong, powerful waves in the Luna beaches, the diningding, the freshly harvested rice, white and appetizing after a swim, the chicken barbecues, the buco and its sweet juice. He remembered the plastic portable phonograph and the music of Trio Los Panchos. Then there was the yearly Good Friday procession in Luna and the Salvat being sung in Latin.

Frankie mused on the rituals of the summers of his youth and he remembered his mother reminiscing one evening in the Langley townhouse: "When you were children, those summers in the beach, Poro Point, the picnics, how happy we all were."

He now remembered Marquez their driver in Lipa who drove for them many times to Poro Point and the driver whom they called Apeng Daldal and Remulla. He wondered where they all were now. Lipa and Nichols, his happy childhood, and Ben from Pagsanjan. He remembered meeting him in one of those guarded outposts right outside their home in Nichols. He climbed up and they would chat and look at the fields, at pump hill in the distance, and even farther away, Laguna de Bay. A few years later, Ben invited him to Pagsanjan to meet his son. He told his son that Frankie was his godfather. Frankie wondered nostalgically what had become of Ben and his godson.

Frankie visited Nichols again in the summer of 1992 and walked the streets of his neighbourhood. How sad, how changed, he thought. He remembered the streets, the conset huts that once was his boyhood home—there was the Abano home, behind them the Laurons, the Diazes on the left, the Punzalans on the right.

As he walked he remembered his grandmother. He remembered the summer of 1965 right before he left for Madrid. He had a premonition when he kissed her and said goodbye that it was going to be the last time he would see her alive. He was in Bowling Green in 1972 when he received the sad news of his grandmother's death. His spirits were dampened that day. That same evening, he wrote a poem and mailed it to his mother. His father wrote him a month later to tell him the family received the poem and were very appreciative. He also informed his son that his mother had suffered a stroke. Her grief was too much for her to handle. He also told him the stroke was also caused because his youngest brother, Albert, had become a drug addict.

He reminisced happy memories of his grandmother—how she rolled her own tobacco to make her cigars like the traditional ilocana that she was; how she avidly read the ilocano version of Liwayway and faithfully follow the serials, and without eyeglasses at age 85; how she cooked the beefsteak only she could make with her magic touch, the steak so tender.

He remembered how she would get up and cook when he came up from Manila and prepare Frankie his favourite dishes—steak with toyo, dinengdeng, pinakbet and fried potatoes. His aunt Aida would comment: Apay ni Frankie laeng ti linulotom na espesyal, mamang.

And his grandmother would say Kayat ko.

Indeed, she did like Frankie; Frankie was his favourite grandson. And she would always attend to him when he came up to Baguio during his Christmas and Summer breaks, always gallant to his lola, kissing her hand to greet her and she would always ask him Que quieres comer? And after Frankie would tell her what he wanted, she would pick a few bills wrapped in her handkerchief inside her saya and call Tina to run to the market and buy the groceries for Frankie's lunch and dinner. Beside her bed, she kept Frankie's picture as Oedipus Rex when Frankie played this role in his freshman year in college.

Frankie remembered how his grandmother would keep all kinds of goodies under her bed, and only took them out when we would all come up from Manila to spend our vacations with her. She had mangoes which, unfortunately, were oftentimes overripe because she would forget she had them kept there; she had homemade chorizos, barbules, and all kinds of goodies she would keep for her "special guests" from Manila.

But she had a good memory and she knew where she kept everything.

Now, his aunts Luz and Aida would do the same when he came over to visit them in the traditional house, la casa solariega.

Frankie was now 50 and all his memories came and went—his childhood, his teenage years at the Ateneo, the worst year being his third year in high school when he suffered a nervous breakdown because his classmates called him muta and all sorts of names. He felt they were envious of him because of his popularity as an actor and public speaker; they also hated him because he was an officer for the PMT. During his breakdown, he lost all appetite to eat; he went to school half-heartedly; his mind would wonder. He remembered drawing grotesque pictures during his biology classes of animals in torture; he remembered his Latin teacher, Mr. Esguerra—he was the only kind person and he perhaps saved him from the harsh boys in his class. He somehow was able to uplift his spirits when he was down and out, and even gave him a perfect score in one of the Latin exams. He got out of this depression when his father was assigned to Baguio as Commandant of Cadets in the Philippine Military Academy. He enjoyed Baguio—he enjoyed the cadet dances, especially the ones where the Plebes were because they were more or less his age. He longed to join the Academy but he failed the physicals because he was nearsighted. Baguio relieved him of his breakdown, and he was living and happy again.

His life many times would pass before his very eyes in seconds as though the 50 years he lived in this planet were mere seconds— his childhood, his teenage years, his scholarship years in Spain, the fellowships for graduate studies he garnered in Canada and the US, remembering how proud his grandmother was of his grandson, how proud his mother and aunts were of this "genius" of a son, the old house in Abanao would would now flash back, then the marijuana and the LSD during those psychadelic years in Bowling Green, and then back to those teenage and childhood years in Nichols and Lipa and San Juan. Now he understood why, in the last months of her life, his mother didn't want to live too long away from her homeland. Now he realized that no matter what, the old adage 'there's no place like home' is a truism, we want to go back to that comfortable cuna where we were born, where we also want to die. Death, like birth, in your own native land, no matter how long you've lived abroad. Only in one's own native land, thought Frankie, where he was born, where he grew up, those formative years, happy, sad, nostaligic years, will death's contentment be realized.

"I want to be buried beside you and mom", he remembered telling his father the day his mother was buried.

# IV.

"Casla uki ti nuang ti rupa na", his tita Antonia commented. Frankie was only 14 then, and his moustache was beginning to show. His aunt was teasing him. Puberty. They would tease boys and girls reaching puberty. An inititation to life and adulthood.

—Sabes, Frankie, a tu mama le llamaron 'ugang' porque su pelo parecia a los igorotes y el barbero igorote que le corto el pelo se llamaba 'Ugang'. Asi que a tu mama se quedo el nombre 'ugang'.

Tita Antonia loved Frankie's mother; she was like her second mother because his grandmother had just given birth to his mother just about the same time tita Antonia gave birth to her first child, Munding. That was why Munding who was Frankie's eldest cousin was very close to his mother, and despite the fact that they were the same age, he would still respectfully call his mother "tia Pepa". They were so close in birth and death, so close that Munding died one year after his tia Pepa died. Frankie recalled that last conversation over the phone he had with Munding in January 1989. Munding was in Alaska and called to find out if his mother was still in Langley.

"Frankie, happy new year. Como estas, hombre?" Munding still had that happy go lucky tone in him despite the fact that he was physically suffering.

382

"She just left, Munding, for the Philippines two days ago. Are you going back too?"

"Not now. I've just come out of the hospital."

"Why?"

"I was just diagnosed for cancer of the pancreas."

That was the last he heard from Munding. Frankie never found out whether Munding saw his mother alive once more after that conversation with him a month before his mother died.

He heard from his cousin Migueling that Munding did return in 1989 to celebrate the last months of his life, announcing to all his relatives that he was dying and that he was spending the rest of his life the way he had always lived—happy-go-lucky. Indeed, Munding died a happy man.

Death, death everywhere. He remembered Migueling's conversation over the phone when he called to greet Frankie on his birthday, "The old generation—they're almost all gone."

Frankie replied sombrely: "Yes, we're next."

"And yet, just 20 years ago, how time flies, everyone was alive and happy. There were no deaths, and then, suddenly, Death stalked the family. Happy times had run out. Conchita in 1984, Antonia in 1985, Lolita in 1987, Pepa in 1989, Miguel in 1991."

"Only tita Luz and tita Aida are left. Who's next?"

"Too many unanswered questions in life. We'll probably know answers in the next life. Most of the time we say kuma the sana susana syndrome."

"I remember my father reciting a poem, I don't remember now. It had something to do about unfinished business in this lifetime, and how it's always the case that we never finish what we want to accomplish in this lifetime."

"I guess the attitude should be that's life, that's how life was meant to be—so many unfinished symphonies. And if we can convince ourselves of that, perhaps we'll have peace of mind in our deathbeds."

"I know what you mean. That feeling of guilt. And oftentimes, when your loved ones die, you hear yourself saying 'I should have done this to him or to her before she died' and then you feel guilty, but then it's too late. I'm trying to come to terms with myself and constantly telling myself 'If God can forgive, why can't I forgive myself?' And sometimes, I find peace."

"Yes, I know what you mean. You wonder why you have to leave this world without finishing so many projects. There are so many things to do, so many, and yet so little time. Just have peace of mind. Just to be content to say that if you lived this life and you leave it with unanswered questions, they'll most probably be resolved in the next life."

"You know, my dad said 'Don't be obsessed with things you can't change. It'll only frustrate and drive you crazy.' I always remember that when things get tough. Do you remember Nichols? We often went swimming in that pool in the Officers' Club, and one time, the water was shallow and you jumped head first and had a big bukol on your forehead, and then we had hot dogs for lunch."

"Oh, yes, it seemed like yesterday. Then you would visit in Baguio and we would march like soldiers in Abanao and Session Road, doing 'Right Oblique and Left Oblique marches. We were happy and crazy teenagers. We were also doing judo one day in my room and I ended up giving you a sprained ankle."

Frankie laughed. "But going back to the pool incident. I think we were only 7 or 8 and were at tita Luz's house in San Juan, and it was a hot day and apparently, the German neighbour was out of town but we were invited to swim in that nice pool of his. Remember? I almost drowned in that pool and you were like my guardian angel. You just pulled me up from the water."

"Well, I saw you couldn't come up so I yanked you up."

"You know I still remember those days in Lipa. There was this big fire in a cornfield near the Air Base, and Juancho who was the cousin of the Laurons, gave us a silindro in exchange for roast corn. Or was it the other way around?"

"I remember that incident but I don't remember if we gave the silindro to him or the corn. Well, anyway, compadre, best friend, favorite cousin and best man, I'll have to go. Have a nice birthday."

"Thanks, Mike."

# V.

Frankie was reading his diary:

Delta, January 14/93

Is writing a privilege? Or a leisure? Or work? Or all? I lie to say all of the above, I want to keep it that way. Retirement. Retirement is a privilege. Reading is a leisurely activity. Taking a vacation is leisure. Shopping is a leisurely activity too.

Am reading Animal Farm by George Orwell. Reminds me of Fabulas Zoologicas by Antonio Martinez Ballesteros, topic of my dissertation 20 years ago. Probably was reading this book too when he wrote his play. Translated and directed it in Maryknoll two years later.

Hell. Looking at my books, I came across an ilocano version of Dante's Inferno Ti nadiosan a comedia translated by Victorino Balbin in 1932, San Fernando, La Union. I need to see the English version to follow the Ilocano. I can only pick up a few words—the numbers, phrases like "Nacadanon dagitoy" or numbers like "Maicatlo". Ilocano, my mother was ilocana, and I spent my vacations in Baguio and I know Ilocano, but I'm losing it. I'll pick it up when I go back to Baguio.

Hell. What was that about hell? "The road to hell is paved with good intentions" or in Spanish El infierno esta lleno de personas con buenas intenciones, from the words of Senor Felix as recounted to me by Dad. My dad, a man of a few words but a lot of good deeds. A good man. Heaven will be happy to have him.

**Caveat emptor**. Buyer beware. Oh death in life! The days that are no more!

Thursday, February 18/93

JAL 741, en route to Manila from Tokyo, 11:25 a.m.

I remember mom saying that when I was 5, in Lipa, one of Major Adecer's boys, Sonny I guess his name was, the eldest, also 5 like me, hit me, and I went home crying. She said that dad told me to go back and hit the boy which, she said, I did. I don't remember. I only remember she told me that. A tooth for a tooth. Old testament teaching. Should I have given the other cheek?

No, I think dad was right.

What I remember now is Nichols. I was 10 or 11. Rolly Ledesma, our leader. I liked him; I somewhat admired him even if he was hated by the other kids in the Base. He was the terror of Nichols and the MPs were always running after him. But I liked him; he was a natural leader. Once he told me to beat up Ondo, which I did. And he cried after I beat him up. Five years later, Ondo became a black bolter in Karate, and no one, including myself, dared even challenge him in a friendly fight!

There was Rafael Leon, another boyhood friend in Nichols. His father was a pilot in a crash when he was only 10 or 11. he had a sister called Linda. Where are they now?

Rafael and I were at the Ateneo, and there was one of those "boy-gang" tease and challenge things again. We called a fight "square" then. I fought him, hit his nose and it bled. I didn't feel like fighting again after that. I sort of chickened out after seeing that bloody nose; the other kids stopped the fight. I never fought again after that.

BF Homes, Paranaque. Feb 19/93

I was with dad this afternoon, recalling military days. He was telling me how in 1944 he went through a rigorous training in Texas in 1945. He was only 28 then. I told him how I also went through hell during the Basic Officer Training 2-week course in 1991 at Ipperwash, Ontario for the Canadian Armed Forces Reserves. But I was 48! I told him those 2 weeks sent a message to me: I was too old for this sort of stuff. So, I quit. I stayed for two years though. I had fun—went to gun camp too and tried grenades, bazookas, and other weapons. Got paid for it too. I guess I have better things to do with my life. Like writing about my grandfather Don Paco, and my aunts, my parents, cousins. I was joking the Montecillos 10 years ago saying I was going to write about them, and now it's no longer a joke. In fact, ten years ago, I wrote a short story about the twins and it was published in Nuevo Horizonte as Las gemelas. Then came the poem Angeling de los angeles, then Calubcob, about my brother-in-law and sister's beach place in Batangas.

I've been condemned to be a writer. It started when I was 10 or 11. There was a full moon shining over my face in my bedroom. hat woke me up. I couldn't sleep anymore, so, I composed a murder story, with knives and the whole works. I don't remember where that story is now. All those moves. Spain, USA, Canada, etc. Couldn't carry all my manuscripts all over.

I started seriously in 1967 as a poet in Madrid with the publication of my first book of poems Lluvias filipinas. My "writing career" didn't even begin seriously. It started as a joke when I won an award at the Colegio Mayor de Guadalupe for writing a short essay entitled: "Different ways on how to peel oranges for dessert". After that, my career as a writer was launched.

\*\*\*

Twilight now. Just across is Manila Memorial.

"I can't leave mommy all alone", I remember my sister telling me that when she decided it was not meant for her to immigrate to Canada.

Nena my little sister. My 5-year old sister in Kansas. I remember the pictures with her in Leavenworth and West Point. Nena now in my little girl Alexandra.

Mi difunta madre, I again think of her as I look towards the west, in its dying orange horizon, as a warm humid wind blows waiting for twilight's death into night.

Feb 20/93

6:30 a.m. Birds twirping. Quiet morning today. Sun's orange rays in the east as I lie awake in my room.

Feb 24/93

Ash Wednesday. Mom's death anniversary. I looked blankly at her grave as Nena said the prayers. I left purple orchids; dad left a variety of flowers. Nena and boy left sweet-smelling jasmine. Too windy. Candles couldn't light. Estabas soplando el viento y las velas 'mang?, I monologued.

Picked up plane ticket. Leaving tomorrow for Iloilo. I fasted all day. I'm getting hungry. Fasting and abstinence today. Will have full meal tonight. Prayed the rosary. Corrected my manuscript.

# VI.

## OLD FRIENDS AND RELATIVES

Metro Manila, March, 1993

Old friends are haunting memories, Frankie thought. His sentimental trip back to the Philippines after 20 years was to seek out old friends and relatives—the parapeptones united in the ROTC cadre days, appropriately at the Nichols now called Villamor Officers' Club. Efren and Ding were missing, but the others laughed and reminisced old days; they went to the "scenes of the ROTC crimes". Boy remembered that this was the nurse's quarters; Frankie remembered the barracks and "Where the hell were those makeshift toilets?" Ernie answered: "They were makeshift for the summer cadre. No longer there."

Then they went to Frankie's old home the real scene of the crime where Toting met Mira, and Ernie, Helen. Pictures were taken in front of the house, the parapeptones arms on each others' shoulders. Then to Baby's house. Baby was Helen's older sister, and she was now fat after her stroke and talkative, as usual.

"Frankie, you were a conceited son of a bitch when you were a teenager!" was Baby's warm greeting to Frankie.

Frankie laughed. "Ateneo training. We had to uphold the virtue of chastity impregnated in our brains and beings by the Jesuits."

"Goddam Jesuits", commented Boy. "They were Marcos tutas!"

"Or the other way around, those sneaky bastards", interjected Frankie. "Vargas Vila, the Colombian writer, spoke so highly of them in Aves de Rapiña. You'd think Machiavelli was second string!"

***

Then there were the Montecillos, the beloved cousins of Frankie, his cousins whom he loved so dearly from his boyhood days. They would tease him and remember when he was a baby and would make pangkek, or that one picnic day when he was 5 or 6 an ant bit his pitinggoy and they had to take his pants off to look for the ant. His tia Luz commented: Naanseg laeng.

There was Nenet who lived with them in Nichols. Frankie remembered him as the start of the New Year's Party; he was the matador, giving lessons in bullfighting in his funny, entertaining and comic way. Nenet was just operated for cancer of the throat and he was commenting: "It feels like someone stuck a needle in my throat."

Frankie half-joked: "You must get an X-ray. There probably is a needle the doctor left there by mistake."

Nenet was recounting and acting out how fast a typist he was; he was excellent in his Marcel Marceau imitation of a typist, and also that of a bus conductor when he did this for a while.

"God, how could you remember all those passengers and the different fares you charged them?"

"Yak, yak" laughed Nenet in his signature guffaw.

Half of the Montecillos were there—Nenet, Nenita, Carmencing, Charito, Tony, the twins Milag and Merced; the other half—Nena, Angeling, Pepit and Teresing had just left for San Francisco; and two had passed away: Duarding and Manoling.

"Falta Tito", said Frankie, looking at Tito's picture with his cataract thick lensed glasses. "Lakayen".

Frankie looked at Nenita. "Pues Nenita, our champagne dream of riding a motorcycle cross-country seems to be fading away".

Nenita laughed her familiar asthmatic, strong laughter from her heart. "Yes, Frankie, we planned it but never got to do it. Now it's too late." She embraced and kissed his cousin.

"Never too late, prima. If Tia Luz who"s 88 can still run around with her broken shoulder and a cane, why can't we ride our Harley Davidsons?"

Everyone laughed. Frankie enjoyed entertaining the Montecillos. They were a great audience. The actor in him was fulfilled.

"That Karaoke was terrible", he remembered. Frankie had gone with Tony and Merced to that sing-along club but there was a drunk who hugged the mike all night singing all the songs in the most out of tune fashion.

"It's good George got it for a while", commented Tony.

"I couldn't stand him. Besides, we were too far from the mike, it couldn't reach and we couldn't sing", said Merced.

"And I couldn't read the letters on the TV screen anyway,", added Frankie.

"Oh well, next time."

"Yeah".

***

Then there was Guillermo who talked all day about the plight of Spanish and real estate in the Philippines. He laughed about his Tia Loling Vidal whom Frankie remembered as Lola Lolita.

"Ay, que mujer. Hijas con diferentes hombres. Me acordaba de sus bromas escandalosas 'No puki-puki English' decia alguna vez a un americano que le invitaba."

"Me acuerdo cuando ya tenia casi 80 o 90 años. Se urinaba levantada!"

Guillermo, the quixotic hispanist, the indefatigable person that he was, controversial but always active, writing consistently of his dreams to return the Philippines back to the Hispanic roots, where his utopia was to listen to every man, woman and child speak Spanish, or even chabacano.

"Get into politics, Guillermo. That's the only way to have clout."

"I'll consider that seriously."

"I'll be your campaign manager. I'm sure you'll sweep Iloilo."

***

# JOSELING, THE "TURK"

He was called the "Turk" because he looked like a middle-easterner, with his nose and curly hair, taken most probably from his mom, my tia Rita, who had the semi-crooked nose and the black curly hair.

"Tell me something about our grandfather, primo."

Frankie and his cousin Joseling were sitting under a mango tree in Palali one hot afternoon in March.

"What I know is that he worked as a Forest Ranger when the Americans took over the Philippines. After the Filipinos lost the war against the Americans in 1902, he left his job at the Tabacalera."

"Most of the Spaniards left for Spain when they lost to the Americans in 1898. There was an amnesty. They were allowed to return to their homes."

"And our grandfather was one of them".

"Yes, the so-called "ultimos de Filipinas, or the last stragglers left in the Philippines.

"Los últimos de Filipinas". Yes, they made a movie with the same title.

"Spain after the Treaty of Paris in 1898, was allowed to get her soldiers back to Spain."

Frankie showed Joseling an old photo. "Look at this photo taken in 1900 at the Escolta, in Manila. That's our "lolo" with "lola" and their three children: Antonia, Maria and Abelardo."

"Exactly. Lolo was about to leave for Spain. He was about to board the boat, but when he saw lola with the three children, he couldn't leave them alone by themselves. So he decided to stay on."

"And then what happened?"

"They got married".

"What? You mean they weren't married?"

"Yes, they were married civilly. But not in church Your uncle Paquito, my dad, was the first legitimate child, in the eyes of the church. He was the fourth child, right after tia Maria. He was born in 1902."

"They got married, but it wasn't a church wedding"?

"Yes, it was a church wedding."

"So lolo decided to stay, they got married and your dad was born in 1902."

"Yup".

"And then he left?"

"Yup."

"I think he went back to Spain because there was a death in the family."

"I don't know about that. I just know he left."

"I think he left because his mother died."

"I don't know that part of the story. But I know he left after my dad was born. I don't think it was a death in the family. He went to Spain with lola to let her meet his parents and family in Ronda.

"In 1905, tia Luz was born, followed by tia Conchita, then, tía Lolita in 1909, tío Miguel in 1911, tía Isabel in 1913, who died when she was 4 because of pneumonia; then tía Aida in 1915; tía Josefina in 1917; and tío Diego in 1919.

"But you know, Frankie, lola was really in love with lolo. And lolo likewise. Graciano, the father of lola, didn't like lolo at all. There was some kind of hatred of the Spaniards, as you know, during those days. el padre de lola, no quería para nada al español. And Graciano wasn't an exception. And lola, because she was very much in love with lolo, lied to her father and said she was pregnant and naturally, her father forced them to get married."

"A civil wedding."
"I believe so. Because they got married again in church before my dad was born."
"They were really in love, eh?"

"Of course. Why do you think they had 12 children, if it weren't for love?"
"You're right. That's logical. But I didn't know he became a Forest Ranger."
"When the Spaniards lost the war to the Americans, he had to leave the Tabacalera because the Spaniards left, and it closed down.

"That's true, and obviously he had to look for work to support a family of four."

"As a forest ranger, he was assigned in the Benguet region. And because of his position, he was able to buy land in Palali and Baguio. According to my parents, he boulght lands from the natives: sometimes, bartered. With this igorot, he'd give a pipe, with this other one, he'd give shoes, clothes, etc. In exchange for a few hectares, and so forth. Finally. He was able to accumulate as many as 200 hectares. He was also able to claim some public land as during that time, you could do that."
I didn't know whether Joseling was making up these stories about lolo, but I heard no other version from other family members. The last time I saw Joseling was in Palali in 2009; he couldn't walk nor talk because of a stroke that left him half-paralyzed.

\*\*\*

"Let's forgive and forget", said Frankie's cousin Tony Sandico whom he didn't see for more than 30 years. He made good in Hong Kong and was now a multi-millionaire, holding architectural offices in Hong Kong and Manila.

"Your parents are gone; my dad is still alive. Your proposal is great, but my dad still feels sensitive about Allen."

Tony had just proposed the construction of condominiums financed by him in the Allen property the Sandicos and Narcisos owned. They were adjoining lots, but Frankie's father felt that there was bad faith involved when the adjoining lot was sold to the Sandicos.

"Frankie, let's forget about this", insisted Tony. "Let's look at this as a business deal. Forget the sentimentalities of our parents. That's the past. Let's look at the future."

"I see your point, Tony. I'll talk to my dad about it again and see what he says."

Tony was always a go-getter, but he confessed, as they were drinking their San Miguel Super Dry beers at Kamayan Restaurant that he had become less aggressive in his mid-fifties.

"That's part of life. You're no longer as aggressive as before.

"You're right. I'm getting there too."

Tony was always the meticulous, detailed person; always well-groomed, well-dressed, popularly known in his youth as the Rock Hudson of the Philippines. His architectural designs were impeccable to the last detail. He married an architect from Hong Kong and they zoomed up to wealth and fame.

"Despite all this money, I just have to keep working. It keeps me alert. I'm sure I'll deteriorate if I stop."

"I know what you mean."

"You won't call me 'bully' in your novel, will you?"

"No, don't worry. I'll say nice things about you, primo."

## AUNTS LUZ AND AIDA

Aunt or tia Luz, the gypsy girl, "la gitana", that's how her father Don Paco called her, because she was born with black curly hair. For this "gitana", life was a divine mystery. She lived according to the words of Jesus from the book Imitación a Cristo, a big -letter edition which her nephew Frankie sent her when he was a student in Madrid in 1966. *Fe, Esperanza y Caridad. Pero la mayor virtud, la caridad.* (Faith, Hope and Charity, but the greatest of all, Charity.) She told everyone that she was going to leave all her money to the orphans of the world, with the exception of Carlitos, Frankie´s son who would inherit a million pesos.

She didn't have any children, but she took good care of her nieces, the daughters of her deceased sister, Maria and in particular Angeling, whom Frankie referred to in his poems as "Angeling de los angeles". Frankie still had memories of his tia Maria; she was very sick at V. Luna hospital . Frankie was only five or six then, and he remembered her charming face, so much like Charito's, her daughter. She died a few days later and Frankie's dad piloted the C-47 that took her body back to Baguio for burial. Tia Luz or tia Lui as Angeling would call her was an extremely generous person. After Angeling had married, she then cared for Maria, the daughter of her deceased brother, Diego.

The generous Angeling inherited tia Luz's traits, and like her, didn't have any children. So, like her, she took care of the children of her favorite sister, Charito. These two sisters had the good fortune of marrying successful military men, men of principle and integrity, products of the Philippine Military Academy. Angeling married the hero and famous guerrilla leader who later in his career obtained the highest military rank, that of 4-star general, and upon retiring was made Secretary of Defense under Marcos. But because of his integrity, he didn't last long and resigned after seeing the corruption of this man and his greedy and capricious wife.

Frankie remembered that one time, in his younger years, when he visited his tia Luz in Angeling's house, the retired general whom tia Luz affectionately and jokingly referred to as "el matador" asked him, "Frankie, what do you want to do with your life?" And Frankie simply answered, "I want to be a writer." That was the only question he was ever asked from the retired general, and there were no more conversations between the two of them after that. Tía Luz in her joking mood would call the General "el matador" (the bullfighter).

The other niece, Maria, also had the fortune of being cared for by tia Luz and received the Midas touch from her. When her father, tío Diego, died, her mother, the young Lydia with the help of Frankie's sister who was working in the Canadian Embassy in Manila, helped her obtain a visa to go to Canada to work as a nurse in Montreal.

After Maria finished her high school in Baguio, Frankie took her to Montreal where Maria completed her studies in Computer

Engineering. She went on to the Silicon Valley in California to work for various computer firms.

Tia Luz was the anchor of the family after Dona Adela died. In her moments of sadness, teary-eyed, she would remember her mother and would hum Lara's song... *Somewhere my love, there is a song to sing* from the film Dr. Zhivago.

She dedicated her entire life to serving her mother whom she cared for with so much affection, in the same way she took care of her brothers and sisters, her nephews and nieces, an in particular, the Montecillos who revered her for all she had done for them. She treated Frankie in a special way, particularly because he was the eldest son of his favourite sister Pepa.

She was always proud of him, and talked about him especially to her friends in the mahjong table, saying that he was the most intelligent nephew with his university titles, etc., as though Frankie were a saint on a pedestal in church.

The nephew, on the other hand, listened attentively to his gypsy aunt, following almost every advice she would give him. It was because for him, he considered his aunt like his mother, his adopted mother, as his mother had already passed away and she was happy and proud to be both the aunt and adopted mother of this talented nephew she endeared so much.

Frankie's other aunt, the spinster Aida, was named thus from her mother Adela. Her baptismal name was Adela, but everyone called her tia Aida.She was also named after her aunt Adela, her father's sister from Malaga, the elegant tia Aida who inherited the Andalusian beauty of her aunt and her grandmother the Countess. She was courted by men of different nationalities, but she didn't accept any of their marriage proposals because she always found some defect in the character or personality of her admirers. Thus, she didn't like the Russian because he didn't brush his teeth, and the Swiss had dirty fingernails and didn't wash his hands, and so forth and so on. She was a perfectionist, an idealist of old, in search of the perfect prince from Fantasy Island riding in his spotlessly white horse to take her away to the magic world of Camelot.

Frankie's old aunts were gourmet cooks, each in her own way. They always took care of their nephew who, like them, liked eating well. Whenever Frankie arrived from abroad to visit, he would always bring them ingredients for their gourmet recipes: dark chocolates, dried figs, olives stuffed with anchovies, virgin olive oil, Spanish ham, red wine, etc.

They would sit in the dark living room of the third floor of the ancestral house in Baguio and they would recall stories of their feared and beloved father, Don Paco. Then they would laugh as they recounted stories of the *querats,* or eccentric members of the family, and then with tears in their eyes, recall sad memories of a sister or brother who passed away. But then, after a short silence, would break out again with jokes, laughing. Now, the spinster aunt would go to her room and come out dressed up like a cowboy, or in some exaggerated costume to imitate a certain person; then, the gypsy aunt would do the same, go to her room, and do her dramatic entrance, and we would laugh, while the old and faithful deaf-mute servant Sara, with a cigarette in her mouth, would look disdainfully at them, and look at Frankie with that look saying "They're crazy!"

"Pues, aqui, la marquesa de Sablan, la duquesa de Abanao, y el principe de Palali." And they laughed again.

Another man they revered and respected was their brother-in-law, the writer's father, the professional soldier, the ex-brigadier, diplomat and flyer.

*El aviador*, was how the grand old man Supreme Court Justice and Spanish Academican Alfonso Arguelles referred to him. There was mutual admiration between the old justice and the flyer because both were men with integrity and high principles.

The nephew grew closer to his aunts Aida and Luz after his mother died, as he felt like an orphan, and he only had his aunts to take his mother's place, his two kind aunts who had taken care of him since his infancy and childhood. They liked telling stories about the world wars, especially World War II when the Americans were bombing Manila during the 1945 Liberation, and how his mother held him nervously in her arms while the "dogfights" with the Japanese were taking place in the skies above. Tia Luz would remember the many cans of KLIM milk she kept in her pantry for her infant nephew, in that gigantic house she owned in San Juan. She would reminisce about Kamakubo, the Japanese officer they befriended. Tia Aida would tease her nephew and say that he was Kamakubo's son, and that his mother was Valentina, his *yaya*. She would remember one time when the guerrilla Tony Garcia (who eventually married Alice, Frankie's cousin) entered the house and frightened Valentina in the drugstore owned by tia Luz in Ermita. He wanted to catch a few winks as he was tired from running away from the Japanese patrols during their occupation of Manila, and he wanted to hide there and rest a bit.

Frankie remembered how, during one summer vacation, he would go with her to the movies almost every day. He had just arrived from the US after finishing Grade I in a primary school in Kansas. Tia Luz had just sold her house to the Limcacos, and was renting the Laurel house in Alfonso XIII. Frankie's cousins, the Alunans were also living here. A year later, Frankie's dad was assigned to Nichols air Base (now called Villamor) and the Narciso family moved there and stayed at the officers' quarters.

During the summer holidays, his tia Luz who was a movie fanatic would open the freshly delivered Manila Times in the movie section. Frankie could still recall that fresh smell of newsprint ink and right away he knew it was movie time. His aunt would dress up in her black dress and they would walk to the corner and catch the jitney to Avenida Rizal and sometimes pass by Quiapo first to visit her lawyer, Fat Gonzalez, and then to the movies. On the way back, they would pass by the store of Aling Ayong in Santa Mesa where she would play a few rounds of mahjong while her 10 year old nephew would wait in the corner eating barquillos and reading comic books.

This was tia Luz's routine. Sometimes they would visit the Hocsons in Pinaglabanan. They had this beautiful family compound near St. John's, a private school.

Frankie now remembered his other favourite aunt, tia Aida. He remembered how she would tease him because of his English. She would notice that Frankie and his sister would say "wader" instead of "water" as they had recently arrived from the States and carried the American accent.

Tia Aida was a great storyteller, especially ghost stories. One time, in Baguio during summer vacations, she would tell stories that really scared Frankie and the other children. Frankie remembered a particular story that gave him goose pumps and scared the pants off him.

It was a story about a man who was punished and was imprisoned in a high tower. For some reason, he stuck out his tongue and it was so long that it reached the ground below. She told the store in such a way that really scared him. He remembered his sister almost peed in her pants, and Pilaring was also there and the Montecillo twins, as well as Migueling, all seated by the fireplace in the Hocson house in Baguio. Frankie was around 10 or 11 then.

His tia Aida also took him to a lot of places…the Muller mansion house which was just a block away from the Abanao house. Mrs. Muller was a native Igorot of Baguio married to a German miner who made lots of money in the gold mines of Benguet; they also visited Mrs, Hendry, a Filipina mestiza friend married to an American. She had a beautiful house in Manila, and after selling it, moved to San Francisco.

Frankie remembered a call his tia Aida made in 1974 when Frankie was living in San Francisco. She told him to look her up, but when he did, she wasn't around. Years later, his tia Aida told him that Mrs. Hendry had already passed away

He also remembered accompanying her to visit American friends who were in the diplomatic corps, a very nice family, living in Ermita. Tia Aida's life was surrounded by foreigners and foreign food, whereas tia Luz was happy being with family, the movies, and mahjong.

Thus it was that the nephew kept alive all these memories of the little adventures with his two aunts, and so when he left for Spain in 1965, thanks to Justice Felix, an intimate friend of tia Aida, who recommended him for a scholarship there, his nostalgic thoughts of them grew more and he continued sending them letters and gifts such as the Imitacion a Cristo which he sent his tia Luz and a can of olive oil for his tia Aida. He had all these memories of his aunts well kept in a corner of his mind and heart.

## THE MONTECILLOS

"Garbage!" exclaimed Jess Diaz, the retired judge, husband of his cousin Carmencing Montecillo. *"Basura!",* he repeated.

"Look outside! In every corner here in the Philippines, you see garbage. I'm ashamed to be a Filipino!"

Frankie agreed, and said: "I live in Canada and it's exactly the reverse. The problem there is it's too clean and hygienic that you need garbage to maintain your sanity."

They both laughed. Carmencing was preparing dinner with her sisters Teresing and Charito: *pansit, pinakbet, diningding, lumpia,* and fried rice.

"Well, Frankie, I'm preparing all this because you said you wanted native food."

"Thanks, cousin. In Canadá, the Filipino food is not as fresh as it is here."

They then went to the air-conditioned acoustic room of Jess to see a film on the life of Sinatra which Frankie brought along from Vancouver.

After the film, Carmen, Teresing, Jess and Charito had a picture-taking session, and then Frankie brought out from his bag some old photos, first, a family photo when tía María, was only two years old then, pictures of the Spanish relatives from Ronda. He pointed to a photo of the elegant great-grandmother, the countess, and photos of the Corrales family married to one of the de Paula sisters during a funeral.

"Look, this one looks like Nenita", exclaimed Teresing pointing to an aunt.

"And this one looks like tía Luz", commented "General" Charito, looking at an aunt with the same white hair and posture of tia Luz.

"Well, her name is also Luz, Luz Engracia, who married the war hero Rafael Corrales; this is him in uniform holding his crutches, wounded after returning from the Civil War. When I was there, around 15 years ago with tia Luz and my mom, they told me that they were pairing him off with your mother. Just imagine, if they did get married, there would not have been any Teresing, Charito or Carmencing Montecillo."

The three sisters laughed. They looked at the other photos.

"Look at this one", said the charming Carmencing. "She looks like you, Teresing, and this one looks like Nena, when she was young."

They were looking at the photos of the Izquierdo aunts from Ronda.

"*Wen gayam*," answered Charito. Teresing agreed and said:

"Well, you can obviously tell that from their noses."

Everyone laughed. "Oh yes, the Montecillos. The Montecillos of my childhood", thought Frankie. His cousins who took care of him from birth to childhood, these Montecillos of his life.

"Tía Aida was the one who corresponded with the family in Malaga and Ronda, and she got all these photos," Frankie said. "She met them also a couple of times when they were still alive. In 1966 and again sometime in the seventies. They're all dead now."

Charito affectionately put her hand over Frankie's head and said: "Oh, Frankie, how the years have passed; you're getting bald, and your beard is all white, but you're still handsome."

"Thanks, prima. And you're so much like your mom, tia Maria. I have vague memories of her when I was a child. Everyone said she was the most beautiful of the de Paula sisters."

The cousins smiled, happy to see Frankie after all these years.

"Tell me, Carmen, what's happened all these years? How's Nenita and Nenet and Pepit and the twins?"

"Nenet passed away. He lived for a while in the apartment where our brother Manoling used to live, near Pepit's house in Cubao. Later he was diagnosed with throat cancer and he moved in to Nenita's house in Cainta where he died. Nenita also died of lung cancer."

Frankie was choked. He tried to hold his tears. He remembered the last time he saw Nenita and Nenet…

"So, cousin, when are we going cross-country on motorbike?"

Nenita laughed with gusto. She had that hoarse laughter from her chain-smoking.

"We're too old for that, Frankie. But it's nice to dream. I'm always happy when you're around. You always make me laugh."

"That's the De Paula trait."

Frankie got together also with the twins Milag and Merced, and Tony who lived with Nenita. They kissed and embraced.

"It's been a long time, cousin.

"Well, yes, a really long time since we got together like thus.

"But what are you doing in Canada? There's nothing for writers like you there."

"Yes, you're right. It was supposed to be temporary but then you get stuck with your job and family…you have to support your family… house, cars, the whole middle-class North American lifestyle, 'the whole catastrophe', as Zorba the Greek pointed out in that movie.

"Yak yak, Frankie. It's been quite a while."

That was Nenet with his special way of laughing.

Nenet and Frankie embraced each other. Nenet just had a throat operation for a malignant tumor. They recalled old times in Nichols, when Frankie was still a child, and Nenet had a job there. He was always the life of any party. In one New Year's Eve party, he placed the "matador" at the Officers' Club of Nichols, and Nenet was known in the officers' circle as the "star entertainer" whenever there were other parties. He was hearing the echoes of his laughter…. "Yak, yak, yak…"

"Frankie, are you okay?" Carmen brought him back to the present. "By the way, Pepit wants to see you. She married again and has a beautiful house in Quezon City. She's inviting you for lunch. She's asking what you want to eat.

"When I think of Pepit, I'm reminded of my mom. That's probably why they also called her Josefina because she reminds me of mom. You too, Teresing. You have the de Paula look like mom. *Karurupam ni mamang ko.*

He still remembered bits and pieces of his ilocano.

Teresing remembered how bad Pepit's Spanish was. "She looks like a española but she doesn't speak Spanish. One time, Jess's mother asked her: "¿Tienes hijos de pecho?"

You know how she answered? "Sí, estoy satisfecho".

Everyone laughed.

"The twins", continued Carmen, "continue living in Cainta in Nenita´s house with our brother Tony who's retired now."

Pinky arrived. Pinky, a stewardess with Philippine Airlines, daughter of Carmen, her perfect image. She was with her baby, so white like her.

"What a pretty lady. A real Montecillo," said Frankie.

Jess and Frankie later returned to the air-conditioned room, leaving the women with their female chatter, just like the old days where the men would get together alter dinner and have their polemics. So, Jess and Frankie excused themselves and went to the air-conditioned music room to hear and talk about Julio Iglesias, Frank Sinatra, Nat King Cole, jazz music, and so forth and so on.

"Nice acoustics!" commented Frankie. "It's like you're in the middle of the orchestra."

"Precisely. Listen to this Julio Iglesias song. It's my favorite, *Felicidades.* What beautiful lyrics! Listen to this— *Ya se ve que el hombre le gusta ser esclavo de la mujer".*

"What passion! Beautiful indeed. I wouldn't want to be a woman's slave, though," interjected Frankie. They both laughed.

Carmen entered to offer merienda to both music *aficionados*: hot chocolate and ensaimada. "I'm sorry, Frankie. I only have cheese, Danish and chocolate for merienda. Later, we'll have dinner. Not much, just Chinese noodles, roast beef, lumpia, diningding, pinakbet and assorted tropical fruits after. I hope you don´t mind. It´s not much."

"Not much?? Cake, cheese, chocolate for snacks and noodles, beef, rolls, dinigding, pinakbet and tropical fruits for dinner! You've prepared a feast for the king of Spain. Well, why not? It's Mardi Gras! Carmen and Jess laughed.

The next day Frankie visited Nena, the eldest of the Montecillo sisters. They spoke about the escapades she and Frankie's mom had in those days when they were single.

"Your mama and I escaped many times. The late Montenegro was my date, and together with your mom and dad we went to Trinidad for a lauriat. We almost lost our way. We walked with your mom to meet our boyfriends in the road to Trinidad, close to the river. We had to cross the river. It was an adventurous date, but that's how we were. Daring. Adventurous, always looking for adventures: youth always in search of adventure. Montenegro and your dad were cadets in their third year in the Military Academy. That was 1939. Could you imagine? We walked all the way from Baguio to Trinidad!

She laughed with that special idiosyncratic laugh of hers.

"How about your parents, Nena? Tell me about them, tía María and tío Manolo."

"My father was going to marry another Maria from Manila. The wedding was already prepared, but he left her to marry mother."

"Sounds like a romantic novel."

"Tía Antonia found out that my father was going to elope with mother. Lola had hidden in her house dress the letter of father telling mother where to meet him, but it fell and tia Antonia picked it and gave it to grandfather. When he found out, he immediately called the Justice of the Peace and there in the house in Abanao they got married; the next day, they got married in church,. Grandfather then told them after the wedding: —El que se casa casa tiene."

"They lived in Trinidad, in the outskirts of Baguio. Father was the district attorney there. But in those days, the salary of a lawyer was not even enough to support himself, what more a family. We lived in a room of a house in Trinidad, and when I was seven or eight, we moved to Cabinet Hill in Baguio. I studied at St. Louis. That was 1928. Mamá and papa were married in 1917. Duarding, the eldest, was born in 1919. I was born in 1921."

That entire week before returning to Canada, Frankie spent a lot of time with his Montecillo cousins whom he endeared so much, more than his other relatives or friends in Manila. They laughed at Frankie's silly jokes; his cousins were his captive audience; they were also a good audience whenever tia Luz and tia Aida would joke around with them with their Ilocano tales of Alcoz el sadot and the spirit who gave Alcoz the magic cape, and other silly stories that made the Montecillos laugh to their hearts' content.

Frankie had the chance to visit Pepit in her beautiful mansion in Filinvest. Pepit was a gourmet, something she picked up from tia Aida, and she prepared another feast fit not for kings but for sinners, particularly gluttons. Tía Luz referred to her house as "refugio pecatorum".

Pepit was also into karaoke, and Frankie sang his favorites: Nat King Cole and Frank Sinatra.

It was time for Frankie to leave again. They took pictures and said goodbye. "Until your next visit", they said and Frankie, answered, "When I get this novel published we'll have a big fiesta."

Frankie had fond memories of his life with the Montecillos, the Montecillos of his childhood, and his teenage years, and the years when he returned always to visit them....he cherished these memories, these selective memories, a living tribute to their laughter and joy, their generosity and love, the beloved Montecillos of his life.

## DEATH OF DOÑA ADELA

"Apo, alaenakon" (Lord, take me already!), in her dying breath, lola Adela whispered these words, in her hospital bed. George, Frankie's brother, testified to the fact that that these were lola's last words before she expired. Frankie's mother was also in the room during her last agonizing moments.

Tía Luz, with tears in her eyes, recounted lola's last seconds on earth:

"She was agonizing. I was rubbing her head. She opened her eyes and asked, "Where's Luz?"

The nun beside lola said: 'She's right here.' Lola looked at Tia Luz and said: Husto data. I stopped massaging her head, and I went towards her. Just as I was walking towards her side, I noticed she closed her eyes and her head fell to her side. She had just expired. I asked one of the two nuns who were beside me why she looked so youthful in her death. One of them said: 'She lived her life according to God's will, that's why.'

***

## EDSA, March 20, 1993

His father just picked him up, and they were driving home to Parañaque. He was driving carelessly now, since his wife died. Maybe

413

it was his father's way; maybe he always drove that way, but only slowed down and was careful when his mother was with him.

"Today should have been your Golden Wedding Anniversary."

"Yes", he answered quietly. Nothing else was mentioned. He didn't want to remember or talk about her. He quickly changed the subject and talked of his cataracts.

"In Canada they diagnosed me for symptoms of cataract. I sometimes begin to see things blurry."

"You're probably just tired. Driving all day."

"Could be".

They were quiet the rest of the way. There was nothing Frankie could talk about. He was tired too from the long trip from Baguio. He just wanted to reach home, take a shower, and sleep.

He thought of his mother in the silence. His father probably was quietly thinking of her, but they didn't talk. It was a silence they understood and communicated with, a silence of someone dear they could now only remember.

## FAT DOG

"My philosophy is Satanic. It's the impulse that forced me to murder. I was called "fat dog' by the Godfather. When you see the movie, The Godfather, it's too sensationalized. Pure gangsterism. Here, it's survival. A matter of survival."

Roy Torres known among the mafiosos as "Fat Dog" had been involved with the underworld since he was 16. He was now the Godfather of Barrio Gisi, a small pueblo in the island of Nueva Valencia off the coast of Negros.

"There was this English pirate who came to look for treasures from sunken ships off the coast of Gisi. Do you know what that English pirate told us about our culture? Damaged, he said. 'You Filipinos have a damaged culture'. That son of a bitch. He doesn't know that England has a more damaged culture than us with all their Jack the Rippers and pirates."

"Sometimes these foreigners make comments like that to make us feel bad and destroy our morale. Divide and conquer, the old adage. You shouldn't believe them."

"I believed him. I look at myself and I see a symbol of the damaged culture of the Philippines."

"Heal yourself. Don't believe them. Believe in yourself. You're a Filipino, a Christian, you're superior to these pagan foreigners who think you're damaged, because they themselves are damaged."

"But I don't regret anything", Fat Dog continued. "I realize after I do something wrong, I always say 'I did it impulsively'…"

"If there is love, impossibilities will become impossible", Frankie interjected.

"Did you enjoy the sabungan?" Fat Dog changed the subject.

"Yes, I did. If only I didn't have a bad stomach, I would have enjoyed more and joined you for a few beers. I don't know. I must have picked up some kind of food poisoning when I was in Manila. But other than that, I enjoyed it. I liked the drama, the bets aisco, deste, biya, agaw…Seemed like most of the winnings went to the biya. The Cristo Mayor was a good entertainer."

"He's the janitor in the local school. Tonight, we're going to a lamayan. My bodyguard's brother. The kid was only 25."

"What happened?"

"Drank too much. Burned his liver. They just brought the body in from Manila the other night."

Fat Dog and Frankie headed there around 8 p.m. after having their sinigang and chop suey dinner in Fat Dog's house. They went over to his bodyguard's house, and along the way, Fat Dog recounted to Frankie what a loyal fellow his bodyguard was:

"He's a stand-up guy. Real loyalty. He's been my bodyguard for 30 years. He saved my life thirty years ago. He was 14; I was 18. He put himself between me and the policeman. Sonuvabich policeman. He disappeared after that. Never heard from him again."

Fat Dog and Frankie reached the lamayan. The deceased was ignored, as was the case in wakes, Filipino, Irish or Italian.

"That's the way it should be. Let the dead be left alone", quipped Fat Dog.

The living ones were outside playing bingo, pusoy (or Black Russian), and mah-jong. Nestor, his bodyguard, was at the back with his San Miguel. He offered us cold cervezas; I refused. I said I still had an upset stomach.

"You know, Frankie" started Nestor, "Fat Dog and I go a long ways back. Sometimes, there's bad blood between us but we've been together too long to kill each other. There's a magnetism that doesn't allow us to kill each other."

Around us were breeding cages. Two or three month old cocks being bred for the Derby.

"I need capital. There's more demand than supply, but I don't have the money to buy the feeds. Too many buyers. I can't keep up. No money for maintenance."

"I'm looking for business here. I like it here. Quiet and peaceful. Away from the rat race of the city. Nice place to retire. I'll be a misanthrope. I played that role when I was in school. I just like the sea, that's all. Old man and the sea, that's probably what'll happen to me. I like the sound of waves, sea waves, and the winds from the sea."

The next day Frankie went to his island. It was now the dry season. Dead leaves and branches scattered all over the shell and corral-covered island. It was an islet, 400 square meters. He remembered the greenery during the rainy season; now it was all dry, but the siniguela tree was beginning to green. The tide was low; the clouds were beginning to hover. Windy and cold for this time of the year, thought Frankie. Cold at nights, early March, still cold from the Siberian winds that just killed 16 in Aparri up north.

Frankie fell asleep and dreamt of his mother again.

Pues aqui 'mang solo otra vez con lagrimas de tristeza, de soledad, en esta isla, aislado del resto del mundo, recordando Ipil, Surigao, (qué playas tan bonitas como la tengo aquí! Ay, mang, si estuvieses aquí para ver mi pequeña isla! Qué triste estar solo! No vuelvo más aquí sin Carlitos y Alex. A lo menos en Manila está papá, Nena, las tías, los Montecillos. Vine no mas aquí para salir de la sofocación de Manila, bañar un poco en el mar, escribir mis poesías, respirar el aire del mar, cambiar de ambiente, "ambience" como dice Andre, de Brother Andre, así le nombró Nena...

Frankie awoke from his afternoon siesta. Damned these drunk fishermen and their big mouths! No sé, estos visayos.

Frankie picked up his pad but couldn't write. Aquí espero en la cabaña hasta que venga alguna inspiración para que pueda yo continuar escribiendo. 'Mang, oigo tu voz en mis recuerdos, que triste, ay que triste, llamando tu nombre, tu existencia que ya no se puede volver a este mundo efímero. O Filipinas de mis tristezas!

## THE NARCISOS

It was Josefina Narciso who kept the family together. After her death, the family fell apart. But it was all part of the Divine Will, as biblical as the words of Pope John XXIII who, in his diary before he died in the sixties, predicted, after various apparitions of the Virgin Mary, that families will fall apart, catastrophes and epidemics will occur in this planet until 1995, when the saviours from heaven, odd-looking in their appearance, would descend and clean up this planet of all catastrophes, epidemics and family problems to prepare for Christ's second coming on December 25, 2000.

Tía Luz recounted the veracity of these prophecies, saying that the saintly pope had revived a dying nun by just placing his hand over her. She revived and said she wanted to have something to eat. The saintly pope then told her: "Remember this miracle." Tía Luz also observed how Christ had two fingers before his ascension which she interpreted as the year 2000 when he would return to give peace and tranquillity to this planet of believers.

Frankie Narciso, the eldest of a family of five, felt, as he had always felt, a fervent filial love for his mother, and a strong admiration and respect for his father. He had always adhered to the fourth commandment: "Honour they father and thy mother".

His father was, to him, the anchor of the Narciso family, as any head of a family should be. He never could fit his father's footsteps, but he tried to follow his example. His father was a successful military man, rising to the highest level in the military, a General in the Armed Forces. Although his dream was to at least match his father's achievements, he could not live up to his success and fame. He was content in knowing that he had a great father whom he admired and even if he could not live up to his high standards, he was content in being his son.

In his sad moments, thinking of his wife who had recently passed away, Frankie's father would confess to his children, especially to George who followed in his footsteps by being an officer in the Air Force, remarking: "No one to call me Ching anymore."

George, or Joji, as he was called affectionately, was conceived in Washington D.C. when "Ching" and "Ping" were with their first born children, Frankie and Mila in the United States. In 1951, he was assigned for training at the Command and General Staff School in Leavenworth, Kansas. The third child, Nando, was left behind with tía Luz in Baguio. He was too young to take along.

These were happy years for the Narcisos. The Major and his family travelled first class on the USS President Wilson Lines First Class, and Frankie remembered being bullied by a big blonde child his age. He remembered also being frightened while watching one of the movies aboard ship: Wizard of Oz. He closed his eyes when the witch appeared. This was one of the films shown to the children aboard ship during this one month cruise from Manila to San Francisco.

In San Francisco they stayed for a few days at the military base fronting the Golden Gate Bridge. During this time, the Major bought a two-door green Chevrolet convertible, and they made their cross country trek to Kansas.

The Major's wife recalled years later how her children, Frankie and Mila, after getting tired of eating oranges along the way, started playing with the leftover oranges throwing them out the window to passers-by. Mila would sleep on the backseat while Frankie slept on the floor that was padded with sleeping bags, clothes and pillows.

The children who were only 7 and 5 respectively went to school there and easily picked up the mid-Western American accent and started pronouncing WATER like WUDER and PATIS as PAYTIS. Naturally, when they returned to Manila, after less than two months, their mid-Western accents rubbed out again with the Filipino English pronunciation.

Frankie remembered being lost in the streets of Kansas after walking back home from school by himself. He was picked up by a kind police officer who tracked down where he lived. He was given an ice cream cone in the police station while waiting for his mom to pick him up. He also recalled when the snow first fell and he went out to play without ear muffs on. He came back to the house with his ears swollen, which hurt like mad but which later unswelled after a few minutes by the fireplace.

**There was the house with the forbidden apple tree behind. Frankie knew it was wrong to go there, but the apple was tempting.**

There was Tom Cross, his friend. They met again a few years later in Manila when his father was assigned in the US Embassy. There was also that Mexican boy in Leavenworth who played cards so well that he won all the marbles of the kids who played against him... Frankie had moved to the officers' quarters inside the military base in Leavenworth until his father finished his CGSS training. They visited West Point and Washington after that. After his schooling, the Major went ahead to the Philippines while his wife and two kids took the PAL flight back to Manila via San Francisco and Hawaii. Frankie remembered buying the comics book "Felix the Cat" at the airport.

Then there was San Juan where they stayed in Tita Luz's house until they found their own place in San Juan. There they waited until they were given quarters in Nichols. They stayed there until 1967. Frankie had already left in 1965 for Spain. They all got together in Montreal when the Major, now a retired Air Force General, was assigned to the ICAO there.

After that, Frankie married a British immigrant to Canada, got divorced, and returned to the Philippines to teach Spanish at his old alma mater. He was disappointed with the new Filipino Jesuits, left for Canada again and stayed there for another 5 years. He returned home again, remarried, brought his wife and son to Montreal, and became a widower when his daughter Alexandra was born.

"Sometimes I wonder whether, in the confusion of time and eternity, souls were infused at wrong moments. I'll probably be in the body of Ted and you'll fall in love with me, and I'll say 'I'm not Ted; I'm Frankie', and you'd think I was joking because I would look and sound like Ted."

Cornelia laughed. "And of course, Ted will be you, the hopeless romantic", she chided.

"Anything is possible", said Frankie. "In this planet, in this universe of mysteries, somewhere in time, sometimes..."

They looked at each other, deeply into each other's eyes, into each other's souls. It was a beautiful magnetism of of destiny and possibilities that somewhere in time and space they had once lived or would live as lovers, **perhaps again, perhaps for the first time.**

In another time, thought Frankie, when souls will be recycled **by St. Peter and company, the magic would return...in Palali, perhaps in another time...**

## FINALE

In another time…

The days that are no more. Palali, gone to wasteland; Palali, the joy of Don Francisco de Paula, gone to foreigners to build their pollutant factories. Gone are the mango trees, the coconut trees, that idyllic, bucolic life. Dreams gone. Progress must go on. Industries. Money.

Where now can peace and quiet be found? Where can dreams be remade? Paradise lost. Paradise regained perhaps only in the peace and quiet of death.

Just to let go. Towards the light at the end of the tunnel. Into the freedom of eternity.

## THE END

# Would you like to see your manuscript become a book?

**If you are interested in becoming a PublishAmerica author, please submit your manuscript for possible publication to us at:**

**acquisitions@publishamerica.com**

**You may also mail in your manuscript to:**

**PublishAmerica
PO Box 151
Frederick, MD 21705**

# www.publishamerica.com

CPSIA information can be obtained at www.ICGtesting.com
Printed in the USA
BVOW082015211112

306220BV00001B/77/P